THE PACKARD STORY

THE PACKARD

The Car and the Company

NEW YORK: A. S. BARNES AND COMPANY

STORY

y Robert E. Turnquist

ONDON: THOMAS YOSELOFF LTD

A. S. Barnes and Co., Inc.
Cranbury, New Jersey 08512

Thomas Yoseloff Ltd
108 New Bond Street
London W1Y OQX, England

Fourth Printing

6242
Printed in the United States of America

To My Wife Sunny

Preface

This book is for the man who enjoys every facet of this country's fabulous automotive heritage. Among the hundreds of makes that have passed from our automotive scene, there was once a small group of marques that were built to a high quality standard and not down to a price. These cars were to become known as classics, and king of them all was Packard.

Looking back over the years, Packard was more than a car, more than a status symbol; it was part of our American heritage. Packards were the transportation of the people that made America the complex, highly industrialized society that we know today.

If we went to Washington during the first half of the nineteenth century, we would see government-owned Packards and privately owned Packards belonging to Supreme Court Justices like McKenna, Stone, Sanford, and Butler. Most presidents during the Twenties and Thirties had Packards before and after their stay in the White House. Most legislators drove Packards.

If we went to the theater we would see row upon row of Packard town cars and limousines owned by such peoples as John Astor, Howard C. Brokaw, Reginald Barclay, Mrs. David K. Bruce, E. Farrar Bateson, Mrs. Winthrop Dwight, E. S. Gorham, Jr., William B. Leeds, Henry Luce, and Arthur Hayes Sulzberger. The actors, like Al Jolson, George M. Cohan, John Charles Thomas, and Ezio Pinza, all owned Packards.

At a sporting event, we would see Babe Ruth, Phillip K. Wrigley, and Dwight F. Davis all driving Packards, and in Hollywood the list reads like a Who's Who in the film capital. A partial list would include Tom Mix, Gene Autry, Buck Jones, Ken Carpenter, Ben Lyons, Turhan Bey, Dick Powell, Robert Taylor, Clark Gable, Stuart Erwin, Burl Ives, Errol Flynn, Gloria Swanson, Pola Negri, Jean Harlow, and Irene Damiti. Louis B. Mayer of Metro, Cecil B. de Mille, and Hedda Hopper all drove Packards, and in the movies more Packards were used as props than any other make. Paramount's "Reaching for the Sun" was a movie actually done in the Packard plant in Detroit. The movie was the film version of the novel F.O.B. Detroit.

Packard dealers like E. C. Anthony of Los Angeles also left their mark on our lives. It was Anthony who put gasoline pumps on the curb and the attendants in uniform. The "Red and White Filling Stations" he founded are now on every street corner in America.

While in Europe, Anthony met Claude Neon and invested in his neon lighting principle. As a result, E. C. Anthony imported the first three Neon signs in America. Lastly, he built the KECA radio broadcasting chain which was sold to NBC in 1944.

Packard's Detroit plant designed by Albert Kahn was the first reinforced concrete factory in the world. Packard's faith in this young architect revolutionized industrial construction in America. Kahn went on to design and build the River Rouge works, the Willow Run plant, the General Motors Building in Detroit, and the New York Times Building.

For six decades, Packard helped build the American automotive industry into the undisputed leader of the world. For those readers who are fortunate enough to still own these rare gems of the Golden Age of Motordom, there has been included in this book classic automobile restoration material.

The history of the Packard Motor Car Company has many other facets. The Custom Salon Shows of the Twenties, the National Automobile Shows, the history of the great custom body builders, and the problems common to all automotive manufacturers to stay in business have all been included in this book.

Contents

THE PACKARD STORY

First Series Eight, Model 143 Touring. Price at Detroit $3,850. Packard's first straight eight. Production started June, 1923. The granddaddy of all Packard Eights.

1

The Second Series Eight and the Third Series Six

The year is 1925, the halfway mark in the decade known as the "Roaring Twenties." Cal was in the White House and the prosperity bandwagon was shifting into high gear. In a position of honor rode the automobile manufacturer. His hour of destiny had arrived. By this time, there were plenty of paved roads and the landscape was dotted with garages and gas stations which permitted the motorist to venture forth without fear of having to get out and get under. The boxy, drab models of the vintage era were beginning to be replaced by softer, more stylish lines. Bodies were slung lower and the custom-body companies were beginning to set the styling level for the industry.

It had been twenty-six years since the first motor carriage designed by the brothers James Ward Packard and William Doud Packard had rumbled down to No. 2 High Street in Warren, Ohio. The original car was called the Ohio, but soon after the name was changed to Packard. History shows November 6, 1899, as being the time when the first Packard saw light of day, but as early as 1893, J. W. Packard,

assisted by E. P. Coules, made drawings for a horseless carriage. The Panic of 1893 came, however, and the matter was dropped. In 1895, W. D. Packard went to Europe and brought back a DeDion-Bouton Tricycle to see how it would perform on American roads. The next car purchased was a Winton. The brothers drove the car for about a year and then suggested to the makers some changes which they thought would improve it. "Well, if you think you can build a better car, why don't you do it?" was the reply of the gruff old man who controlled the factory.

In July, 1899, the Packard brothers and two Winton men, George L. Weiss and W. A. Hatcher, organized the partnership of Packard and Weiss. Packard put up $6,000 and Weiss contributed $3,200. On September 10, 1900, capital stock of the company was increased to $100,000 and the name was changed to the Ohio Automobile Company. J. W. Packard was elected President. On October 13, 1903, the capital stock was increased to $500,000 and the name was changed to the Packard Motor Car Company. On September 5, 1903, the

Directors of the Packard Motor Car company decided to move the factory to Detroit. William Doud Packard elected to remain in the electrical business in Warren, Ohio.

From 1903 to 1911, the growth of the factory was healthy and continuous. In 1911, there were 6,000 employees and the factory was using 33 acres of floor space. By 1925, the Packard plant was the most modern automobile manufacturing facility in the world. With the profits from World War I and the sales of Single Sixes and Twin Sixes, the company had completely rebuilt the existing plant on East Grand Boulevard and then had made major facility additions to this. There were eighty-one separate trades under one roof. Precision equipment, some of which was the company's own design, turned out precision parts that were superior to the best that Europe or America had to offer. This modernization and expansion program cost $36,000,000, and $21,000,000 more would be spent in the next three years. In addition to the production of automobiles, Packard was also one of the largest engine producers for land, sea, and air vehicles. The World War I engine contracts fostered this early diversification with Colonel Vincent in charge.

In the air, 1921 saw a Packard-engined airplane set a new world's altitude record. The PN9 seaplane with two 600 h.p. Packard engines later established seven new world's records, which included doubling the previous record for continuous flight. Later Packard built and successfully flew a diesel-engined transport plane. The famous and ill-fated Navy dirigible *Shenandoah* was one of the two dirigibles that were powered with six Packard twelve-cylinder aircraft engines. As a result of these accomplishments, Packard was a heavy supplier of engines to the military and commercial plane manufacturers. By 1925, Packard had marketed an x-type 24-cylinder 1250 h.p. engine which developed one horsepower

for each 18 ounces of weight, and an inverted V-type for better visibility in aircraft applications.

On the water, Packard marine engines outperformed and out-sold those of all other manufacturers. The speedboat *Rainbow III* with a standard marine engine captured the endurance record by traveling 1,064 miles in 24 hours. *Miss America X,* piloted by Gar Wood, set a world's speedboat record of 124.91 mph during the 1925-26 season. The boat was equipped with four Packard Twin Six engines that developed 6,400 h.p. Packard-engined boats had become so popular that those less fortunate financially were equipping their inboards with used Packard automobile engines.

On land, the army was buying 200 h.p. Packard V-8 engines for their new 23-ton tanks and were delighted with the performance. The Packard heavy-duty truck was extremely popular and their sales had been good. However, production had been discontinued in late 1923 when management decided to concentrate on passenger car production.

Another venture also discontinued in 1923 by Packard management was racing. Competition had begun in 1902 when J. W. Packard entered five Model C automobiles in the 475 mile New York to Buffalo run. All five completed the trip, which was a great boost in prestige. However, Packard's interest in prestige was secondary to his burning desire to whip the pants off Alexander Winton. In May, 1903, Winton had one of his cars driven from San Francisco to New York in 64 days. Packard promptly equipped a Model F (old Pacific) and knocked three days off Winton's record.

In 1904, Packard took a Model K chassis and fabricated the famous Packard *Gray Wolf*. The *Gray Wolf* was taken to Daytona Beach where it made new one- and five-mile records. The one-mile record was 8.8 miles faster than the Winton *Bullet*. Later in the year, the *Gray Wolf* was entered in the First Vanderbilt Cup

DRIVER RALPH DePALMA
CAR PACKARD
300 MILE RACE 1923
INDIANAPOLIS MOTOR SPEEDWAY

PHOTO #4320
BY
KIRKPATRICK
23.

Ralph DePalma in Packard entry No. 1. Packard's second and third entries were piloted by Dario Resta and Joe Boyer, respectively. The event was the 7th Annual "Brickyard" run.

Race and came in fourth. Charles Schmidt, who had helped supervise the construction of the *Gray Wolf* and had raised hob driving it to these new world records, next appeared in Grosse Pointe, Michigan, to drive a Model L around a 1-mile dirt track 1,000 times in 29 hours, 53 minutes and 37.6 seconds at an average speed of 33.5 mph. Winton blew the whistle and retired his cars from racing. With Winton gone, Packard lost interest and the *Gray Wolf* was retired.

It was not until 1917 that Packard again re-entered racing. Two cars were constructed; however, to win trophies again was only secondary. The primary reason for the cars' existence was to test aircraft engines for military use. The first racer was called *299*, which was the cubic displacement of its twelve-cylinder engine. Ralph DePalma piloted *299* and in 1917 and 1918 nailed down just about every loose trophy. He set a 116-mile lap record at the Maywood Speedway. In the 1919 "Brickyard" event, he came in sixth; he was leading the pack until a pit stop was necessary to replace a wheel bearing. The second racer was called the *905*. It had a larger twelve-cylinder engine with a 905-cubic-inch displacement. If the *299* was "hot," the *905* sizzled. In Daytona in 1919 it clocked 149.9 mph for the one-mile straightaway record. Ralph DePalma did the driving. Also while at Daytona, the *905* did the standing mile at 92.71 mph, a record that held for 30 years in the unlimited class.

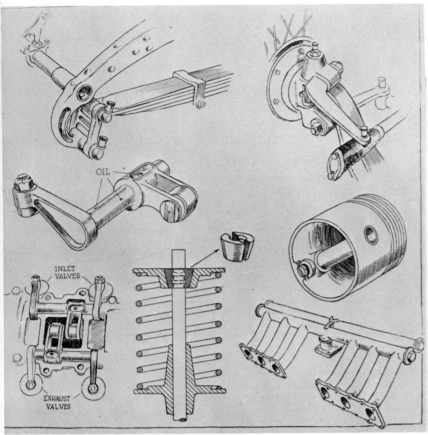

Some mechanical details of the Packard Twelve. The valve rocker in the center is machined from one piece and has a hollow shaft through which the oil flows from the small well at the top. Below is shown the arrangement of the rockers in position over the camshaft. A special form of split conical retainer is used to hold the valve spring seat on the valve stem as shown below in the center. The aluminum inlet manifold is in two halves, clamped together at the center, from which point the carburetor is suspended.

OIL

INLET VALVES

EXHAUST VALVES

In 1923, Packard, with the urging of Earl C. Anthony, commissioned Ralph DePalma to build three 122-cubic-unit specials for the Memorial Day event. The cars were built in Los Angeles and shipped to Indianapolis for the event. All three qualified, but halfway through the racing Classic their head gaskets began to disintegrate, causing all three to retire from the race.

Although Packard never raced again in competition, this mishap at Indianapolis was only coincidental with the management's decision to discontinue racing. As when they discontinued truck production, they felt that the funds and facilities would be better utilized in passenger car production.

At Packard, the new in-line Eight had been in production for two years. In this short time it had become the American motorist's new sweetheart, the epitome of automotive excellence. This new nine main bearing high-per-

formance engine had successfully filled the gap left in the public's heart when the Twin Six, the Boss of the Road, had been discontinued in June, 1923. In passing it should be said that the Twin Six introduced the American motorist to high performance engines. It was not only America's first twelve-cylinder engine (1915), but it was the world's first aluminum-pistoned automobile engine.

February 2, 1925, saw the introduction of the Second Series Eight and the Third Series Six. Technical improvements were numerous. The most important was the Bijur chassis lubricating system. This chassis lubrication system, which is still incorporated in the new Rolls Royce and was optional on the 1955 Lincoln, is in good measure responsible for the many classic Packards that are still running today. The oil reservoir was bolted on the firewall, and, when the driver pulled a plunger on the dash, it automatically greased thirty-

Second Series Eight Model 243 Convertible Coupe by Phillips of Ohio. Price was $5,500. Packard's first production convertible coupe would not be introduced until January 1928, during the Fourth Series run.

two chassis parts. Also incorporated in these two new series was a new Bendix three-shoe internal expanding four-wheel braking system. Prior models had internal rear brakes and external shoe front brakes. The oil rectifier made its appearance in these two series. It was excellent but complicated and was dropped at the end of the model run in favor of the simple can-type oil filter. The spring setup was changed. The shackle assembly was re-designed to allow bumper brackets to be integral with the frame horns. A new crankshaft was installed in the Six with seven larger main-bearing surfaces. Also a unique counterweight setup was fitted to the Six and the Eight crankshaft. The connecting rods were drilled for oiling the wrist pins. The phaeton model in both series was the first American car to introduce English Burbank top material which made for easy-folding compact tops. Fender flanges were made wider.

The Second Series Eight had new 21″ wheels. Disc wheels, which were introduced in the First Series Eight, remained. In April, 1925, a two-passenger coupe, called the Holbrook, and a Club sedan were added to the line. The Club sedan as a body style is now the most popular closed car among classic car collectors. For the Holbrook Body Company, founded in 1921 in Hudson, New York, this was their first big order from a luxury car producer. They continued to supply custom and semi-custom bodies to Packard until bankruptcy closed their doors in the winter of 1929.

The Third Series Six had increased horsepower (7 h.p.), a heavier frame, disc wheels, and a new 23″ tire size. Bumpers, tools, spare tire, etc., were made standard equipment. The Club sedan was added to the Six line in March. As a result of these improvements and the reputation gained through the owners of the 116, 126, and 226 Series, the Third Series Six broke all previous sales records. Although it was Packard's volume classic in the luxury market, the delivery wait was four months. When the Third Series production ended, 40,358 units had been sold—four and one-half times as many as its predecessor, the Second Series Six.

Packard's plan was to make the Six their volume car. Thus, the Eight was not to be produced in quantity. It was to be designed and equipped without regard to cost. As Alvan Macauley said in his Annual Report:

Second Series Eight Model 243 Roadster by Dietrich.
Price was $4,600. The entire Fourth Series Big Eight
production would eventually incorporate the styling
of this vehicle. Dash-mounted temperature gauge was
a factory option.

The Eight in its standard form is equipped with
every luxury and embellishment the markets of
the world afford. It is the most powerful and
usefully active car in the market. Its riding qualities are unsurpassed, due to its long wheelbase,
its long flexible springs, and to its scientific weight
distribution. The broadcloths, silks, and fabrics
with which the body is trimmed are the finest
obtainable. In order to cater to the wishes of an
exacting clientele which often desires bodies built
to respond to some unusual personal preferences,
we offer a complete line of custom bodies. We
have not sought quantity production in connection with the Eight. We think it best to keep
them on a plane where they will always be in
demand and where in normal times the demand
will be somewhat greater than the supply.

The straight eight engine continued to gain
popularity at the 25th National Automobile
Show. Better steering systems were offered in
1925 models to compensate for the balloon

tires. The high point of the show was the
introduction of pyroxylin finishes on the cars
displayed. With the advent of synthetic lacquers, motor cars were offered in a rainbow
of colors. Other popular features shown were
rumble seats, one-piece windshields, mohair
upholstery and crank-type window lifts. For
the first time, the sale of closed models surpassed the open models. Front and rear
bumpers had now become standard equipment. Accessories on the must list for car
owners included stop lights, heat indicators,
balloon tire jacks, locking radiator caps,
trunk racks, and all-weather enclosures for
touring cars.

Fisher body (not yet owned by General
Motors) acquired Fleetwood, a custom body
building company in Fleetwood, Pennsylvania. Fleetwood, up to this time, had been
one of the biggest suppliers of custom bodies
on the Packard chassis.

Oldsmobile introduced chromium plating
creating a new industry literally overnight.

Second Series Eight Model 236 Phaeton. Price at
Detroit $3,750. Deluxe emblem and tonneau wind-
shield were factory options. Burbank top cloth was
introduced to the U. S. on this model.

The luxury car owners specified it for custom classics immediately. New plating plants were constructed with inside garages so customers could drive their present transportation to the platers and have the nickel parts removed and plated in chrome. As a result, today's restorers of classic cars may specify chrome for all parts without loss of authenticity in open competition or resale value.

Since Packards were not manufactured on a yearly model basis until 1935, it becomes extremely important to understand that models built prior to 1935 can only be identified by SERIES rather than by year. When a new series was introduced, it was because of a mechanical and/or a styling improvement rather than for styling obsolescence. As a result, new series were introduced at any time during the year. Production of these series would end only when a significant development was incorporated. As a result, some series had as little as a nine-month duration while others had an eighteen-month duration. Thus, proper identification can only be made by series to avoid confusion. As an example, Packard introduced the Second Series Eight and a Third Series Six on February 2, 1925, and discontinued them on August 2, 1926. This was an eighteen-month model run. For further identification the Eight came in two wheelbases, 136 inch and 143 inch. The Six also came in two wheelbases, 126 inch and 133 inch. The model numbers assigned by Packard to the Eight were 236 and 243, and to the Six, 326 and 333. Now the key to identification becomes apparent. The first digit represents the SERIES and the second two digits represent the WHEELBASE and the size of the wheelbase tells whether it is a Six or an Eight. The delivery date stamped on the vehicle plate on the cowl was put there for insurance and registration purposes and cannot be a guide to identifying the series.

Third Series Six Model 326 Sedan. Price at Detroit $2,585. The first year drum headlights were used on the Six. Painted bumpers with plated strips were standard equipment through the Fifth Series.

2

The Third Series Eight and the Fourth Series Six

The management team in 1926 was the best in the industry and it consisted of the following men:

Alvan Macauley	President and General Manager
J. G. Vincent	Vice President of Engineering
Russell A. Alger	Vice President
E. F. Roberts	Vice President of Manufacturing
H. H. Hill	Vice President of Distribution
J. J. Marks	Comptroller
Merlin A. Cudlys	Secretary
Richard P. Joy	Treasurer
Hugh J. Ferry	Assistant Treasurer
Milton Tibbets	Patent Conusel
Henry E. Bodman	General Counsel
H. N. Davock	Service Manager

The Board of Directors consisted of the following men:

Frederick M. Alger
Russel A. Alger
Henry E. Bodman
Alvan Macauley
James T. McMillan
Truman H. Newberry
Richard P. Joy

Advertising was handled by Austin F. Bement, Inc. It was his agency that was responsible for the beautifully colored Packard advertisements of the era which appeared in *Country Life, Vanity Fair, Saturday Evening Post,* etc. Mr. Bement had made his contact with Packard when he was Vice President and Secretary of the Lincoln Highway Association. This non-profit Association promoted the extension of paved roads in America, and was a pet project of the Packard Motor Car Company executives. Together, they did as much to put America on wheels as did the Model T.

Packard also had subsidiary companies,

Packard's internal publications. Many Packard sales brochures, which were given free to prospective customers, cost the company up to $50 each to produce.

Third Series Eight Model 343 All-Weather Cabriolet by Dietrich. Varnished finish was still available on special order through the Fourth Series. Price $6,574.

Third Series Eight Model 343 Coupe. Price $4,750. Multi-colored automobiles are now in vogue.

Packard Motor Car Company of New York, Packard Motor Car Company of Chicago, Packard Motor Export Corporation, and Packard Motor Sales Company.

Packard was also a leader in merchandising and service. Seminars were held constantly for salesmen and servicemen. A house organ called *The Inner Circle* came out weekly to encourage and educate the salesmen. Each year the top salesmen of the country were brought to Detroit for a Packard Master Salesmen Convention. The winner would receive a new Six of his choice.

the fantastically beautiful sales brochures for customers. These beautifully colored catalogues were the finest promotional material that has ever appeared in any industry. Today, they are collector's items not only for car enthusiasts but for historians in other fields.

During the classic era, automobile shows were anticipated by the general public as eagerly as a World Series is today. It was not uncommon for a wealthy automobile *aficionado* to go to the show and purchase a limousine for the family, a club coupe for his wife, a roadster for his son, a coupe for his daughter,

Third Series Eight Model 343 Club Sedan. Coachwork by Dietrich of Detroit. Price $5,890. The sun visor on this automobile became standard equipment on the Fourth Series Production Sedans.

The servicemen had a house organ called *The Packard Service Letter* which was used for the dissemination of factory service information and service information gained from the men in the field. *The Packard Service Letter* was published every two weeks and contained a wealth of information that is invaluable for the present-day restorer.

A third publication was the *Packard Salesman's Data Book* which was a critique on the present series car and sales suggestions. This came out once a year and was the salesman's bible.

Last but not least as a salesman's aid were

a club sedan for himself, a phaeton for his summer house, and a spare sedan for use while one of the other cars was in the garage for maintenance. The 26th National Auto Show held in January, 1926, was no exception to the rule. It was here that new motoring innovations were seen and discussed. One safety feature was better and safer vision. Through the use of narrow steel pillars better vision was achieved. Safety glass also made its debut. Stutz "shockproof" safety glass had wires running horizontally through the glass at intervals of several inches. The Rickenbacker windshield was a sandwich of transparent celluloid between two sheets of glass. Other engineering features discussed at the show were heavier crankshafts, shorter strokes, and faster engines. Hot water heaters were also introduced at the show and were enthusiastically received. Soon the purchase of hot water heaters all but killed the hot air heater industry.

The Rickenbacker sport sedan displayed was one of the high points of the show. The car was low with no running boards and had a fender-mounted spare. The radiator, wire wheels, lamps, and other exterior trim were finished in brass. The bumpers were mahogany, shaped in the form of propellers and bound in brass. The interior had beautiful plush upholstery and the hardware was gold plated.

Drake Hotel in Chicago in January, the Biltmore in Los Angeles the first week in February, and at the Palace Hotel in San Francisco the third week in February. These salons were open only to foreign chassis and body builders and American custom body builders and were by invitation only. From these displays, orders were taken for reproductions, modified reproductions, and special one-of-a-kind customs. Because of the four locations,

Third Series Eight Model 336 Phaeton. This was the last of the Big Eights to use six-lug wheels. $3,750 at Detroit.

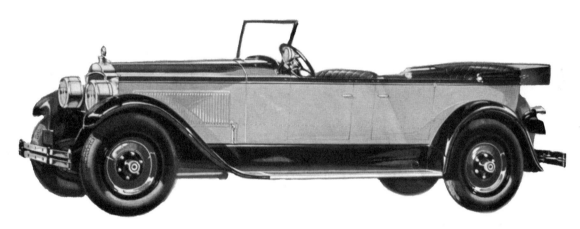

Other automotive events of the year included the acquisition of the Fisher Body Corporation by General Motors. This was a fat plum, for it gave GM control of the Fleetwood Custom Body Corporation in Fleetwood, Pennsylvania. Cadillac would now be in a position to compete with the other luxury manufacturers in the sale of custom-bodied cars. During this same year, Dr. Graham Edgar devised the octane scale for gasoline. Regular gas for 1926 was rated at 60 and premium at 74 octane.

The Custom Salon Shows which started in 1904 should never be confused with the Annual Automobile Shows which began in 1900. These salons were held at the Hotel Commodore in New York in December, the

body builders and manufacturers usually had their custom units constructed in triplicate and sometimes in quadruplicate and then shipped by rail to the salon. The cars were not shipped from salon to salon. This is why collectors who often feel that they have a one-of-a-kind classic soon discover upon research that there are at least two more copies of their prized possession. After the salon closed the manufacturer or body builder sold the cars either to private individuals or to factory branch distributors for display and eventual sale.

The Third Series Eight was introduced on August 2, 1926. Among the technical improvements offered in this series, one was to revolutionize the automotive styling industry.

1927

Fourth Series Six Model 426 Phaeton. $2,585 at Detroit. Chromium cowl band and drum parking lights were factory extras.

This technical improvement was the hypoid differential. This new low-slung trouble-free rear end made it immediately possible for designers to create low graceful body lines. The classic era of body design had now been ushered in.

Other technical improvements included the introduction of the Turbo Head, which increased the compression and turbulence in the combustion chambers. A new manifolding and carburetion system that gave increased fuel-air distribution to the cylinders was added. The cylinder bore was increased from $3\frac{3}{8}$ inches to $3\frac{1}{2}$ inches, and Nelson Bohnalite pistons were installed. The stroke remained at 5 inches. These innovations increased the Eight engine's output by 22 horsepower. A single disc clutch was also incorporated which replaced the more complicated multiple disc type. A can-type oil filter, replacing the oil rectifier, was mounted at the lower left side of the engine. For restoration purposes modern cartridge-type filters may be used to replace this filter, provided it is done in an esthetically pleasing and workmanlike manner. Air compressors mounted on the transmission were optional equipment. The hose and compressor connection were kept under the front seat for emergency tire changes. The 136″ and 143″ wheelbases were continued with six-bolt 700 x 21 disc wheels, as in the previous series.

Body changes were practically non-existent. The roof line of the closed models continued forward over the windshield, forming an integral visor. The inner lines of the radiator shell were slightly modified and the fenders became full-crowned.

Watson stabilators, which were not snubbing devices but actually shock absorbers, were optional equipment. Each stabilator consisted of a small brake which held in check the recoil force stored in the springs when they became compressed from the car's hitting a bump. The Packard-Lovejoy single action hydraulic shocks were also available.

Packard limited production on the Third Series Eight to 9,630 units.

The Fourth Series Six was also introduced on August 2, 1926, and was produced for 11 months. Its mechanical improvements included the hypoid rear end, the turbo head, new manifolding, carburetion, Bohnalite pistons, and the single disc clutch. In general, it had cleaner lines than its Third Series counterpart, but its interior appointments were identical. Small drum headlights were added. The cylinder bore had been increased from $3\frac{3}{8}$ inches to $3\frac{1}{2}$ inches. The stroke remained at 5 inches. This, plus the other new mechanical innovations, boosted the horsepower from 61 h.p. to 81 h.p. The 126″ and 133″ wheelbases were continued, as were the 650 x 23″ six-bolt disc wheels.

The Fourth Series Packard Six continued its reign of popularity. Delivery wait was still four months. The delivery wait was not by design, as in the case of the Packard Eight, but rather due to the inability of the factory to keep up with the orders. Packard dealers

Fourth Series Six Model 426 Sedan. $2,585 at Detroit. This was Packard's volume classic.

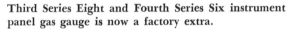

Third Series Eight and Fourth Series Six instrument panel gas gauge is now a factory extra.

clamored for more and more cars, but the factory refused to lower standards to increase production. In the eleven-month production run, 25,355 Packard Sixes were sold.

The Packard Six and Eight engines and running gear were without doubt the most visually pleasing that ever graced an American automobile. Since the American motoring public was then more mechanically inclined than it is today, engines were as much a part of a car's appointments as the upholstery. Also, since so much of the chassis was exposed, its color treatment and mechanical decor had to be integrated with the body lines.

The basic factory engine was finished in nickel, enamel, black vitreous glass, and polished aluminum. The engine block and head were green enamel. However, the shade of green varied, running the gamut from olive green to gray-green. Starter and generator end covers were also green, as well as the valve covers. The crankcase, crankcase pan, fan, oil breather, and oil filter were polished aluminum, the last three items being polished to a mirror-like finish. The starter body, generator body, vacuum tank, Bijur oiler, ignition harness conduit, steering column, splash pans and firewall were black enamel. All fuel and oil lines plus engine acorn nuts were nickeled. When restoring these items, you can authentically rechrome them, since chrome was available from the year 1925 and could be had on special order. The manifolds were cast-iron and protected with a black vitreous glass coating. Present-day stove manufacturers can restore this glass coating at minimum expense.

426 and 433 engine room.

Carburetors were usually black enamel to match the manifolds, the exceptions being the Second and Third Series Six and First and Second Series Eight (carburetor with spark ping), whose carburetors were nickeled. Chassis were usually painted to harmonize with the body colors in the Packard Eight. There was no charge for this option until July, 1929. The Sixes and small Eights, which will be introduced later, usually had black chassis. When restoring a chassis, it is best to refinish as outlined here (particularly if you have a production-bodied classic) to avoid arguments with the uninitiated.

For the record, there are show chassis, special-order chassis, and custom-bodied chassis that deviate. When one of these rare deviations are found, you must find out from a

recognized authority the answer to this one simple question: were the modifications made prior to delivery to the first owner or were they made after delivery? If the modifications were made by the manufacturer or body builder prior to delivery to the first owner, you may restore it as found. A letter of verification should also be obtained testifying to this. If the modification is in doubt as to time, or known to be done after delivery to the first owner, it is a bastardization, and engine and chassis must be redone to conform with the factory standard. To violate this basic tenet will result in loss of points in open competition and, more important, a financial loss in the sale of the classic if disposal is ever necessary.

Now, how do show chassis, custom-bodied

chassis, and special-order chassis differ? The first and most obvious difference is in the use of chrome. Any and all of the following were often chromed—water jacket cover, valve covers, Bijur oiler, ignition harness conduit, fuse block, water outlets, generator and started covers and inspection plugs, and, on the chassis, king pin dust covers, transmissions and differential cover plates, and steering columns. The

426 and 433 used the 650 x 23 tire and wheel.

aluminum crankcase was often highly polished to a mirror-like finish. There is also one engine of record done by the factory that had a damascened aluminum crankcase. Engine color, however, was green. A repeat word of caution: a letter of authenticity from a recognized source should be obtained before restoring a suspected special chassis.

The accessories that could be purchased for the Packard in 1926 ran to well over one hundred items and was illustrated in a thirty-one page brochure. Trunks, of course, were the most popular and the most needed. The second most popular item was the Packard Deluxe Emblem which symbolized speed, grace, and power. Dubbed the Flying Lady by Packard owners, it was made of Britannia metal and was triple silver plated. A triple-lensed tail light, which consisted of a red, white, and green lens, was also available. Cowl parking lights and driving lights called Saf-De-Lites were popular. Leather spring covers were also in demand. These accessories to modern-day collectors are the icing on the cake and very much in demand.

Author and his 443 Custom Phaeton, cost at Detroit
$3,875. Standard factory equipment included side
mounts and chassis in color.

3

The Fourth Series Eight and the Fifth Series Six

The 27th National Automobile Show held in January, 1927, saw the introduction of more small cars. Chevrolet had made such inroads into the Model T sales that other manufacturers thought the time was right to follow suit. The new small car offerings included the Erksine by Studebaker, the Whippet by Willys, the little Marmon, and the Jordan Little Playboy. In 1927 there was also introduced the LaSalle V-8 and the famous Model A Ford.

Graham-Paige Motors Corporation succeeded Paige-Detroit Motor Car Company and Studebaker celebrated its Diamond Jubilee. The automobile business was booming. General Motors paid $134,836,081 in dividends, Chrysler paid $10,000,000 and Packard $7,195,363. The truck manufacturers were also busy improving their product. Mack adopted vacuum boosted four-wheel brakes. Concrete mixers mounted on White heavy-duty trucks appeared on the Pacific Coast. The Fageol brothers organized the Twin Coach Company.

There also occurred at this time a portent of the future; Carl Breer began the study of aerodynamics in relation to automobile body design, which led to the "Airflow" design and uni-frame type of body and chassis construction. E. M. Frazer developed an electric drive with no gearshift. Lockheed (Malcolm Loughead) introduced an internal expanding hydraulic brake system.

To the motor-minded American people, the first showing of the Packard 443 on July 1, 1927, was a real event. This Big Eight came in one wheelbase (143″) and two models, Standard and Custom. The Custom models, which were introduced on January 3, 1928, would normally have been a new series. However, management had decided that to avoid any possible merchandising confusion, only one series at a time would be introduced, starting August 1, 1928. As a result, there is no Fifth Series Big Eight. In addition to the Custom line being introduced, a rumble seat coupe and convertible coupe also made their debut on January 3, 1928.

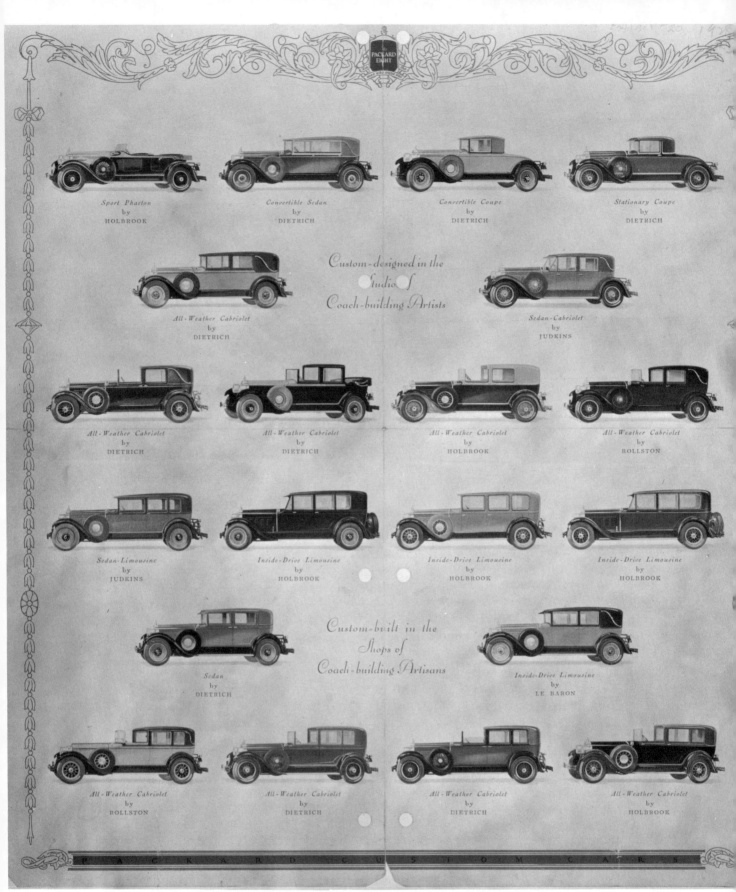

Sport Phaeton
by
HOLBROOK

Convertible Sedan
by
DIETRICH

Convertible Coupe
by
DIETRICH

Stationary Coupe
by
DIETRICH

Custom-designed in the Studio of Coach-building Artists

All-Weather Cabriolet
by
DIETRICH

Sedan-Cabriolet
by
JUDKINS

All-Weather Cabriolet
by
DIETRICH

All-Weather Cabriolet
by
DIETRICH

All-Weather Cabriolet
by
HOLBROOK

All-Weather Cabriolet
by
ROLLSTON

Sedan-Limousine
by
JUDKINS

Inside-Drive Limousine
by
HOLBROOK

Inside-Drive Limousine
by
HOLBROOK

Inside-Drive Limousine
by
HOLBROOK

Custom-built in the Shops of Coach-building Artisans

Sedan
by
DIETRICH

Inside-Drive Limousine
by
LE BARON

All-Weather Cabriolet
by
ROLLSTON

All-Weather Cabriolet
by
DIETRICH

All-Weather Cabriolet
by
DIETRICH

All-Weather Cabriolet
by
HOLBROOK

PACKARD CUSTOM CARS

Examples of custom coachwork on the 443 chassis.

Fourth Series Eight Model 443 Convertible Sedan by
Dietrich. Cost at Detroit $7,409. Wire wheels were
$110.00 extra.

Fourth Series Eight Model 443 Roadster. Cost at
Detroit $3,975. Spotlight was standard equipment on
the roadster, touring, and phaeton.

Fourth Series Eight Model 443 Four-Passenger Coupe. Cost at Detroit $4,450. Metal tire covers were introduced on this series.

The Standard models, which were the first introduced, can be identified by a hard-maple steering wheel and a choke and spark unit mounted above the dash. The Custom models had slightly modified drum headlights, a new type headlight and parking light lens, a hard rubber steering wheel, and the choke and spark controls were part of the instrument panel. Also, chrome was introduced on these later models. New engineering features for the 443 included a new cylinder lubrication system. Oil was sprayed in the cylinders automatically when the engine was choked. This protected the cylinder walls from being scuffed, and compression was maintained when starting the engine cold. Twin ignition coils were added for fast starting and high speed driving. The lighting switch appeared on the steering wheel in place of the spark lever for the first time in the 443. Performance-wise, the 443 was extremely agile, fast handling and powerful. The open cars sported a 4 to 1 gear ratio which made them excellent for cruising at high speeds. The closed cars had a gear ratio of $4\frac{1}{3}$ to 1. The 443 was fitted with eight-lug 700 x 20 wheels, and fender-mounted spares were standard equipment. Wire wheels became an option.

Distinctive innovations on these models included doors instead of louvers in the hood and a three-lensed tail light which incorporated a back-up light. On the open models, a

Fifth Series Six Model 526 Convertible Coupe. Cost at Detroit $3,350. This model was introduced as a production body style January 1, 1928.

Fifth Series Six Model 533 Sedan. Cost at Detroit $2,685. This was Packard's last six-cylinder automobile until the introduction of the 110 Series in 1937.

new one-piece swinging-type windshield with a walnut finished panel between it and the cowl made its appearance. The instruments were clustered in an embossed center panel.

The 443 production models were the most individually stylized Classics. It is the exception rather than the rule that there are any two alike. There were three distinct reasons for this. First, since there was a four-month delivery wait, most customers took advantage of the situation and selected their own body and chassis colors, upholstery, and accessories to match their individual tastes. Second, since Packard would allow any color and any upholstery material at no additional charge, it was like ordering a custom car at no additional cost. Lastly, those cars which might have found their way to a show room floor without a customer waiting were usually sporting four-tone color combinations. All black cars accounted for only 6 per cent of the 443 production.

The 443 can also be credited with the rise in popularity of the custom body, for it was this car that embodied the long, sleek lines that added so much to Packard's beauty. The public as well as the Custom Body Builders wanted this chassis for their custom creations. The 443 catalogue offered twenty semi-custom creations by Holbrook, Dietrich, Judkins, Rollston, and LeBaron. For one-of-a-kind bodies, the builders listed above plus Brewster,

Derham, Murphy, Earl C. Anthony, Waterhouse, Biddle and Smart, Phillips, Brunn, and a raft of foreign body builders stood ready to execute at customer's slightest wish. This was the beginning of a long procession of triumphs in the Concours D'Elegance in Europe for Packard. It was also the 443 that made coast-to-coast journeys prosaic, uneventful trips. It brought the use of the motor car for long trips into popular favor.

The Fifth Series Six, which also was introduced on July 1, 1927, represented the end of Packard Six production. This series came in two wheelbases, 126″ and 133″. The 526 had five different body styles and the 533 consisted of seven body styles. These two models represented many refinements over the previous Packard Sixes, but perhaps the greatest distinction of this series was in appearance. The cars of this series were hailed as America's most beautiful automobiles and had a sales record to prove it. There were 41,750 units delivered, an increase of 16,415 over the previous Fourth Series Six sales. Mechanical improvements included the cylinder lubrication system and an oil filter. In many respects, it was a miniature 443. 650 x 20 six-lug wheels were added to give it a lower look. Optional

Fourth Series Eight. Note the twin coil ignition system and priming cups.

Fourth Series headlight and hood louvers.

equipment included wood or wire wheels, fender mounted spares, cowl lights, hood doors (three per side) instead of louvers, and special colors. Production ended on August 1, 1928, after a 13-month production run.

The Fourth Series Eight and the Fifth Series Six would be the last series to have priming cups on the cylinder head. Gas had reached a quality and distribution nationally that made priming cups obsolete. The outside motometer, cowl lamps, drum headlights, and painted bumpers would also disappear. It was also the last Series for which a varnish-finished body was available.

The Annual financial report for the period

ending August 31, 1927, was unequivocal evidence that the plan embarked upon by Packard's management three years earlier was a resounding success. Basically, the plan was to enter the luxury automotive market as a quantity producer with the Packard Six. The Eight, on the other hand, was purposely held to 500 units per month and no attempt was made to get it to the public at a price. This 500 unit figure had remained constant since the Eight was first introduced in 1923. To illustrate the success of this plan, the figures for 1925–1927 are compared with the corresponding figures for the preceding nine years.

Fourth and Fifth Series instrument panel. Note fluid level gas gauge.

Fourth Series Cowl Parking light.

	3 Years 1925-1927	9 Years 1916-1924
Earnings	39,778,166	39,449,824
Average Earnings per year	13,259,722	4,383,314
Percent of earnings to sales	18.9	9.8
Dividends paid—cash	22,006,770	18,101,941
Plant Expenditures	20,623,723	36,268,006
Percent of earnings to Plant investment	57	36.5
Percent of earnings to invested capital	29	11

Management's next three year plan was to replace the Six with a Standard Eight. They knew that soon there would be no place for a six-cylinder car in the luxury market. The timing would be perfect. Also on the drawing boards was a speedster.

Packard now outsold Cadillac 3 to 1. It was the undisputed leader in the prestige field. In every corner of the earth it was recognized as the symbol of wealth and success. Management had seen to it that there was no com-

Fourth and Fifth Series tail light.

promise with quality for the purpose of underselling.

The famous Packard proving ground was completed in Utica, Michigan. It covered 500 acres, and contained in addition to sand traps and rough test roads the world's fastest concrete track for endurance and speed tests. Packard now had the finest craftsmen, ultra-modern plant facilities and the best proving grounds in the world to insure a quality motor car. Their engineering labs were ahead in metallurgy, precision tools, and in an advanced development program. It was an unbeatable combination.

Paint, like the automobile, made rapid technological improvements during the Classic era. In 1925 pyroxylin finishes (synthetic lacquers) were invented. Opalescent paint was introduced in November, 1927, at the Custom Salon. It appeared on several 1928 Fleetwood-bodied Cadillacs. The catalogue given out at the show verifies this date. This early iridescent paint was made from a fish scale base. In 1929 metallic paints were introduced to the public by E. I. Dupont via Fleetwood-bodied Cadillacs.

The retired paint superintendent of Fleetwood relates the following story of how E. I. Dupont got into metallic paints. The story may not be completely accurate but is very interesting. Cadillac commissioned Fleetwood to build three channel-maroon and Paris-gray formal bodies for the November, 1928, Custom Salon. Fleetwood in turn ordered the special maroon paint from Dupont. Dupont made the small special batch and delivered it to Fleetwood. Time being of the essence, the paint was immediately applied to these three rush custom orders. The paint superintendent became furious, for there before him lay three beautiful metallic-maroon bodies. His first order was "get me that Dupont salesman," and his second order was "start removing the paint from those bodies." A crowd of Dupont people arrived on the scene immediately. A quick discussion

Fourth Series 700 x 20 tire and wheel. The Fifth series uses a smaller version, 650 x 20 tire and wheel.

followed and the following facts came out. In crushing the japan, the basic paint pigment, the steel balls in the crushing operation had flaked, sprinkling the red japan with metallic particles. Two of the bodies were repainted, but due to the shortness of time the third was not repainted and brought much favorable comment at the Custom Show.

However, metallic paint did not come into general use until 1932 because of cost and difficulty in applying it. By 1931, nearly every color and shade of paint that now appears on today's automobiles was available. In fact, there were colors then that are not used today because of changes in taste. The real difference in the paint of the Classic era and the paint of today was durability and resistance to fading. It was because the former colors did not keep their true color many classic enthusiasts think that all color was lifeless and of drab hues. Nothing could be farther from the truth.

In Packard, as in all other prestige makes of this era, the color and color scheme was a personal selection. Certainly there were factory-suggested colors, but in the final analysis the luxury car was tailored to the tastes of the

individual buyer and not to a factory production schedule. When repainting a classic, it is impossible to paint it an inauthentic color (with certain rare exceptions or the use of acrylic laqueurs). One word of caution when restoring: the use of enamel paint on a classic that was originally lacquered will result in a mandatory loss of points in competition and, more important, seriously hurt the car's resale value. Some organizations feel so strongly against enamel that if enamel is used on a classic that was originally enameled, it must be of the same quality as the original, which is next to impossible to duplicate. The reasons behind this are extremely sound. Classics when new were known for their lustrous depth of finish. This finish could be compared with the reflection of a clear crystal pool of water. Modern enamels and application techniques leave a classic with a high shine but no lustrous depth of finish. To add insult to injury, the more you polish them the faster the shine disappears. On the other hand, the more you rub lacquers, the more beautiful they become. To get depth of finish, one should apply six-

Fourth and Fifth Series were the last series to use the outside motor meter. 50,000 Packards were sold in the calendar year of 1928.

teen light, consecutive coats and then compound down to eight and finish with a clean lamb's wool buff. A sprinkling of corn starch on the last buffing will prevent swirls or lines in the paint. General collision shops, however, are not set up to do this type of perfection painting.

Color is a wonderful tool and, used carefully, will make a beautiful classic even more beautiful. Color will also affect the competition scores and the resale value of a classic. In eleven years of judged competition, it has been shown that a black car will receive fewer points than a non-black car of identical make and body style. Yet, the judging forms have no category for color preference! It is also suggested to the restorer that the use of metallic paint on pre-1932 production classics be avoided, for the same reason.

Some of the judges' preference can probably be explained by the fact that over the past half century the color of cars has reflected the economic condition of the country. When we are prosperous, the cars are colorful. During times of war and economic depression, the colors are somber.

4

The Sixth Series

In January, 1928, the 28th Automobile Show opened in New York City. The trend to straight-8 engines continued. The trend had been sparked earlier in the decade by Duesenberg and Packard. Also, with better gas available, higher compression engines were offered.

Cadillac offered safety plate glass and Ford offered shatterproof glass as standard equipment. Safety glass was an English development which was quickly adopted by the American manufacturers. The big problem with early safety glass was that it turned yellow quite readily due to the plastic sandwich material drying out. It was not until 1935 that the glass industry had perfected a non-yellowing plastic that would remain pliable. In restoring a classic, yellow safety glass or plate glass must be replaced with new safety glass. Classics without safety glass are barred from all national club meets.

Nineteen twenty-eight was also a big year for transmissions. Ford gave up the planetary transmission, Graham Paige equipped most of its models with four-speed transmissions, and

Cadillac introduced a Synchromesh transmission.

In the low price field, Ford had their new Model A. Chevrolet, not to be outdone, switched from a four-cylinder to a six-cylinder engine. Chrysler introduced the Plymouth, and a new automotive term was coined—"The Low Price Three."

Chrysler was really on the move in 1928. In addition to the Plymouth, Chrysler introduced at the show a new medium-priced entry in the form of the DeSoto. In July of 1928, Chrysler purchased Dodge Brothers. In later years, Chrysler, Ford, and General Motors would become the "Big Three" and dominate the automotive scene.

Other events of the year included Buick celebrating its Silver Anniversary. David Buick, founder of the firm, is also credited with the porcelain bathtub, which gave him the capital to enter the automotive business. Studebaker, one of America's oldest vehicle builders, purchased control of Pierce Arrow, a manufacturer of luxury classics.

Sixth Series Standard Eight Model 626 Five-Passenger Sedan. Packard's first small eight. Cowl lights were an option on this model. Cost at Detroit $2,435.

Sixth Series Standard Eight Model 633 Four-Passenger Coupe. Cost at Detroit $2,735. Thermostatic radiator shutters and Packard's coat-of-arms were introduced on this series.

Packard introduced the Sixth Series on August 1, 1928. The prospective customer had his choice of five basic models. The Standard Eight 626 and 633, the Speedster Eight 626, the Custom Eight 640, and the Deluxe Eight 645. The least expensive Standard Eight sedan sold for $2,275 f.o.b. Detroit. This was a sizeable price when you consider the Model A roadster sold for $435 f.o.b. The Sixth Series Standard Eight represented Packard's change from six- to eight-cylinder engines for its smaller classics. There were ten distinct body types mounted on the Standard Eight chassis. The wheelbases of these two chassis were 126½″ and 133½″. The first Standard Eights had a side mounted water pump to save space between the fan and radiator. The pump proved very unsatisfactory and a conventional type pump was installed after two months of production. The Standard Eight was extremely popular with the rising young executive and as a second car for the now well-to-do middle income family.

The Speedster Eight was designed as a personal sports car. In today's car market, a personal sports car is old hat, but in 1928 it was a revolutionary concept. The Speedster Eight came in a phaeton and roadster body style, and the basic construction of the speedster consisted of the following:

Sixth Series Standard Eight Model 633 Roadster. Cost
at Detroit $2,535. Standard eight can be identified by
louvered hood. However, a three-door hood was available at extra cost.

1. 126½″ Wheelbase.
2. Big Eight engine with high compression
   head and high lift camshaft.
3. Big Eight transmission and 3.31 to 1
   differential.
4. Special phaeton and roadster body with
   rear mounted spare.
5. Standard Eight hardware.

Seventy Speedster Series cars were sold. Only
one has been found and restored.

The 640 Custom Eight was introduced on
August 1, 1928. In had a new 140″ wheelbase.
For the most part, the bodies were identical to
the Fourth Series 443 with the exception of
the new Dietrich semi-customs that were
added to the line thirty days later. For the

first few months of production the open cars
also had the stationary swinging-type windshield that had been introduced in the 443.
Later, a completely folding windshield made
its appearance. The Sixth Series exemplifies
what every classic Packard owner knows: not
all models in a particular series are the same.
Packard in this respect is much like the Rolls
Royce. If a new engineering feature was developed, it would often go right into the
present series rather than wait for a new
model. To further complicate series identification, the converse of the above occurred. If they
had a large supply of parts at introduction
time, they would continue to use them on the
new series until the supply was exhausted.
This was a standard operating procedure in
the manufacture of luxury classics.

Added to this complexity of series identification is one more factor which causes enthusiasts to argue far into the night. Packard

Sixth Series Eight Model 645 Club Sedan. Cost at Detroit $5,785. An identifying feature of the 645 is the trunk rack with vertical cross bars.

was very proud of its evolutionary versus revolutionary changes and, therefore, they encouraged their customers to bring back their older series Packard and have it brought up-to-date. This ran the gamut from having current headlights added, current fenders and radiator shells installed, to engine modifications. In open competition and for good resale value, it is incumbent on the present owner to convert his car's equipment back to the original. Any deviation from the Series must be confirmed by an official letter from a known authority that the changes were made prior to delivery to the first customer or were made during that current series production.

One month after the introduction of the 640 Custom Eight, the 645 Deluxe Eight made its debut. This chassis had a choice of eight factory bodies and thirteen semi-custom bodies. Of the semi-customs, four were by Dietrich, seven were by LeBaron, and two by Rollston. The best selling semi-custom was the dual cowl phaeton by Dietrich, and the most admired was the expensive convertible sedan by Dietrich.

Ray Dietrich had been spirited away from New York and his partnership in LeBaron in 1925. Dietrich Incorporated was located on Clay Avenue in Detroit, and in 1928 was the

Sixth Series Eight Model 645 Convertible Victoria. Cost at Detroit $7,064. The Big Eights are easily identified by the round jewel in the rear of the headlight. At night these indicate high and low beam. By now Dietrich had become the top producer of custom bodies.

Sixth Series Eight Model 640 Sedan (early). Cost at Detroit $3,750. Early 640 bodies can be identified by belt line, location of door handles, and windshield visor.

biggest supplier of custom and semi-custom bodies to the luxury car manufacturers. Ray was also a design consultant to P.M.C. His styling concepts influenced Packard production design during the early thirties more than those of any other single individual. Ray's semi-custom Sixth Series designs became the factory production styling of the Seventh and Eight Series.

Styling and mechanical innovations that identify the Sixth Series are as follows:

1. Packard family crest carried on the radiator.
2. Thermostatically controlled radiator shutters.
3. Cone-type headlights with matching cowl parking lights. The big Eight has a round green jewel in each headlight to indicate high or low beam.
4. The instruments on the dash board are spread out with the clock on the right hand side. A heat gauge has been added.
5. Single coil ignition system.
6. Oil capacity gauge on left side of the engine.
7. External fuse block on firewall to protect wiring system.
8. Seven optional gear ratios including a 3.31 to 1 for the speedster and the 640 and 645 Series.

Sixth Series Eight Model 640 Sedan (late). Cost at Detroit $3,750. Packard introduced a new line of bodies during the Sixth Series. The reason for this was that the Fourth and Fifth Series bodies were used on Sixth Series chassis until the stock was exhausted.

9. New Houdaille shocks are installed on the axle with shock arms mounted to frame.

10. Trunnion block attached to rear of right front spring to eliminate road shimmy and shock transmission to steering column. This trunnion block consisted of four coil springs mounted in a block that is riveted to the frame and connected to the spring shackle. This device can be found on some late 443

The number of Packard accessories continued to mount. You could order just about anything. There were fat round "Jumbo" bumpers at $100 per pair, and three different types of stoneshields at $27.50 each—the basket weave, the box mesh, and the vertical bar type. You could have a right-hand tail light assembly and an assortment·of metal and cloth tire covers. The no-charge options of the 443 Series were curtailed. Six wheels and a luggage rack were now $45 extra. Six wire wheels were

Sixth Series Eight Model 640 Roadster. Cost at Detroit $3,175. Wire wheels were $80.00 extra and the wooden artillery wheels were $102.00 extra.

Series. The trunnion block was invented by a Frenchman and the right to its exclusive use was purchased by Packard.

11. Bumpers are all chrome. A deluxe edition was mounted on the 640 and 645.

12. Radiator filler is wider and lower with detachable radiator cap.

$80 additional and wood wheels were $102 more. An onyx horn button was $1.85, and an onyx gear shift knob was $2.50. A monogrammed lap robe was $115.

In December, 1928, the custom salon was held in New York City. There was much money in the economy and, therefore, the attendance was unusually heavy. The foreign entries were fabulous and their coachwork was the best that European and American designers had to offer. The one subtle point of the show that could not be denied was the fact that the American luxury car had taken over the automotive leadership of the world. The American Luxury cars now excelled their European cousins in mechanical performance, roadability, and styling. This trend was accelerated by the desire of wealthy owners and their wives to drive their own classics.

The most popular body style at the salons was that of the convertible sedans, and the most popular convertible sedan was designed and built by Dietrich. It was displayed on many American and European chassis. The

From these salons, a second observation was made by the automotive writers; Packard and Cadillac were the leaders in color styling, with Packard having the edge on Cadillac.

Packard's custom catalogue given out at the Show contained seventeen custom bodies and only one was all black. The Cadillac custom catalogue had twelve semi-custom bodies and not one was black. The economy was bright and so were the colors of even the most formal body styles.

Sixth Series Eight Model 640 Custom Roadster by Dietrich. Cost at Detroit $4,675. The side mounts are now $240 extra. Forerunner of the Seventh Series production roadster.

Lincoln convertible sedan by Dietrich, which was shown at the New York show, had black fenders and undercarriage with a royal-blue body. The wire wheels and pin striping were red. The Packard convertible sedan by Dietrich at the Hotel Drake Salon had pheasant green fenders and undercarriage with a partridge cream body. Disk wheels and pin striping were green. Cadillac's Fleetwood entries were three formal town cars. Two were Paris gray and channel maroon. The third was Paris gray and metallic maroon (discussed in Chapter 3).

Most of the body builders now owned their own plating departments and, therefore, the use of chrome on the engine components and chassis was prominent on these custom cars.

The Packard crest, which was the family coat of arms, first appeared on the Sixth Series automobiles. This crest was placed on the famous Packard radiator in memory of James and William Packard who had founded the company and had built the first Packard literally with their own hands. This family crest and coat of arms goes back to the Middle Ages. In the language of ancient heraldry the crest was described as follows, "Gules a cross lozengy between four roses or. A pelican in her piety." In modern terminology this translates as follows: a field of crimson, a cross of diamonds between four yellow roses, and a pelican representing loyalty to family. The pelican is plucking blood from her breast to feed her open-mouthed brood. The family crest was

Sixth Series Eight chassis. The "Luxury Market" in 1929 represented only 10 per cent of all automotive production. Packard earnings reached $25,000,000.

Sixth Series trade marks. Packard stock splits 5 to 1 in ·1929. The 107,000 out-standing shareholders make it the second most widely owned automobile stock (G. M. is first).

brought to America in 1638 by Samuel Packard on the good ship *Diligent* from Windham, England.

The radiator crests were made for Packard by Auld Company of Columbus and the Fox Company of Cincinnati. The crests differ from Series to Series for two reasons: Packard's use of two suppliers and the need for replacing the dies when they wore out. As a result of these differences in crests, they have become sought after by emblem collectors. The unfortunate by-product of this interest is that classic car owners have difficulty in finding a replacement medallion for their classic. The dies having been destroyed for scrap during World War II makes it doubly difficult to find a replacement medallion. Fortunately, if a damaged medallion is found, it can be restored through a complicated process. However, this restoration should not be entrusted to amateurs and low-price foreign firms. The process is an art and the crests are ·in the category of fine jewelry.

The differences in medallions are:

under cloisonne. Bar and knotted rope relief under pelican.

Sixth Series	Flowing plumage encrusted with cloisonne. Shield has mottled filigree background
Seventh Series	Flowing raised plumage (very delicate). Shield has mottled filigree under the cloisonne. Bar and knotted rope relief under pelican. Smaller helmet.
Eighth Series #1	Heavy flowing plumage. Shield has mottled filigree under cloisonne. Shield heavier with rounded bottom. Bar and coarse woven rope under pelican.

Eighth Series #2	Flowing plumage with ends curving inward. Shield is delicate with vertically lined filigree under cloisonne. Bar and fine woven rope under pelican.
Ninth Series	Heavy flowing plumage with ends curving inward. Shield is squat with vertical lined filigree pattern under cloisonne. Four large roses in crest. Large helmet. Bar and fine woven rope under pelican.
Tenth to Seventeenth Series	Large crest used only on Packard Twelve luggage racks and Tenth and Eleventh Series instrument panels. Small crest on oval appears with model designation on radiator of Ninth Series Twin Six and Tenth through Fifteenth Series. Heavy flowing plumage with ends curving inward. Shield delicate with vertically lined filigree under cloisonne. Small helmet. Bar and heavy woven rope under pelican.

All crests were plated in heavy gold with the exception of the tenth and Eleventh Series instrument panel crests. They were silver-plated. All ovals consisted of black cloisonne edged in chrome with the exception of some Eighth Series stoneshield ovals that had satin chrome instead of cloisonne. Ovals have slight differences in art work but are not related to Series.

Stoneshield medallions often differ from the radiator medallions for the same Series. Stoneshields were made by several Packard suppliers and they ordered their medallions direct from Auld or Fox. Depending upon the time the medallion order was placed, they might receive the current medallions or the new medallions for the Series yet to be produced. For example, the stoneshield for the 443 Custom Models, which were introduced six months prior to the Sixth Series, carry a Sixth Series medallion. The 443 radiator shell has no medallion. Some of the Eighth Series stoneshields carry a Ninth Series crest and Ninth Series stoneshields have no provision for a crest. One word of caution: the crest characteristics by Series is to be used only as an information guide, not as a positive rule for authenticity. There will always be exceptions because luxury car manufacturers would continue to use up a large supply of current parts in their new models.

What is cloisonne? It is a surface decoration in fired enamel. The designs are produced by binding wire fillets called cloisons to make a form. Enamel paste is then placed between the wire fillets and fired. This art form goes back to the ancient Egyptians and Assyrians. Unfortunately, the glass-making techniques of this era have been lost to the world. Their glass and vitreous enamel was practically shatterproof. The tempered glass of today is just beginning to approach the glass of this ancient civilization.

From the dawn of history, the Chinese also were active in cloisonne. Later the Romans and Greeks encrusted their silver and gold objects with cloisonne. This method of rekindling of fired enamel in Greece and Rome

Sixth Series Instrument Panel. Note speedometer on left side.

was probably a result of the Western world's contact with China in the 4th and 5th Century, B.C.

When the engraving art was sufficiently ad-

Sixth Series wooden artillery wheel, 640—700 x 20

vanced, an offshoot of cloisonne was developed and called Champlene. Instead of using wire fillets for the form, the form was engraved and then the depressions were filled with paste enamel and fired. However, the generic term for both processes is cloisonne.

The base metal used in striking automobile medallions is oriedie. The metal consists of 87.25 per cent copper, 11.50 per cent zinc, 1.25 per cent tin, and is reddish gold in color. It has a high affinity for cloisonne and is considerably less expensive than silver and gold. The medallion is then filled with enamel paste and then fired at a very high temperature. White and black enamel are opaque, and the greens, blues, and reds are transparent if fired at the proper critical temperature. The medallion is then plated.

The restoration of a medallion involves all of the above plus the preparation of stripping the old plating and removing the shattered vitreous enamel by means of an acid bath.

5

The Seventh Series

Public enthusiasm for new models had reached such proportions that most Manhattan hotel lobbies were filled with new car displays during the 1929 National Automobile Show which was held in January. Highlights of the show were bigger and more luxurious classics, and there was also a larger selection of medium-priced models.

In the classic field, the big Duesenberg J and the front-wheel-drive Cord made their debut. The Sixth Series Packard had been in production for five months, so most of its display consisted of fabulous semi-customs. Cadillac was much in the same position, since their introduction dates did not coincide with the motor shows either. Franklin introduced the le Pirate model with concealed running boards under the door.

The medium price field had several new entrants. Oldsmobile introduced the Viking V-8 and Buick offered the Marquette. Nash offered an eight-cylinder engine for the first time and Chrysler adopted the down-draft carburetor.

Accessory-wise, tail lamps on both sides were introduced and radios were offered as optional equipment on many automobiles.

When the year ended, motor vehicle production had broken all previous records. Output totaled 5,337,087 units. This figure would not be exceeded until 1949. Ninety per cent of this total output were closed models.

Wherever highways existed in 1930 and motor cars were known, the name Packard symbolized but one thing, the prestige leader of the world. There were many marques more expensive than Packard but none were more desired. In fact, Packard sales accounted for· 50 per cent of all prestige automobiles sold throughout the world.

Packards were to be found in the garages of most royal families and in the embassy garages of most foreign officials here and abroad. Outside the United States, Packard is pronounced Pack-CARD and up until the fifties it was the best-known American marque. Packard was the official royal automobile of Belgium, Egypt, India, Japan, Norway,

Seventh Series Standard Eight Model 726 Sedan. Price at Detroit $2,485. Fender parking lights were optional at extra cost.

Seventh Series Standard Eight Model 733 Roadster. Price at Detroit $2,425. This model carried a 650 x 20 tire and a seven-lug wheel, also half-oval bumper bars. Special equipment fender lamps, deluxe emblem, and side mount mirrors. Although not listed in the accessory catalogue the running board spot-light could be purchased from the dealer.

Seventh Series Big Eight Model 734 Speedster Phaeton. Price at Detroit $5,200. Note the non-folding windshield.

bought armored versions for happy motoring around the restless natives.

In the United States, Packards resided in the White House garage for most of the first half-century. White Steamers first arrived in 1909, followed by a Packard and a Pierce Arrow. By 1913 all six cars in the inaugural parade were Packards. President Taft and President-Elect Woodrow Wilson rode in a carriage. It wasn't until 1921 that a President-Elect rode in an automobile to his inauguration. This first went to Warren G. Harding in a Packard Twin Six. Seven Packards were in the White House garage through the term of Coolidge. Hoover's administration added two and F.D.R. added nine. During Truman's administration, the classic Packards were replaced with four new Packards and two new Lincolns. One of the Lincolns was built by Ray Dietrich, Inc., in Kalamazoo, Michigan. After a long absence, Ray was having another go at the custom body business.

The Secret Service continued to use several V-16 Cadillacs purchased in 1938. New V-8 engines had been installed for reliability. The decision to keep them was based on the fact that they had running boards for the Secret Service men to ride on.

Packard phaetons and touring cars were used as high-speed pursuit cars by state and local police. Since police radios were still in their infancy, speed was essential. Movie stars and industrialists bought Packards by the baker's dozen and hospitals and funeral parlors bought Packards and fitted them with exquisitely ornate ambulance and hearse bodies.

The mighty Seventh Series which had made

Romania, Saudi Arabia, Spain, Sweden, and Yugoslavia and in the constitutional governments of Chile, El Salvador, and Mexico. Just a partial list of Packard's royal owners would include King Alexander of Yugoslavia, King Farouk of Egypt, King Alfonso of Spain, King Al-Faisal of Saudi Arabia, the late Queen Marie of Romania, and Queen Astrid of Belgium. Prince Eugene deLigne of Belgium in 1931 drove two 740 Packards from Brussels to the Belgian Congo via the Sahara desert. The return trip was made via Juba, Khartoum, Luxor, Cairo, and Alexandria. The Maharaja of Gawilor used his Packard for tiger hunts.

By 1910 there were forty-eight Packards in France. Many Packards were among the cars used to transport troops from Paris to the battle of the Marne. The war lords of China

Seventh Series Big 8 Model 734 Speedster Victoria. Price at Detroit $6,000. Note the hood hardware.

Seventh Series Big 8 Model 734 Boat Tail Speedster. Price at Detroit $5,210.

Seventh Series Big 8 Model 740 Custom Phaeton. Price at Detroit $3,190. Seventh Series Big Eights can be identified by the large half-oval bumper bars, which are mounted with the cast tapered bumperettes.

its debut in August, 1929, came in four series and five wheelbases. There was the Std. 8 (126½″ and 133½″ wheelbase), the hot Speedster 8 (134½″ wheelbase), the Custom 8 (140½″ wheelbase), and the Deluxe 8 (145½″ wheelbase).

The Standard Eight was the bread and butter classic of the Packard line. The shortest wheelbase (126½″) would hereafter have only one four-door sedan body available. The obvious reason for this was that through standardization comes volume, and with volume, a lower price. However, lower price is relative and in no way reflects poor quality. You could still buy five Model A sedans for the price paid for a 726 Packard Sedan. There were ten bodies offered on the 733 chassis, including a glamourous phaeton. This Standard Eight was extremely popular with all ages and both sexes. It had gained this popularity because of its light handling qualities and peppy performance. Its prestige was not tarnished in the slightest by comparison with its larger and more powerful family members. Its quality, construction, and reliability gave it a time-honored place in the "Halls of Classic Immortality."

The 734 Speedster Series was now a full line of cars. The specially designed short, lower, and narrow bodies were built in Packard's

The Seventh Series panel has been re-designed to incorporate two glove compartments and a reading light. Burled walnut finish and ivory color pull handles make their appearance. Bezels are heavier and "pull daily" has been added to the chassis lubrication handle.

Seventh Series Big Eight engine compartment. This is the last series that used the integral intake exhaust system and the vacuum tank. Northeast ignition systems were used on the Sixth through the Eleventh Series inclusive.

own new custom body shop located right on the plant site. These specially built speedster bodies and the individual customs on the longer chassis were built in this shop; they carry a black and red body plate on the lower right cowl.

The Speedster Series used 745 components in conjunction with its own specially designed bodies. The open speedster had a solid brass non-folding windshield without wind wings, just like its Sixth Series predecessor. In the engine room, one saw a glimpse of the future. It carried an engine which was to become standard equipment in the 840 and 845 series cars. Its exhaust manifold was a separate unit mounted at 45°, and finned. It boasted a large vacuum booster in conjunction with a double-sized Detroit Lubricator carburetor. The brake drums were finned and it had an optional 3.31 to 1 or 4 to 1 gear ratio. As a personal sports car it was a complete success. However, only one hundred fifty cars were sold, which would indicate that the Packard clientele wanted posh cars. This, coupled with a tightening money situation after the crash, is why Packard management discontinued the Speedster.

The 740 and 745 introduced on August 20, 1929, were the flagships of the Seventh Series

fleet. The best production and most of the custom bodies appeared on these chassis. A summary of the principal changes, listed below, indicate that Packard, like Rolls Royce, continued to improve its product, and yet to the casual observer the car retained its distinctive and ageless classic line.

The wheelbase has been lengthened a half inch. Frame side members had been changed to provide for a deeper seat cushion and a larger gas tank (25 gallons for the 726-33-40 and 28 gallons for the 745). The front cross member had been changed to provide more clearance for the vibration damper and fan pulley. The rear intermediate cross channel had been redesigned to obtain greater rigidity. The steering gear mounting holes had been slotted to provide adjustment of the steering gear with relation to the front seat. New front and rear motor brackets had been designed for model 745, made necessary by the motor's having been moved back five inches in the frame.

The frontal appearance of the radiator appears unchanged although it slopes toward

Seventh Series Big Eight Model 745 Five-Passenger
Convertible Sedan by Dietrich. Price at Detroit $5,275.
This was the last series to use the piano spoke wire
wheel which was now a $90.00 option. For approxi-
mately $250.00 more these wire wheels could be had
in stainless steel. The Big Eights used an eight-lug
wheel fitted with a 700 x 19 tire.

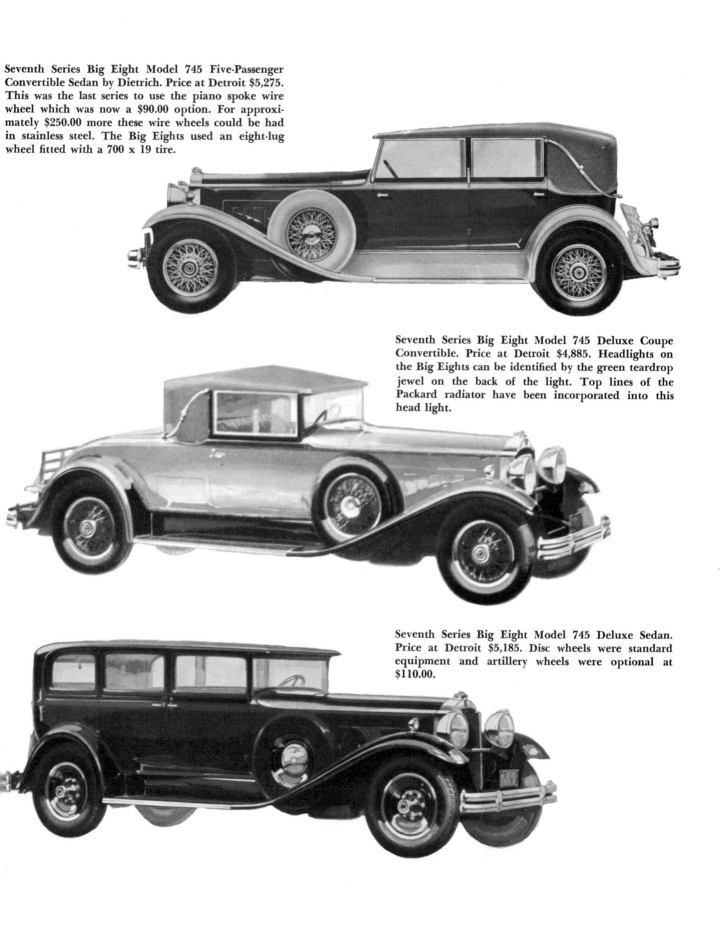

Seventh Series Big Eight Model 745 Deluxe Coupe
Convertible. Price at Detroit $4,885. Headlights on
the Big Eights can be identified by the green teardrop
jewel on the back of the light. Top lines of the
Packard radiator have been incorporated into this
head light.

Seventh Series Big Eight Model 745 Deluxe Sedan.
Price at Detroit $5,185. Disc wheels were standard
equipment and artillery wheels were optional at
$110.00.

the rear 1½°. The 734 and 745 radiator shell is 1½" lower than the 745C (C stands for chassis) and is the same as the 726-33-40 except for the filler neck. The 734, 745, and 745C have a triangular filler neck which extends down over the front of the radiator shell and contains the Packard Crest. The 745 hood is five inches longer than the 745C hood and is the same height as the 740, which is 1½" lower than the 745C. Two hood handles are now standard and small knobs have been added to the louver doors for opening them from the outside. The molding terminates in an arrowhead for the 734 and 745. The fender and brackets have been designed for interchangeability with the 726 and 733 fenders except for the battery box opening. A four-speed transmission is introduced, plus a new S51 carburetor and double fan belt pulley system.

Additional styling innovations that identify the Seventh Series are as follows:

1. Rounded type headlights with matching fender parking lights, with a radiator outline at the top of the light. The big eight had a teardrop green jewel in the back of each headlight to indicate high and low beam. Fender parking lights were an accessory on the Standard Eight.
2. Three-lens tail light redesigned with the red running light in the form of a Packard radiator outline.
3. Dash board incorporates a glove compartment on each side.
4. Bijur dash lubricator handle redesigned with "Pull Daily" wording.
5. Gas tank has sheetmetal enclosure.
6. Adjustable drivers seat and adjustable sun visors.

Custom coachwork reached its zenith in 1929. Never again would there be the selection of semi-custom and custom built bodies from such a variety of custom body manufacturers. The decline of the custom body suppliers started in July and August of 1929 when they tried to borrow capital for their fall line. The problem was accelerated by luxury manufacturers like Pierce Arrow and Franklin embarking on a retrenchment program. This immediately resulted in the bankruptcy of quality body builders like Holbrook.

Dietrich, Inc., at Hamilton and Holden Avenues in Detroit, was still in fairly good financial shape. Their Detroit location plus Ray Dietrich's personal friendship with Edsel Ford and Alvan Macauley in no small measure extended the life of the Dietrich firm. Dietrich's specialty, which coincided with the Luxury car trend, was the convertible coupe, convertible sedan, and sport sedan. Only the roadsters, phaetons, and dual cowl phaetons built by Packard were selling, which, of course, was a paradox to the over-all industrial statistics on the trend to closed cars. However, the practicality of the all-weather body styles could not be denied.

Packard was the last luxury car to feel the pinch. Its own custom body shop, started in 1928, was now producing semi-custom and custom cars of the highest quality. Management had embarked on this program to share in the greater profits of a custom built car. This was a very real consideration when you consider that chassis were sold to the custom body builders at dealer's cost and the profit on the completed car went to the body builder. Packard also increased its selection of semi-custom offerings by adding six Brewster-built semi-customs and continued with six LeBaron and one Rollston semi-custom.

The technical definition of a custom, semi-custom, and stock body is as follows:

A custom body is a one-of-a-kind body built to the personal taste of an individual customer. This type of body starts at approximately $9,000.

A semi-custom body is a non-stock body made

Seventh Series Big Eight Model 745 Deluxe Coupe. Price at Detroit $4,785. The Seventh Series 734 and 745 can be identified by their triangular radiator cap and arrow lead belt moldings on hood. In addition to this, the 745 had a larger trunk rack with vertical bars.

King George VI and Queen Elizabeth on their first trip to the new world arriving at the Parliament building in Victoria, B. C., in a 740 Tonneau windshield phaeton.

The 1930 Custom Salon
in New York City.

in quantities of two or more but limited in total number produced. They differ from a custom body only in method of assembly but not construction.

The Packard stock body should not be confused with the word "production." The Packard Senior Series stock bodies were assembled with the same meticulous care that characterized the construction of the semi-custom bodies. A group of craftsmen worked as a team on each stock body. Often point of origin was the only distinguishing factor in whether it would be called stock or semi-custom.

When the annual Custom Salon opened at the New York Hotel Commodore in December, 1929, it was like the opening night at the opera. It was by invitation only and was considered one of the high points of the social season. The show ran for a week, and each day was set aside for a different type of function. One day was for the manufacturers who were the suppliers of leather, trim, paint, and hardware to the custom body trade. In the evening, a banquet was given, again by invitation, to these suppliers and the exhibitors. The banquet was actually an informal seminar on new styles, trends, new auto accessory items, and a general bull session on the coach work on display. Another day was set aside for the automobile manufacturers and their engineers. It was here that volume manufacturers picked up ideas that could be fitted into their mass production techniques. Many a consulting fee grew out of this show. Another afternoon was set aside for chauffeurs, who were the automotive consultants of every estate. They could make or break a deal, so they were really given the red carpet treatment. Naturally, the chauffeur received a commission for influencing his employer to make the "right" decision. It was not uncommon for a chauffeur to make $10,000 a year in salary and trade commissions on cars, tires, and other acces-

sories. It was much the same as an expense account today, and it was common practice and generally accepted. The balance of the the week was subdivided into one afternoon and evening for the "400," and the balance for the newcomers with money, such as movie stars, wealthy industrialists, etc.

The Director of the Salon was John R. Eustis, who was in charge of the New York Rolls Royce branch. The exhibitors, like the guests, were there by invitation only. The Salon was restricted to the exhibit of European coach and chassis builders and to American custom coach builders. If you were selected as one of the exhibitors by the Board of Directors, you then paid $500 for each car exhibited. Engraved invitations were then allotted to the exhibitor for distribution to his clientele.

Seventh Series sales reflected a troubled automotive industry. The stock market crash was only one facet of this problem. Automotive manufacturers had put 5,000,000 new cars on the road in 1929. Under normal conditions consumer credit would have been saturated for at least three years. Add to this the radically different buying habits of the 1929 automobile consumer: he bought a car to last at least five years. To trade in every year just wasn't in his thinking; it would have been the epitome of wanton waste. The manufacturer didn't have the slightest idea of what built-in obsolescence was, and he produced cars to last. The carriage trade would often add one or more cars to their stable each year, but they too would never trade a one-year-old model in on a new one. If it was a custom bodied car, it was kept like a rare family jewel, and often a new chassis was purchased for the body before any thought of trading the car in crossed their mind.

When August, 1930, arrived and the Seventh Series became a statistic on an annual Packard financial report, 36,364 units had ben manufactured. A drop of 18,638 units. Packard

Note that the center section of the Seventh Series tail light resembles the top contour of the radiator.

management had seen the handwriting on the wall and had reduced the selling price of the Standard 8 by $400 on May 28, 1930, and reduced the last six months' production by 1,968 units. The Big Eights for the first time were now in oversupply due to the cancellations of orders from custom body builders and from some of Packard's own wealthy clientele who wished to wait and see the economic outcome. As a result, at Eighth Series introduction time, there were some Seventh Series 740 and 745 Eights still awaiting customers. The factory reduced the price by $500, which cleaned up the surplus nicely but cut into the sales of the new Eight Series.

Eighth Series Standard Eight Model 826 Sedan. Price
at Detroit $2,385. This was Packard's volume classic.
The 826 had only this body style.

6

The Eighth Series

There were many visitors but fewer buyers at the January 1930 National Automobile Show. The high point of the show was the new twelve and sixteen offered by Cadillac. The multi-cylinder race was on. Cadillac was pulling out all the stops in an effort to close the sales gap between the prestige leader Packard and itself. At the end of the year, with LaSalle thrown in for good measure, total sales equaled 25,991 units, which was still 10,373 units less than Packard.

General Motors had many new innovations in their cars, among which were hydraulic silencers for the Cadillac engines and tin plated pistons and a pressed steel axle housing for the Pontiac.

Chrysler offered their first eight-cylinder engine. Studebaker introduced free wheeling. This was one of the few automobile innovations that would eventually be discontinued because of legislation in many states branding it as dangerous. Studebaker also presented a new carburetor silencer. Cadillac, Chrysler, Dodge, LaSalle, Marmon, and Roosevelt were wired for radio installation. Other automotive events for the year included Plymouth franchises being given to all Chrysler, Dodge and DeSoto dealers; the American Austin Car Company was organized to build the Austin Bantam; and police cars were being equipped with two-way radios.

In July, 1930, Packard management was moving swiftly to modify their three year plan in light of declining sales, the Carriage Trade interest in twelve- and sixteen-cylinder engines, and the well-to-do middle class wanting well-built medium-priced automobiles.

The first part of the plan was to produce a medium price Packard that would invade the market dominated by the Buick 32-90 Series and the LaSalle. It would be called the Packard Light Eight and its introduction was scheduled for January 1, 1932. Packard designers and production men had eighteen months to learn and accomplish an entirely new concept of car assembly called mass production. Could they do it?

The second part of the plan was to design and build a multi-cylindered classic. The twelve-cylinder engine design was easy to agree

Eighth Series Standard Eight Model 833 Seven-Passenger Sedan. Price at Detroit $2,785. Standard Eights can usually be identified by their louvered hood. A three-door hood was optional. Parking lights were now standard equipment.

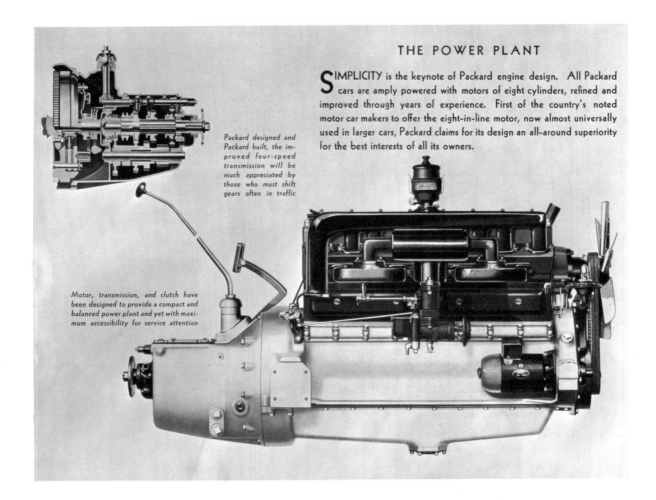

THE POWER PLANT

SIMPLICITY is the keynote of Packard engine design. All Packard cars are amply powered with motors of eight cylinders, refined and improved through years of experience. First of the country's noted motor car makers to offer the eight-in-line motor, now almost universally used in larger cars, Packard claims for its design an all-around superiority for the best interests of all its owners.

Packard designed and Packard built, the improved four-speed transmission will be much appreciated by those who must shift gears often in traffic

Motor, transmission, and clutch have been designed to provide a compact and balanced power plant and yet with maximum accessibility for service attention

Eighth Series Standard Eight Model 833 Club Sedan. Price at Detroit $2,675. The standard engine had flat lensed headlights and cast bumperettes. Dual windshield wipers are now standard equipment on all closed body styles.

SHOCK ABSORBERS AND
STEERING GEAR

ONLY an hour back of the wheel can disclose the ease of Packard riding and car control. A complete shock absorbing system, including a device for the elimination of front wheel "shimmy" and steering wheel "whip" together with finger-tip ease of steering control, reveal more than mere words can tell. It is the Packard engineering formula of building a smoothly fitted ensemble rather than a single feature, that gives such outstanding results of riding and driving comfort.

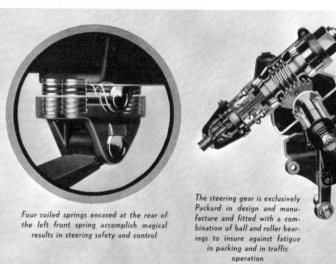

Four coiled springs encased at the rear of the left front spring accomplish magical results in steering safety and control

The steering gear is exclusively Packard in design and manufacture and fitted with a combination of ball and roller bearings to insure against fatigue in parking and in traffic operation

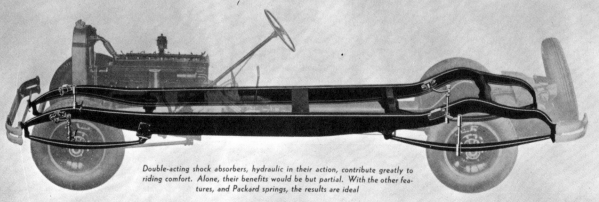

Double-acting shock absorbers, hydraulic in their action, contribute greatly to riding comfort. Alone, their benefits would be but partial. With the other features, and Packard springs, the results are ideal

upon. Since Packard was one of the biggest military and commercial engine producers, its experience had taught it that the twelve, being inherently balanced, had much more to offer performance-wise than the sixteen. The Packard engine plant was then requisitioned to build two prototype twelve-cylinder engines. One engine was to be designed for a front-wheel-drive car and the second engine for conventional drive.

The handling characteristics of the front wheel drive automobiles had impressed the Packard engineering staff. The styling group didn't need any selling, since to them it meant longer and lower body designs. As a result of this interest, money was appropriated for one experimental front wheel drive automobile. Packard's engineering staff went to work and constructed not only a front wheel drive but a segmented frame which, when unbolted, left the engine and front end easily accessible for repair work. The prototype twelve-cylinder engine was then installed. The engine had twin distributors mounted back by the fire-well, L-shaped heads with the plugs set vertically and the gear shift linkage running directly through the center of the V-shaped block.

In the meantime, the styling department commisioned Alex deSakhnoffsky to build the body. When the body was completed and fitted to the chassis, it sood just 5′ 6″ high. The car was elaborately disguised to protect Packard from any wild rumors which might damage the current sales program.

The new front wheel drive car was then reviewed by management with mixed emotions. Much discussion followed and finally it was agreed, and rightly so, that the design was just too radical to be readily saleable in the now vanishing luxury market. This automatically firmed up the decision that the new twelve-cylinder car would be of conventional design. Introduction was tentatively set for late in 1931.

In order to implement this program, it was decided to curtail the Eighth Series production schedule and to limit the number of production bodies. In this way, part of the facilities could be revamped for the projected Light Eight production. For greater flexibility, the 840 Series bodies were designed to be interchangeable with the 833 Series bodies. The 845 Series was reduced to two body styles, a seven passenger sedan and a seven passenger limousine. To round out the selection, a group of semi-customs was made available for the 833 Series.

On August 14, 1930, the Eighth Series was introduced to the motoring public. Although it bore a close resemblance to its Seventh Series stablemate, upon close examination one could see the evolutionary changes that had been incorporated. The new changes included:

1. A redesigned transmission to give a quick shift from third to high. The third-speed gears are in constant mesh. A sliding sleeve is used in shifting into high or third.
2. The radiator shutter thermostat and linkage had been redesigned to allow the assembling of the thermostat from the rear of the radiator.
3. The front and rear fenders had been changed to give a one inch deeper outer skirt.
4. A fuel pump has been specified for all models.
5. Automatic Bijur system. New drip plugs were specified due to automatic operation of tank.
6. The cylinder block had been redesigned to provide improved intake and exhaust passages similar to those used in the Seventh Series Speedster engines. New intake and exhaust manifolds had been incorporated. A heavier fly wheel was used to improve idling.

The Eighth Series now has wide chrome instrument bezels. Pull-handle on chassis lubricator is eliminated due to automatic operation. Note the thin rim, three-spoked steering wheel integral with the hub.

Eighth Series Big Eight Model 840 Custom Phaeton. Price at Detroit $3,490. The windshield has now been raised one inch to allow for more head room. Bumperettes are pressed steel.

7. A new type of shock which mounts to the frame had been added.

8. Springs were longer and wider.

Economic conditions grew worse, and the once lush luxury automotive market had fallen from a high 10 per cent of all automotive production in 1929 to a new low of 2 per cent seventeen short months later. Cadillac's initial success with its Twelve and Sixteen had cut deeply into the available 2 per cent. Add to this the large number of Sixth and Seventh Series sold which in turn cancelled out any need for their owners to purchase a new Eighth Series car. As a result of this combination, Packard sales on the new Eighth Series fell to an all-time low.

Packard management was quick to recognize the situation and the following course of action was taken. The timetable for the in-

700 x 19 tires were used on the Eighth Series Big Eights. Locking lugs have been placed inside hub. Wire wheels were $60.00 extra and wooden wheels were $70.00 extra.

troduction of the new Ninth Series, which included the new twelve-cylinder car, was rescheduled for June instead of late August. This rescheduling they knew would result in a large surplus of Eighth Series cars at Ninth Series introduction time. On the other hand, it was hoped that by shortening the Eighth Series production schedule to ten months, this known surplus would be kept to the minimum.

To protect their dealer organization from undue financial hardship, a special modification kit was made up by the factory for the Eighth Series. The kit consisted of a special veed radiator shell and headlight bar, outside horns, and the Ninth Series twin taillights and bumpers. The purpose of the kit was to make the Eighth Series superificially resemble a Ninth Series model and thereby more readily saleable. These kits would be made available to the dealers at no cost when the Ninth Series was introduced. The kit helped, but it was no panacea. Eighth Series cars were delivered through August 1932, which was fourteen months after the introduction of the Ninth Series.

For authenticity purposes, no Eighth Series car delivered before July, 1931, can have this kit because it was not available. In addition, Eighth Series cars delivered after 1931 do not necessarily have to have this modification kit since its use was at the option of the dealer as a sales aid. The authenticity of these cars cannot be questioned since their modification was done prior to delivery to the first owner. However, when the kit was used, it was always used in its entirety. This special Eighth Series modification can be positively identified by the post-July, 1931, delivery date on the firewall plate, the veed radiator that has no provision for bolt-on outside horns of the Ninth Series, and the special top receptacle for the single piano-type hood hinge. The special outside horns are bolted to the light bar. There was also a special stoneshield available

Eighth Series Big Eight engine. Note the new intake-exhaust manifold system and fuel pump. Carburetor air cleaner was optional.

for this car. These parts are not interchangeable with Ninth Series parts. The tail lights and bumpers are interchangeable with the Ninth Series. Records show that 25 per cent of the Eighth Series production carried this modification kit.

The Eighth Series incorporated a new vehicle serial number system which would be used with slight modifications right up to World War II. This vehicle number on the firewall plate indicated the body style in the first three digits and the production number of the body style in the last digits. For example, the vehicle number 472-137 indicates that it is the 137th Eight Series Big Eight roadster. When chassis were sent out of the factory for custom body installation, a different numbering system had to be used since it was impossible to know what kind of body would be ultimately mounted. These vehicle numbers start with the series designation followed by the number of the chassis being consigned outside the Packard plant. The vehicle number 840-89 indicates the 89th 840 chassis being sent out of the plant for exhibition purposes or for a custom body. 840-89 happens to

be a Dietrich convertible sedan, 845-89 is a LeBaron convertible coupe, and 845-94 is a Rollston convertible victoria. In other words, nothing more can be read into the digits following the series number. Packard did not keep body production figures as a permanent historical record. Today this type of record would be mandatory for production scheduling, since dealers are told what they are going to sell. In the classic era, Packard production was scheduled on the basis of orders from dealers.

Today, the only way the number of body types produced for each particular series can be ascertained is by a statistical analysis of all the remaining cars in that series. Eventually, the highest number of each body style will show up. Addition of the highest body number of each body type will give you the total number of cars produced. Since the numbers of cars produced in each series is a matter

Eighth Series Big Eights have ribbed running boards and chrome strips. New hood-locking clamps make their appearance.

of historical record, this becomes the double-check on the accuracy of the tabulation.

The tabulation that follows is the analysis done by the writer on the 840-845 Series. Of the 3,345 cars produced, only 497 are unaccounted for in this tabulation. A calculated guess tells us that the missing cars are in the 840 sedan and club sedan category. The survey confirms the club sedan as the most popular body style on the 840 wheelbase. The analysis also shows that Packard produced far more open cars than the industry average of 10 per cent.

Body Style #	840 Series Body Style	Amt. Produced
476	Sedan Club	467
473	Sedan 5 Pass.	304
479	Coupe Conv.	194
472	Roadster	154
471	Phaeton	114
478	Coupe	103
491	Phaeton D. C.	97
477	Coupe-Club	84
470	Touring	45
840	Chassis	233
	Total	1,795

Body Style #	845 Series Body Style	Amt. Produced
474	Sedan 7 Pass.	522
475	Limousine	437
845	Chassis	94
	Total	1,053
	Grand Total =	2,848

All the prices listed in this book are for the five-wheel models at the factory. The only exception is the 443 Series which had fender mounted spares as standard equipment. For the delivered price structure, let us take the 840 phaeton, vehicle number 471-9, delivered in Morristown on September 16, 1930.

$3,490.00	Packard phaeton (471) f.o.b. Detroit
148.00	Additional charge for fender mounted spares and luggage rack
60.00	Additional charge for six wire wheels
27.50	Stoneguard
10.00	Deluxe Emblem (flying lady)
25.00	Windwings (2)
125.00	Trunk
104.50	Freight charges, make ready, etc. (compute at 3 per cent)
$3,925.00	Delivered Morristown, New Jersey

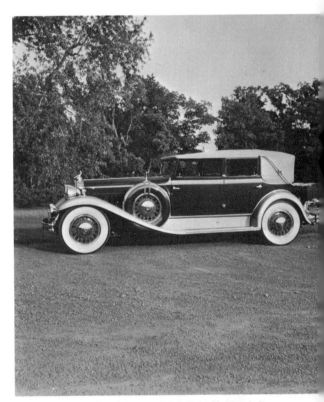

Eighth Series Big Eight Model 840 individual Custom Sedan Convertible by Dietrich. Price at Detroit $5,275. These automobiles were assembled at the Dietrich Plant under Ray Dietrich's personal supervision. A few months later Ray sold 50 per cent of Dietrich, Inc., to the Murray Body Company. This particular car was built for the New York Custom Auto Show.

In December, 1930, the 26th and last of the exquisite salon shows was held in the Hotel Commodore in New York City. The salons in Chicago, Los Angeles, and San Francisco would also end. Never again would there be such a display of the world's finest coachwork. This salon represented the zenith and also heralded the beginning of the end of the independent custom body builder. Holbrook, United, and Phillips were dead. Fleetwood was now a General Motors subsidiary in Detroit turning out short-run body types for Cadillac and LaSalle chassis. LeBaron was also in Detroit and was now a subsidiary of Briggs Body Company. Dietrich, Inc., would soon be absorbed by the Murray Body Company, which had always owned half the stock. Over the next 12 years, all of the major custom body builders would disappear. Only Derham of Rosemont, Pennsylvania, would survive as a living legend of a bygone era.

Packard was heavily represented at the salon in that their chassis had been selected by Derham, Dietrich, Rollston, and LeBaron for their creations. These cars were owned by the body builders and their chassis had been purchased by them from Packard. As was stated in an earlier chapter, it was from these salon shows that the custom body trade received their annual new orders from individual clients as well as lot orders from the luxury car manufacturers.

Derham was represented by several bodies, the most popular of which was a sport sedan. It looked exactly like a convertible sedan but had a fixed top. LeBaron's most popular exhibition piece was a beautiful convertible sedan. Everything above the belt molding was chrome, and it carried twin rear mounted spares. The interior had four individual pigskin upholstered seats. The finish was all black with chrome disc wheels. After the show, the car became the personal possession of Mrs. Walter Briggs of the Briggs Body Company.

Rollston had several town cars plus a beautiful convertible victoria on an 845 chassis. The car was finished in metallic tan with tan upholstery. The car was purchased by Arthur McEwen, a Morristown, New Jersey, industrialist.

Dietrich, Inc., built three convertible sedans for the show circuit that year. The vehicle numbers were 840-87, 840-88, and 840-89. All three cars had identical bodies but the treatment of the finish and the appointments were all different. The 840-87 convertible sedan was powder blue with basketweave trim, red striping, cream wheels, and a driver's

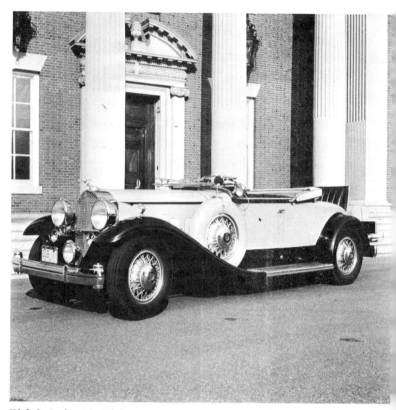

Eighth Series Big Eight Model 840 Roadster. Price at Detroit $3,490. This was Packard's last production roadster. Note the similarity to the Ninth Series automobiles. This effect was achieved by a conversion unit offered to the dealers by the factory to help sell the leftover Eighth Series vehicles at Ninth Series introduction time.

Eighth Series Big Eight Model 840 Convertible Coupe. Price at Detroit $3,595. Factory production bodies are interchangeable between the Standard and Super Eight.

partition. The application of basketweave is now a forgotten art and the material called mastic used in this application is also a forgotten substance. The basketweave was applied with a special spray gun which deposited heavy yellow mastic in vertical and horizontal lines which formed the basketweave pattern. This was striping at its ultimate. To keep the mastic from running, the body was laid on its side for the application. The chassis for these three cars were purchased by Dietrich in late September, 1930. When completed, the following disposition was made. The 840-87 was sent by rail from Detroit to Chicago for the salon at the Hotel Drake. This show was held in January, 1931. After the salon closed, Packard purchased the car and put it on display at Packard Chicago. It was later transferred to New York for display. It was sold on April 17, 1931, and shipped to Sweden. It returned to the States in 1951 in remarkably excellent condition. The car had been purchased by a classic car collector from the original owner in Sweden. It was then restored, then changed hands several times, and is now located in West Lawn, Pennsylvania.

Number 840-88 was shipped to California for the Los Angeles Salon and then to the San Francisco Salon. This car was last reported in 1954 in the possession of a large collector in Wisconsin. The car was subsequently sold and disappeared from sight.

Number 840-89 was shipped by rail to the New York Salon Show at the Hotel Commodore. The chassis had special chrome parts and accessories. It had a metallic maroon body and chassis with tan fenders and individual club chairs done in tan leather. The car was purchased at the show from Dietrich, Inc. When the show closed, it was sent over to New York Packard for servicing and was delivered on January 6, 1931, one week after the show closed. Its history and ownership are obscure. Its trail was picked up after World War II when it was found among the vehicles of a defunct trucking operation. It had been used during World War II as a service vehicle for tractor trailers that were hauling coal from the Pennsylvania collieries to the New York docks. The car is now fully restored and is in Morristown, New Jersey.

MPH'S AND RPM'S

The following table will give us the various motor revolutions per minute at the various car speeds for both ratio axles on Eighth Series Cars.

826-833			840-845		
6.50 x 19 Tires			7.00 x 19 Tires		
4.38 to 1 Ratio		4.69 to 1 Ratio	4.38 to 1 Ratio		4.69 to 1 Ratio
MPH	RPM	RPM	MPH	RPM	RPM
5	230.2	246.3	5	222.9	238.7
10	460.4	492.6	10	445.8	477.4
15	690.6	738.9	15	668.7	716.1
20	920.8	985.2	20	881.6	954.8
25	1151.0	1231.5	25	1104.5	1193.5
30	1381.2	1477.8	30	1327.4	1432.2
35	1611.4	1724.1	35	1550.3	1670.9
40	1841.6	1970.4	40	1773.2	1909.6
45	2071.8	2216.7	45	1996.1	2148.5
50	2302.0	2463.0	50	2219.0	2387.0
55	2532.2	2709.3	55	2441.9	2625.7
60	2762.4	2955.6	60	2664.8	2863.4
65	2992.6	3201.9	65	2887.7	3102.1
70	3222.8	3448.2	70	3110.6	3340.8
75	3452.0	3694.5	75	3333.5	3579.5
80	3682.2	3930.8	80	3556.4	3818.2
85	3912.4	4177.1	85	3779.3	4056.9
90	4142.6	4423.4	90	4002.2	4295.6

7

The Ninth Series

The 31st National Automobile Show was well attended as usual but orders for new cars were few and far between. Most manufacturers had the larger, more powerful, and luxurious classics on display. Most makers were also offering these gems at reduced prices. This would be the last show for some of the luxury makers.

General Motors was busy consolidating its hold in the medium-price field. Buick was equipped with a straight eight engine, Oldsmobile was sporting a synchromesh transmission and a downdraft carburetor, and Pontiac had a six- and an eight-cylinder engine and a pressed-steel radiator grill. Oakland was discontinued. Plymouth offered "Floating Power" and free wheeling. Seventeen other makes offered free wheeling for 1931. A retractable hardtop convertible was patented by B. B. Ellerbeck of Salt Lake City.

During National Auto Show week, the National Automobile Chamber of Commerce passed a resolution favoring the grouping of new model announcements in November and December. It was hoped that factory automotive employment would be more stable. More than this would be needed. Sales in 1930 had dropped off by two million cars and 1931 would see another one million fewer sales. Would it stop?

The Ninth Series Standard Eight and Eight Deluxe introduced on June 17, 1931, were bigger and more powerful. Their compression ratio had been increased 6 to 1. The wheelbases were longer and an entirely new frame had been designed. To compensate for these extra long wheelbases, the driveshaft was jointed and rubber mounted. The cars produced in 1931 had four-speed transmissions. The Ninth differed from the Eighth Series in that it was synchromesh. Beginning with production in 1932, the Ninth Series was equipped with a three-speed synchromesh transmission. All original Ninth Series owners were offered this option. As a result of this option being exercised, it is authentically correct to have either a three- or four-speed synchromesh transmission in a Ninth Series Standard Eight or Eight Deluxe.

The engines were again mounted in rubber

1932 Packard Twin Six front-end drive. An experimental car with body by de Sakhnoffsky.

Ninth Series Model 900 Light Eight Coupe. Price at Detroit $1,795. Packard's first attempt at the medium-priced field. 17″ tires first appeared on this model.

**Ninth Series Standard Eight engine. Manifold and fan
have been re-designed. Engine was also used in the
light Eight.**

supports. This type of engine suspension was last used by Packard in their 443 Series. A new ride control system was introduced in this series. All shocks were adjustable from the dash by mechanical linkage. On special order, you could have a vacuum-operated clutch. It operated as a free-wheeling device and it also permitted the changing of gears without the use of a clutch. Cars equipped with this device had a red throttle knob on the steering wheel.

The bodies maintained their simple enduring lines, but they had been lowered and given a more sweeping appearance. Again a complete line of individual bodies was offered. The cars had a striking new instrument panel of dark burled walnut with the instruments grouped in a blue-black engine-turned sub-panel. Also introduced in the Ninth Series Eights was a drop forged rocker arm with forced-feed lubrication. Ninth Series Standard Eight and Deluxe Eight can be easily identified by the battery and tool boxes mounted in each fender.

The big automotive news for 1931 also happened on June 17th. The nation's old friend, the Twin Six, was back in the Packard line-up. It would not be called the Twelve until the Tenth Series. Its re-introduction caused such excitement among the well-to-do that the news was flashed across the ticker tape on the floor of the New York Stock Exchange. Even at first glance, one realized that this car was the portent of the future. Its graceful veed radiator, its tapered headlights, and chrome aircraft-type instrument panel would set the styling trend for the Tenth and Eleventh Series. When the Twin Six was first introduced, it could only be purchased with a semi-custom body with a price tag of $6600 and up, f.o.b. Detroit. In January, 1932, Packard-built bodies were made available at a price of $3650 and up. In June, 1932, the prices were upped an additional $500.

Mechanically the Twin Six also had many innovations which would be incorporated into future series. Vacuum booster brakes, automatic clock, electric gas gauge, hydraulic valve silencers, solenoid-operated starter switch, downdraft carburation, and an oil dip stick. The Ninth Series Twin Six can easily be identified by its nomenclature on the hub caps, the non-skirted fenders, and its 18″ wheels.

The new stabilizer front bumpers were introduced on the Ninth Series. These front bumpers came in three sizes, the largest stabilizers being on the Twin Six. However, these larger stabilizers could be ordered as optional equipment on the Deluxe Eight, and the Deluxe Eight stabilizers could be ordered as optional equipment for the Standard Eight. The stabilizers consisted of a heavy spring and a weight in a cushioning chamber of oil. These heavy weights, being spring loaded, resisted and canceled out road shock. Technically speaking, they are harmonic dampers which absorb road shock. The rear bumpers are smaller in appearance and are strictly ornamental.

Considerable care should be used when dismantling these harmonic dampers. The top chrome cap is hollow and is held on by a simple spring clip in the top of the dome. Underneath this cap is the real cap which is cast iron and held down by a hex nut. This cap holds the spring and weight in position. When dismantling, strap down this cap and then turn the hex nut until the cap is free and the tension has been removed from the spring.

The January 1932 Automobile Show held in the many Manhattan hotel lobbies was strictly a window shopping affair for most of the motoring public. Cars were bigger and heavier. Packard, Auburn, Lincoln, and Pierce Arrows had new twelve-cylinder models. Most had been previously announced. Con-

The first series to have twin tail lights. Note placement of luggage rack medallion.

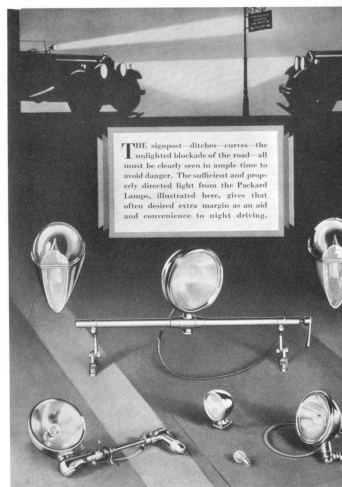

THE signpost—ditches—curves—the unlighted blockade of the road—all must be clearly seen in ample time to avoid danger. The sufficient and properly directed light from the Packard Lamps, illustrated here, gives that often desired extra margin as an aid and convenience to night driving.

For safety and convenience.

Ninth Series Standard Eight Model 902 Convertible Victoria. Price at Detroit $3,395. Packard's first Factory production Victoria. Ninth Series can be identified by veed radiator, re-designed instrument panel, and tool box in left front fender. Horns were an accessory on the Standard Eight.

vertibles with disappearing tops were a new trend. Inside visors began to replace outside shades in an effort to decrease wind resistance. Buick, Cadillac, Chrysler, DeSoto, Dodge, LaSalle, and Packard offered vacuum-operated clutches. Oldsmobile and Packard introduced automatic chokes. Ford was again mad at the world and was having his own private show crosstown. This was the year that Ford introduced the famous Ford V-8. This car would start the trend to inexpensive high-speed transportation. It would also spawn a new speed-equipment industry.

At the official auto show, Packard presented the new Model 900 Light Eight. It was the first truly fine car ever produced to sell below $2,000. It came in four body styles, the coupe, coupe roadster, coupe sedan, which sold for $1,795, and the sedan, which sold for $1,750. It was Packard's first attempt at invading the medium-price field. It had a Standard Eight engine, the angleset rear, which first appeared in this model, two shoe brakes with a star-wheel adjustment, 700 x 17 wheels, an electric gas gauge, and solenoid-operated starter switch. It is not considered a classic because of its low price and, with the exception of the engine, it had little in common even with the Standard Eight. Unfortunately, from a factory cost standpoint, it was a failure. It cost almost as much to build as a Standard Eight Sedan and sold for $690 less. Since there was a $500 markup on the manufacturer's cost to the dealer, the factory, in order to protect the deaker's markup, had to sell the cars at just about factory cost.

Since manufacturers are not in business for their health, management decided it just didn't have the know-how and the techniques of the bucket shops to accomplish low-cost volume production. The new plan was to cease production on the 900, institute an executive recruitment program to spirit away from General Motors and Ford a few brains who knew the bucket mill techniques, and

have a new medium-priced car on the market in two years. It was a tall order, but Packard knew that a medium-priced car was needed to survive.

Packard was in the news several times in 1932. Packard-engined *Miss America X* won the Harmsworth air race for Gar Wood and established a world's record of 124.91 miles an hour. President Hoover, acting for the Aeronautical Association of America, presented President Alvan Macauley with the famous Collier Trophy as recognition of Packard's outstanding achievement in building and demonstrating the practicality of the Diesel aircraft engine. This plane is now in Greenfield Village in Dearborn, Michigan.

Many famous automotive pioneers died in 1932. Hugh Chalmers, Fred Duesenberg, Ray Graham, Henry Leland, George Selden, and

The Packard J. & H. Tonneau Windshields

THESE shields may be extended back close to the rear seats, and the side wings adjusted to any desired angle, affording excellent protection. They fold down and out of the way when not in use. Furnished for Phaetons and Touring Cars, as shown in the left picture, or for the rumble seats of Roadsters or Coupes, as illustrated in the right picture.

The Packard-Hartford Tonneau Windshield

FULL protection is offered in Phaeton and Touring Cars by this shield, which blends beautifully with open car body lines. It may be adjusted so that with the top up it combines the advantages of both open and enclosed cars.

Tonneau windshield.

Standard Eight and Eight Deluxe instrument panel.

Ninth Series Eight Deluxe Model 903 Club Sedan. Price at Detroit $3,890. Spring-loaded vibration deadening bumpers made their first appearance and were standard equipment.

Alexander Winton. All in their own way had contributed much to the dependability and prestige of the American automobile.

The Ninth Series saw the implementation of a new model designation nomenclature. This was due to the introduction of the Light Eight and Twin Six and new wheelbase dimensions for all four models. The Light Eight had a new 127″ wheelbase. The Standard Eight was now on a 129½″ wheelbase and a 136½″ wheelbase. The Eight Deluxe and Twin Six shared the same 142½″ wheelbase and 147½″ wheelbase. One can readily see the confusion that would result using the series designation plus the last two digits of

the wheelbase. It would also be meaningless for differentiating the Eight Deluxe from the Twin Six. It was therefore decided that the last two digits would be an arbitrary code representing the model and the wheelbase. Under this system 900 became the Light Eight on a 127″ wheelbase, 901 was Standard Eight on a 129″ wheelbase, and so on. Number 906 was the highest assigned and it represented the Twin Six model on a 147″ wheelbase. The code quickly caught on because the public as well as the Packard owners had always referred to the Packard car by series, never by year or type of engine.

1932 was the blackest year of the Great Depression. Industry was operating at less than half its maximum 1929 volume. Among the comparatively well-to-do people of the country (pre-Depression incomes of over $5,000 a

Ninth Series Model 904 Individual Custom Stationary Coupe by Dietrich. Price at Detroit $5,900. Wire wheels were still extra equipment. Tire size on the Big Eight was 700 x 19.

year), the great majority were living on a much reduced scale, for salary cuts had been extensive.

It is ironic that the finest luxury cars ever built were produced at a time when even the wealthy were reluctant to invest in any kind of automotive transportation. However, it was probably because of these depressed economic conditions that these fabulous gems of the

In 1932, 1,103,557 passenger cars were sold. Of this figure, 22,071, or 2 per cent were classics. Packard led with 35.6 per cent of this market. The Cadillac Eight, Twelve, and Sixteen settled for 16.9 per cent and LaSalle helped General Motors by contributing an additional 15.3 per cent of the market. The balance of the 30.2 per cent was shared by Chrysler, Cord, Duesenberg, DuPont, Frank-

Ninth Series Model 904 Individual Custom Convertible Sedan by Dietrich. Price at Detroit $6,250.

classic era were produced. The luxury manufacturers were giving their all to maintain a hold in the vanishing luxury market. Only the top craftsmen were still left on the factory payrolls and the finest materials were practically being given away to reduce extensive inventories. This combination produced a luxury car that would never again be financially possible.

lin, Lincoln, Marmon, Peerless, and Pierce Arrow.

Packard's leadership over the other prestige makes did not falter. The habit of years and the knowledge that there was no better automobile to be bought regardless of price kept wealthy Americans coming back to the Packard show rooms and buying. Their customer repeat business stood at 90 per cent, a figure that has never been equaled in the automotive industry. It was the age-old story of when you can afford the best, you can afford what you like. No pressure was exerted on a Packard owner to buy a new model every year.

The Ninth Series saw the introduction of the fourth famous classic Packard radiator cap ornaments. The first radiator cap ornament to appear was called the Packard Motor Mascot, nicknamed the "Wings." As the name implies, it was a pair of wings that locked under the motor meter. It was introduced in the teens

Well," alias the "Adonis Emblem." The famous French sculptor Emil Antoine Bourdelle was commissioned in 1927 by the Packard styling department to execute this new ornament. It would be an accessory mascot for the new Sixth Series scheduled for production in July, 1928. Bourdelle selected "Daphne at the Well," a young nymph from Greek mythology. When it came time for the ad agency in Detroit to illustrate this new

Ninth Series Twin Six Model 905 Sport Phaeton. Price at Detroit $4090. New styling of this model would set the design for the next three years. The pelican and 750 x 18 tires made their appearance on this model.

Ninth Series Twin Six instrument panel and wheel.

and was made of Britannia metal and was silver plated. It was available through the Fifth Series and sold for $20.00.

The second ornament, and most famous one, was called the Packard Deluxe Emblem, nicknamed the "Flying Lady." It represented the trinity of perfect motion—Speed, grace, and Power. It was introduced in 1924. In the twenties, it was silver plated. The Deluxe Emblem sold for $10.00 and, like the Packard family crest, there are six different styles depending upon series and mounting. It was an accessory right up to World War II.

The third ornament to be introduced for the Packard radiator was "Daphne at the

ornament, the name was arbitrarily changed to Adonis. The advertising men felt that Adonis would have better sales appeal than Daphne. It was probably felt that since Adonis was also a legendary figure from Greek mythology, why let the facts mess up a good sales pitch. However, for the record, Adonis was never a child that grew to manhood. As a legendary figure, he was "knit full size" in his early twenties and represented the blossom of manhood. This ornament was last offered in the Eighth Series accessory catalogue at a cost of $15.00.

The last classic Packard radiator cap ornament was the Pelican, nicknamed the "Cormorant." The original quest for a new ornament was actually an advertising campaign started in 1931 to stimulate interest in the new yet unannounced Ninth Series cars. It

took the form of a sculpture contest for young
artists. However, none of the entries were
acceptable to the judges. The project was then
turned over to Packard's own styling department who created the highly stylized pelican
to tie in with the family coat of arms.

After the bird became an accessory on the
Ninth Series cars, Earl C. Anthony, a Cali-
fornian who was a large stockholder, an even
bigger distributor, and a frequent visitor to
the Packard plant, was kidding the Packard
personnel about the cormorant they had designed. As you know, the cormorant is indi-
genous to California. This was a great
standing joke at Packard, just as the GI's after
World War II called their discharge pins with
the eagle "Ruptured Ducks." By the middle of
1938 this standing joke had filtered into the
advertising department and some bright
young account executive decided that it was
a cormorant. Now, like all large corporations,
the wheels ground slowly and eventually the
old management group received some letters
from some families in the Boston and New
York area complaining that they too had a
pelican in their family crest and wanted to
know why the word cormorant was being

Deluxe emblem introduced in 1924 (Second Series).

used. A letter was sent out in 1949 to the staff
explaining the thoughts of management. For
about a year they started calling it a pelican
again. Finally, a meeting was held in July,
1953, with all parties agreeing that it was a
pelican and not a cormorant. However, it was
a rather hollow victory because the 1955 Packards were already on the drawing boards and
they weren't going to have this type of orna-
mentation.

In addition to these four well-known fac-
tory-approved radiator ornaments, there were
the glass ornaments by Lalique of France.
These beautifully cut-glass ornaments were
sold by the larger Packard distributors and,
of course, by the Custom Coach Builders.
Their authenticity is unquestionable. Unfortunately, the Germans destroyed most of the
French Lalique molds during World War II,
which, of course, included all of the radiator
ornaments.

All Packards were delivered from the factory with a plain cap and the owner could
purchase as an extra the particular radiator
ornament that he desired. An owner could
purchase a Pelican for his Super Eight and the
Deluxe Emblem for his Twelve. It was his

"Daphne at the Well," ("Adonis") introduced in 1928.
(Sixth Series).

choice, not the factory's, as to what radiator ornament would appear on his new Packard.

The Ninth Series custom and semi-custom Dietrich bodies were the last of the bodies designed and built under the guidance of Ray Dietrich. In an earlier chapter, it was pointed out that 50 per cent of the stock of Dietrich, Inc., was owned by the Murray Body Corporation. Edsel Ford, who had been instrumental in having Ray leave LeBaron in 1925 and come to Detroit, was responsible for this financial arrangement. Naturally, Ray needed capital to start his new business in Detroit. Edsel, who had become a personal friend, had a financial interest in the Murray Body Corporation and he suggested to the Murray board of directors that they put up half the money in Dietrich, Inc. They agreed and Dietrich, Inc., started business on Clay Street in Detroit. Edsel was also responsible for letting Ray Dietrich purchase in 1927 the old Leland Lincoln plant at Hamilton and Holden Avenues on the most favorable terms. By 1931, Ray knew the end of the custom era was at hand and he requested the Murray Body

Pelican introduced in 1931 (Ninth Series).

French Lalique. The rarest and most beautiful of the ornaments.

Corporation to buy him out. This they did and moved the operation back to the Murray plant as Dietrich, Inc., a subsidiary of Murray Body Corporation.

Murray continued to produce the Dietrich-design customs through 1934, primarily for Packard and Lincoln. These were special-order bodies to fill the specific customer requests. The bodies were mounted at Murray and cars were then shipped to the dealers for delivery. The true Packard-Dietrich semi-customs can be identified by the vehicle numbers stamped on the firewall plate. The first digits carry the series nomenclature rather than the body-type number. The visual aids to identification are the veed windshield, short cowl, extra-long louvered hood, and the doors hinged from the center post in the convertible sedan.

Packard also had the Murray Body Corporation build several production open bodies to round out the factory line. The convertible victoria and convertible sedan bodies, for example, were built by Murray from 1932 to 1939. These production bodies were then sent to Packard for stock and eventual mounting. Since all of these bodies were built by

Murray, Packard had the option at assembly time to use the Dietrich nameplate or leave it off.

If a customer ordered a Dietrich victoria, the factory would then allow him special color and upholstery options at no charge, but naturally the car had a higher asking price, being a Dietrich. The upholstery option was usually a combination of Bedford cord and leather with wider window garnishing. Of course, a Dietrich nameplate was attached to the cowl. In 1936, Murray stopped producing bodies under the name of Dietrich, Inc. A time-honored name had been laid to rest. However, there are 1937 cars with Dietrich nameplates but these were still produced in 1936.

When Ray Dietrich left Dietrich, Inc., in 1932, he went to work for the Graham Brothers to help develop the Graham Silver

C. P. Joy of St. Paul (no relation to the Packard executive). This dealership was established in 1904. Packard's oldest distributors include Alvin T. Fuller, Boston, December 24, 1903, L. R. Mack, Albany, 1904, and E. C. Anthony, Los Angeles, September 19, 1905.

Streak. It was a beautiful car and is now best remembered as a Tootsie Toy series sought after by toy collectors.

Unfortunately, 1932 was not the year to introduce new models. Coincidental to the announcement of the Graham Silver Streak, Ray Graham died. As a result of the economic conditions in the automotive market and Ray Graham's death, the automobile failed to show a profit and the Graham fortune was badly dissipated. However, the remaining two Graham Brothers continued to produce automobiles of unusual design until 1939.

Ray Dietrich was then hired by Walter P, Chrysler for the Chrysler styling department. Twenty years later, Ray would again work for himself as Ray Dietrich, Inc., of Grand Rapids, Michigan, a product engineering firm. His Sales Manager? Tom Hibbard.

8

The Tenth Series

The 33rd National Automobile Show was the first automotive event of 1933. Aerodynamic streamlining was just beginning to touch car design. The skirted fender, veed front grill, sweeping tail lines, and slanted windshields were incorporated in most models. Economy and durability were stressed by nearly all manufacturers. Innovations included the use of the accelerator pedal for starting, the introduction of independent wheel suspension, reflex glass tail and stop lights, and valve seat inserts.

Fisher bodies by General Motors offered "No-Draft Ventilation" with the front section of the side windows pivoted on the top and bottom to control the flow of air inside the car. Packard introduced a similar system, but it was not quite as satisfactory. The front window was divided into two equal halves and pivoted from front and rear with no provision for rolling the window down.

Power brakes were available on many of the medium-priced cars and on most of the luxury cars. Chevrolet boosted its horsepower to 80 at 3200 rpm in an attempt to stay in the ball game

with the Ford V-8. Plymouth decided that speed was not their "cup of tea" and concentrated on a well-engineered low-price car. Packard used the National Automobile Show to introduce their Tenth Series classics and their new nomenclature, the Eight, the Super 8, and the Twelve.

The Packard's advertising agency became overly concerned with the Twin Six designation, fearing that the public would confuse the new twelve as a warmed-over 1923 Twin Six engine. It is doubtful that any such thought ever crossed the public's mind, but the Madison Avenue crowd is very persistent in devising cures for illnesses that never exist.

The Super Eight nomenclature was advanced on the theory that the old Eight Deluxe designation went out with high button shoes. The Standard Eight nomenclature was upgraded to the single noun Eight. After all, "Standard" imparts to the buyer "ordinary," and it was a time when most manufacturers had an eight-cylinder engine, including the low-priced Ford.

The Tenth Series continued to personify

simplicity, grace, and dignity. Packard continued to have more automobiles registered in the world than any other luxury classic. In Europe, Packard had won almost every important Concours D'Elegance, including first prize three years in succession at Monte Carlo. In America, it would win later in the year the top automotive honors at the 1933 Chicago Century of Progress. Bentley would come in second.

The Eight and Super Eight had fresh new evolutionary styling based on the Twin Six that was introduced in the Ninth Series. They were also a trio packed with power. The Super Eight and Twelve would accelerate from 5 to 30 mph in 8½ seconds in high gear. The Eight would do it in 10 seconds. This was exceptional performance when you consider that some of the Twelves tipped the scales at 5,735 pounds.

Tenth Series Model 1002 Coupe. Price at Detroit $2,350. The first series to have skirted fenders, and no-draft windows. Trunk was a $90.00 accessory. Wire wheels are now standard equipment.

In addition, they were packed with many new goodies. They had power brakes with a four-position power selector on the instrument panel. If you wanted full power brakes with an exceptionally light pedal pressure, the selector was set for position no. 3. Position no. 2 had a power application approximately 75 per cent of position no. 1, position no. 3, 50 percent of position no. 1 and position no. 4, 25 per cent of position no. 1.

The Tenth Series was designed on a new x-member frame that would remain basically unchanged for the next two decades. Other engineering features incorporated for the first time were cooling fins on the connecting-rod bearing caps, the diaphragm-type vacuum pump, the long-range and safety-passing headlights, commonly called the three-position headlight system, and an electrically operated oil level gauge on the instrument panel. This was also the first Series to use 17″ wheels.

Most of the innovations on the Ninth Series Twin Six were continued in the Tenth Series Twelve and added to the Eight and Super

Front view of the Tenth Series Standard Eight. Note flat-lensed headlights. Stone shields were $30.00 extra and the deluxe emblem was a $10.00 extra.

the aircraft-type instrument panel with no provision for a radio. Normally the Twelve had a painted shell with chrome shutters, the Eight and Super Eight having the reverse. However, any combination of the above could be had as a $25 option. The instrument panel was finished in burled Carpathian elm with American walnut wood trim. The Eight, Super Eight, and Twelve can easily be differentiated by their head and parking lights. The Eight had flat lenses, the Super Eight had veed lenses, and the Twelve had a veed lens with a raised rib on the headlight shell. The Twelve tail lights were also ribbed with a blue dot lens.

In Chicago, the World's Fair opened and drew tremendous crowds despite the economic situation. The automotive exhibits were like the reincarnation of the famous salon shows. Cadillac had an aerodynamic-designed V-16 two-door which would be the fast-back sedan design of the forties. All the other luxury manufacturers had exquisite creations.

At the Travel and Transportation Build-

Eight. These items included dual down-draft carburetors, automatic choke, and thermostatic carburetor heat control. A dual-coil ignition system, which was last used in the 443 Series, was re-incorporated. The angle-set rear, which meant lower body design, became standard in all models.

The care in construction and assembly of these classics seems hard to believe in these days of mass production. Each Twelve engine prior to installation was run one hour by electric motor and then six hours under its own power. It was then run an additional one hour and fifteen minutes on the dynamometer. After the engine was placed in the chassis and the car assembled, it was then driven to the Packard Proving Grounds for a 250-mile test run before it was released to the distributor. It was carefully tuned under actual driving conditions. Upon completion of the test, a Packard certificate of approval was then attached to the car.

The Tenth Series visual identification marks are the skirted clamshell fenders and

Tenth Series Model 1001 Coupe Roadster. This particular car was custom built by Packard as a short wheelbased high speed road car for King Alfonso XIII of Spain. All series now have 17" tires.

Tenth Series instrument panel was finished in burled Carpathian elm with American elm trim. The V-12 speedometer also has an rpm faceplate. Gas gauge also registers the amount of oil in the engine.

Tenth Series Model 1004 Coupe Roadster. Price at Detroit $2,870. This is the first model designated Super Eight. These models can be identified by their vee-lensed headlights. Chrome radiator shell and painted shutters were standard equipment. Outside horns were also standard equipment.

ing, the Packard exhibit was the sensation of the Fair. People waited in line for two hours to see the "Car of the Dome" which carried off every automotive prize at the Fair. It was a $12,000 Packard Twelve Sport Sedan designed by Ray Dietrich and built by Dietrich, Inc., a subsidiary of Murray. It was painted golden metallic bronze with chrome wire wheels. Its interior hardware from door handle to accelerator pedal was gold plated. The upholstery was beige English broadcloth with a sheared beaver rear rug. The wood trim and the back seat bar were made of burled Carpathian elm. When the bar was opened, it contained four goblets, two glasses, and a glass mirror with gold corner clips.

After the Fair, Packard displayed this car at their local distributors throughout the country. The car was eventually purchased by a classic car collector in 1951. The car was restored and won 1st Prize at the 1953 National Grand Classic sponsored by the Classic Car Club of America. The selection of factory body styles decreased in the Eight and Super Eight and increased on the Twelve. Body interchangeability not only between models

but between series became even more stand-ardized. Since luxury car manufacturers did not and could not have volume, the only way to receive any savings at all was to use the same body types for several years production. Starting with the Ninth Series Twin Six, this became a standard operating procedure.

In an earlier chapter, we noted that the bodies were ordered from an outside body builder or built in the factory on a quantity basis. The bodies were then stored in white (semi-finished). Also, the last bodies to go into storage were the first ones out. The only iden-tification numbers on these bodies were the body numbers embossed on the firewall. It was strictly an identification number and had no relationship to the series. As the bodies were needed, they were removed from storage and finished. At this point, the vehicle num-ber plate was stamped and attached to the firewall. If the chassis was sent out of the factory for a custom body, the vehicle num-

Tenth Series Super Eight Power Plant. Note the dual-coil ignition and down-draft carburetion.

ber plate would have the series nomenclature and would be included in with the chassis specifications kit.

Understanding the key to body interchange-ability is a great help in the restoration process when one has a body and no chassis, or vice versa. For example, let us take a Ninth Series Twin Six factory phaeton body no. 571. This was the same body used on the Tenth Series Eight model 1002 with a 136″ wheelbase, the Super Eight model 1004 with a 142″ wheelbase, and the Twelve model 1005 also with a 142″ wheelbase. Only the interior appointments are different, plus the fact that the Eight has a shorter hood and running boards.

In addition, this same Ninth Series phaeton body was used on the Eleventh Series Eight model 1101 with a 136″ wheelbase, the Super Eight model 1104 with a 142″ wheelbase, and the Twelve model 1107 also with a 142″ wheelbase. Again only the interior appoint-ments were different, plus new hardware, in-strument panel, steering wheel, etc. These items are merely accessories to the body and were converted to the series that the body was to be used in. There is no problem with authenticity since all the bodies are from the

Tenth Series Model 1005 Phaeton. Price at Detroit $3,790. The Twelve's headlights, taillights, and park-ing lights have a raised chrome rib. Note stabilizer bumpers. Normally, the radiator shell was painted and the shutters chromed, but any combination of paint and chrome was a $25.00 option.

Tenth Series Twelve power plant. Each Twelve engine prior to installation was run one hour by electric motor (jacked in), and then six hours under its own power. It was then run on the dynamometer for an additional one hour and fifteen minutes under its own power.

to that used in the classics. The main reasons for this switch to inexpensive leather is high labor cost and the automotive trend to built-in obsolescence. Under general background remarks, it can be said that leather is the most difficult restoration item to buy. Upholstery leather runs between $.45 per square foot to $1.25 per square foot. Between these two figures lies a tale of quality and more important, the wearing life of leather in the car. To the novice, most leather looks just about the same, and in 90 per cent of the purchases that have been investigated, the restorer had wasted his money. The fault lies equally with the car owner and the upholsterer. Most upholsterers do not know the many grades of leather and what the specific uses they are intended for. Since there is not a wholesale retail trade in leather, the only way that an upholsterer can reduce his price to get a job or to make a better margin of profit is to buy a poorer quality of leather. The car restorer is also at fault because too often he pushes

same order. However, one should not use Eleventh Series instrumentation and hardware in a Tenth Series car, or keep the Tenth Series Twelve appointments in a body placed on a Tenth Series Super Eight. Also, be sure to legally change the vehicle number plate so it corresponds with the proper series for registration purposes and future identification for obtaining parts. Most states today register cars on the basis of the vehicle number, not the engine number.

In restoring damaged or decayed wood parts in the body frame use mountain ash. Ash is preferable because it holds its shape. Moisture content should not exceed 7 per cent. The floor boards were constructed of Douglas fir plywood and the top bows in the open cars were constructed of oak. Hickory should be used in replacing spoke wheels.

The leather that was used in the classics was the finest. Today, only 1 per cent of the world's output of leather is equal in quality

Tenth Series Twelve Model 1005 Club Sedan. Price at Detroit $3,880. The Twelve was one of the first automobiles to have a pressurized cooling system. A condensing tank on the right side of the engine would convert steam to water.

Tenth Series Twelve Model 1006 Town Car Landaulet Custom by Packard. Price at Detroit $6,250. Unfortunately, all too often these elegant town cars have been dismantled for parts.

for the better price rather than a quality job. The main cost in the upholstering of a classic is in the labor, the cost of material is secondary.

Most of the leather used in the classic car is known in the trade as Full Top Grain, which has been bark tanned, drummed in an aniline dye solution, and is not embossed with a pattern. This leather is made only on special order by one or two leather manufacturers in the United States. The best manufacturer of this leather is Radel Leather in Newark, New Jersey.* This manufacturer produced most of the leather that was used in the luxury car market during the classic era. It was from their files that the writer was able to locate the famous body builders of the past like Dietrich, Brunn, etc., and they are still supplying leather to the fine custom body shops that are left, such as Derham of Rosemont, Pennsylvania. They also manufacture landau leather for the tops of formal cars.

When hides first arrive at the manufacturer, the hair is removed by a chemical solution

*Radel leather can be purchased from Classic Cars, Inc., of Morristown, New Jersey.

and the hides are sorted as to quality. Cow hides average between 45 and 52 square feet. The hide is then trisected. The top layer of the hide is known as the Full Top Grain. If the hide contains many imperfections such as barbed wire marks, scratches, etc., it is carefully buffed with a sander and later imprinted with an embossed pattern to give it a uniform look. This hide is known as *top grain snuffed*. The center cut of the hide is called *deep buff*. It is considerably less expensive than the top cut, and very rugged, but lacks the gracious beauty of Full Top Grain. It is mostly used in medium-priced cars where large seat areas are covered without the benefit of pleats. This leather is also used for bus and truck upholstery. The bottom cut is called slab and is used for the soles of shoes, etc.

After being sorted, the hides undergo a process known as bark tanning, in which leather is soaked in a solution of tree bark extracts. This solution imparts into the leather the characteristics that are inherent in the living tree. Oak bark is used for harness leather to give it strength and rigidity. Quebracho from South America, Myrabulan from Africa, etc., is used in upholstery leather to give it softness and flexibility. In addition, bark mordant gives leather a roundness and fullness and aids in color adhesion.

Tenth Series Twelve side mount with mirror. The chrome wheel discs were $7.00 each, tire covers $18.00 per pair, and the mirrors were $16.00 per pair.

The next step is to immerse the hides in a chromic mordant, which serves to produce fixed color in the leather; it also imparts strength and softness.

The final step for the best leather is the drumming process, which does not lend itself to high production. This is the process in which the hide is placed in a drum of aniline dye and tumbled. In this manner, the dye impregnates deeply into both sides of the hide. This drumming process also aids in making the leather extremely soft. When you see Full Top Grain leather with dye on both sides (color back) you are seeing the best. The final finish is then applied and the leather is ready for the trade.

Production leather is processed with in-organic chemicals, then the hides are placed on conveyor belts and colored by revolving sprayguns which deposit a heavy paste pigment on one side of the hide (natural back).

In addition to beauty, color back has these additional advantages over natural back: It breathes freely, and therefore adjusts itself to atmospheric changes (warmer in winter, cooler in summer). Natural back can only take up to 60,000 flexings or approximately four years in the field before cracking. Color

Tenth Series Super Eight taillight.   **Tenth Series Twelve taillight.**

back takes 200,000 flexings before cracking. Natural back will crack at 10° below zero, color back will not crack until 35° to 50° below zero.

After you have purchased your Full Top Grain color back leather, you should insist that your upholsterer use horsehair for padding. Armour and Company can still supply horsehair. Horsehair has the resiliency that insures lasting firmness. Cotton wads and loses its shape quickly, and foam rubber is not only unauthentic but deteriorates through heat and dirt.

Car of the Dome. This is the $12,000 Packard V-12 Sport Sedan built by Dietrich for the Chicago World's Fair. It won every automotive prize at the fair.

9

The Eleventh Series

The 34th National Automobile Show opened on schedule despite the heavy snows and chilling cold of January, 1934. Streamlining was here to stay. It was best exemplified by the quite revolutionary DeSoto and Chrysler "Airflow" models which were introduced at this show. Nearly all models were longer, wider, and offered more room inside. Several were even wide enough to seat three in the front seat. Doors were made wider, and in some models the rear doors were cut back over the rear fenders to provide better access.

Cadillac introduced a new high-output generator and voltage regulator. The increased popularity of the automobile radio, heater, defroster, etc., had made this type of heavy-duty electrical equipment a necessity.

LaSalle was a real hit. It had a new streamlined body, a new straight-eight engine, and a brand new price tag. General Motors had downgraded the price of the LaSalle so it would be competitive with Buick and Oldsmobile. It was felt that the money was in the medium-price cars and that with the addition of LaSalle better sales in this range could be obtained. General Motors also hoped that by removing the LaSalle from the luxury market, Cadillac sales would improve. At least improved to a point where Cadillac would break even. The General Motors board was seriously considering the discontinuance of the Cadillac Division if losses continued.

More and more mechanical innovations were being developed. The most interesting to be exhibited at the show was a completely automatic transmission by Reo, an automatic transmission overdrive by Chrysler, and the mechanical supercharger by Graham that forced air into the carburetor. Independent suspension of the front wheels also gained impetus with most automotive manufacturers in 1934. General Motors introduced knee action, and nearly every other make had one of the three forms of independent front-wheel suspension of that time.

Finally, the name of the National Automobile Chamber of Commerce was changed to the Automobile Manufacturers Association, Inc.

The Thirties was a time of rapid automo-

Eleventh Series Eight Model 1101 Touring. Price at Detroit $2,973. This was an export model and is still in use in Secunderabad, India, today.

Eleventh Series Eight Model 1101 Club Sedan. Price at Detroit $3,082. This was a French import, therefore right hand drive was unnecessary. The Eight did not use the large vibration dampening bumpers. The chrome plated wheel covers are now $10.00 each.

Eleventh Series Eight Model 1101 Coupe. Price at Detroit $2,932. Eleventh Series front fenders have been extended forward and down. Rear fenders have been re-designed to follow the wheel contour.

tive technology. Usually this type of accelerated technology is a by-product of war, when manpower, materials, and funds are unlimited. During the Thirties this same combination was present. This country was waging a war for economic survival. There were surplus manpower and surplus materials, and only minimum funds were required to tap this wealth. As a result of this unfortunate combination of economic factors, only those automobile manufacturers who could continue to offer technological advancements in their product on almost a monthly basis could survive.

Packard management was well aware of this situation. Fortunately, they had never produced cars on a yearly model basis, and this gave them complete flexibility for the introduction of new models anytime during a calendar year. Also, their heavy investment in development and research facilities during lush times was now paying extra dividends. To add to this, Packard's acceptance of evolu-

tionary versus revolutionary changes put them in the enviable position of having their cake and eating it too.

As an example of this, Packard produced the Tenth Series for only seven months and two weeks. On August 21, 1933, a new Eleventh Series was introduced. It looked very similar to the Tenth Series but it incorporated a host of new mechanical innovations that were a result of this rapid technological race in the auto industry. These advancements included an oil temperature regulator which permitted the use of the same oil viscosity number the year round and regulated the temperature of the oil to suit all driving conditions. An oil pressure regulator was also incorporated so that the oil pressure could be adjusted from the outside of the engine. The first full-flow oil filter was added, plus a larger capacity oil pump and oil galleries. A Packard Twelve was tested at the Packard Proving Grounds with this new oil system. The results were fabulous for 1933 and nothing to be ashamed of even in light of today's automotive achievements. The car was driven at the sustained speed of 112 mph for 56 hours be-

Eleventh Series Station Wagon interior. These bodies were built by Bridgeport Body Co.

fore connecting rod bearing failure retired the car.

With the increased use of the automobile radio, the instruments were rearranged and fitted with a radio control panel in the center of the dash. The Tenth Series had already a built-in radio reception system which was continued in the new series. To compensate for the increased electrical load, a new heavy-duty air-cooled generator was installed. Another mechanical engine feature was the steel-backed, babbit-lined crankshaft bearings.

Styling for the Eleventh Series integrated many of the features that were designed in the Golden Packard that was displayed at the Century of Progress. Front fenders were extended forward and down to several inches above the front bumper. An improved gutter construction was incorporated under the leading edge of the fender to prevent water being thrown off at high speed. The rear fenders were also redesigned to follow the wheel contour more closely. The mats on the running boards had chromium strips added. The Twelves had been equipped with a combination tachometer and speedometer which in-

The Eight continues to use the flat-lensed headlights. Note standard radiator cap. The Eleventh Series shell and shutter could be purchased in chrome, black, or a contrasting body color at a slight additional cost.

dicated the engine rpm in high gear as well as miles per hour. The Eight and Super Eight now sported brown steering wheels to match the Twelve, and all three had tail lights that illuminated when the car was put in reverse gear. The awkward front window ventilating system had given way to the "angel wing." The advertised gas mileage for the three was: Eight, 10.5 miles per gallon; Super Eight, 10; and the Twelve, 9.

Included in the price of a standard equipped Eleventh Series car was the freight, delivery, tax, five wire wheels, and one metal tire cover for the spare. The Deluxe Equipped Packard carried the familiar side mounted spares and a rear luggage rack. Suggested extra equipment was as follows:

Instruments in the Eleventh Series have been regrouped to provide pleasing control panel for radio equipment. Finish in Carpathian elm with American walnut trim. Note tach-speedometer combination.

Packard deluxe radio	$ 79.50
Deluxe radiator ornament	10.00
Pelican radiator ornament	20.00
Six disc wheels	25.00
Six wood wheels	78.00
Six chromium wire wheels	192.00
Six chromium disc wheels	85.00

Eleventh Series Super Eight Model 1104 Coupe. Price at Detroit $3,406. The Super Eight continues to use the vee-lensed headlights. Six wheels and luggage rack are now $144 extra.

Eleventh Series Super Eight Model 1104 Coupe-Roadster. Price at Detroit $3,498. Note the new bumper design. Raised rubber strips have now been added to the running boards. This automobile was equipped with the optional rumble seat windshield which cost $175.00.

Six chrome wheel trim rings	12.00
Automatic starter	14.50
Side mirrors (pair)	16.00
White wall tires	n/c

Special paint continued to be a popular option. The trend to special paints and special chassis colors started with the 443 Series in 1927. The special paint options offered on the Eleventh Series continued to be tailored to the customer's desire:

Special stripe on body, bonnet, and wheels	$ 12.00
Special painted window reveals	10.00
Special painted window casing and moldings	12.00
Body, bonnet, and wheels	55.00
Chassis parts in color	55.00
Entire car	110.00
Special painted louver doors	7.00
Chrome louver doors	22.00
Special paint on metal tire covers	10.00 ea.

As one can readily see from the above options, there is no such thing as an authentic color or paint scheme for a Packard classic. Incidentally, any and all of these options could be had on a Twelve at no charge.

There was an unusually fine selection of semi-customs listed for the Eleventh Series. However, the number of semi-custom bodies ordered fell to an all-time low, and Packard management decided to call it a day on the truly fine expensive semi-customs. In later series there would be a sprinkling of semi-customs offered but they would be modified versions of factory body types.

The most fabulous of the semi-customs offered in the Eleventh Series were the LeBaron speedster and sport phaeton. These two models are regarded by many classic car connoisseurs as the *pièce de résistance* of the classic era regardless of marque. Three LeBaron speedsters have been found and all

three have been restored. Three LeBaron sport phaetons have been found and two have been restored. One is in the possession of the original owner. The last time the car was shown at a major Classic Car Club Meet, it made a perfect score of 100 points. The second sport phaeton, which was built for Alex de Sakhnoffsky, is now owned by Herb Shriner and is meticulously maintained. The third car is a mass of rust which is patiently being restored by a young enthusiast in Illinois.

Also in the Eleventh Series, three LeBaron sport coupes were built for show purposes. These cars are not listed in any catalogue. They are exceptionally streamlined, and incorporated design features which were the prototypes for the Twelfth Series. Two of the sport coupes are in the possession of the original owners. The third was destroyed by fire in transit to a collector for restoration.

Sixty-seven Eleventh Series chassis were consigned to LeBaron. Most of these chassis were mounted with town car and cabriolet bodies. LeBaron was now a subsidiary of the Briggs Body Corp. LeBaron, Inc., had been started by Ray Dietrich and Tom Hibbard in 1920 after they left Brewster in Long Island City. In February, 1921, Ralph Roberts joined the firm. Their first office was at No. 2 Columbus Circle, corner of Seventh Avenue and Broadway, New York City. Ralph Roberts was bookkeeper, salesman, writer, and general coordinator. In this way, Tom and Ray could concern themselves strictly with designing. In the beginning, being strictly designers, LeBaron, Inc., used most of the well-known body builders such as Fleetwood and Derham in Pennsylvania; United, Locke, and Holbrook in New York; and the Bridgeport Body Works in Connecticut to fashion the actual custom bodies from the renderings.

In 1923, Tom Hibbard went to Paris to open a LeBaron branch office. They felt it would be good promotion to have a Paris

The gas tank mouth for the Eleventh Series is mounted in the left rear taillight assembly. Twelve taillight lenses still carry the blue center insert.

The Packard Eight engine. The outgrowth of Packard pioneering in the straight-eight idea; a simply serviced design developing 120 horsepower. This was the last year that Packard used North East ignition equipment.

The Packard Super Eight engine. The economy and other advantages of eight-in-line design carried to the challenging performance of 145 horsepower. Note addition of oil temperature regulator and full-flow L-6 filter.

Eleventh Series Twelve Model 1106 Speedster Run-
about by LeBaron. Price at Detroit $7,746. These
beautiful automobiles were the advance style leaders
for the following three years of Packard design. The
top disappeared under a metal lid behind the seat.

The Packard Twelve engine. The result of the Packard experience of building more 12-cylinder motors
than any other car maker; 160 horsepower.

office. The idea paid off handsomely. Almost immediately, the importers of Hispano Suizas, Isotta Fraschinis, and Minervas began to look to LeBaron, Inc., for their designs. This helped them to break into the American automotive market, and resulted in orders from Locomobile and Stearns Knight.

It was soon apparent to LeBaron, Inc., that a body plant of their own was necessary to handle the volume of business. It was decided to merge with Bridgeport Body Company. This transaction was accomplished by the issuance of LeBaron, Inc., stock to the Bridgeport owners.

In Paris, Tom Hibbard became fascinated with the luxury European automotive business and left LeBaron, Inc., to team up with Dutch Darrin. Tom's share of the firm's stock was purchased by the two remaining partners, Ray and Ralph.

In 1924, LeBaron, Inc., was given their first really big order from an American automotive manufacturer. The firm placing this order was Lincoln and soon this relationship would develop into a lifelong friendship between Edsel Ford and Ray Dietrich. As a result of this friendship, Edsel persuaded Ray to come to Detroit. Ray first tried to sell Ralph Roberts on the idea of moving LeBaron, Inc., to Detroit. Ralph just wasn't interested in going to Detroit, no matter how much money was involved, for he feared LeBaron would lose its identity. In 1925, Ray reluctantly sold his interest in LeBaron, Inc., and went to Detroit and established Dietrich, Inc.

Ralph Roberts was now the sole owner of a business that he knew inside out, but he had never designed a body. This was a serious situation because of the orders on the books when Ray left that had to be filled and the factory in Bridgeport that had to be kept busy. In order to give himself time to hire at least one good designer, Ralph asked Roland Stickney, staff artist, to sketch out body designs while he verbally guided him. This technique worked, and the needed time to find new designers was found.

By 1928, the Briggs Body Corporation dearly wanted a famous body subsidiary of their own. In fact, they desperately needed one to stay in competition with Murray, who had an interest in Dietrich, Inc., and in General Motors, who owned Fleetwood. Ralph Roberts finally surrendered to Briggs Body Corp. and their fantastic offer. LeBaron headquarters were moved to Detroit and the New York branch moved up to Fifth Avenue. The Bridgeport plant was maintained for individual customs. In Detroit, LeBaron, Inc., a subsidiary of the Briggs Body Corp., was producing customs and semi-customs for Lincoln, Packard, Pierce Arrow, Chrysler, Stutz, etc. After the crash, Briggs closed the LeBaron New York branch office and sold the Bridgeport Body works.

Throughout the early Thirties, LeBaron continued to build stock and semi-custom bodies as a subsidiary of Briggs. One of the most interesting orders was from Ford for fifty Model A Town Car bodies, the first body being for Mrs. Henry Ford. Chrysler ordered 400 bodies for their Custom Imperial line. It took three years for Chrysler to use up these bodies.

Briggs continued to use the LeBaron nameplate right up to World War II. However, the LeBaron subsidiary lost all identity when it was completely integrated into the Briggs staff in 1934. Ralph Roberts eventually moved to California and in the late Fifties he was designing and building fiberglass bodies.

The Bridgeport Body Works was not to die after Briggs, as part of their retrenchment program, sold it back to the original stockholders in 1930. Since they had never employed more than one hundred people, volume would not be needed to maintain a profit. As a result, the B.B.W. decided to

Eleventh Series Twelve Model 1108 Sedan. Price at Detroit $4,762. 700 x 17 tires were standard equipment on Standard Eight and Super Eight. 750 x 17 tires were used on the twelve.

Eleventh Series Twelve Model 1107 Sedan Convertible (Dietrich designed, Packard built). Price at Detroit $4,750. Until 1931 the Murray Body Company owned half the stock of Dietrich, Inc. When Ray Dietrich sold out to Murray, it became a subsidiary of Murray until January, 1935.

Eleventh Series Twelve Model 1108 Victoria Convertible by Dietrich. Price at Detroit $6,701. Dietrich built custom bodies can be easily identified by their vee-type slanting windshields, short cowls, extra long hood with six ventilators, and the doors are hinged on the centerpost. It took until 1934 to exhaust the supply of these bodies which were built in the white in 1931.

become a specialty body business. Their specialty would be station wagon bodies and one of their biggest customers would be the Packard Motor Car Company.

Packard station wagons could be had on special order only. There were never any Packard brochures that depicted these unusually built bodies, so they are truly phantom classics. How many were built is a moot question. Their disappearance is probably due to rapid body deterioration and rough utility use after they came on the used car market.

Only one pre-Seventeenth Senior Series Packard station wagon has ever been found. It was mounted on an Eleventh Series Eight chassis. The car was found on the south shore of Long Island and the salt air evidently preserved the hardwood maple body. The styling of the body was remarkably advanced for 1934. It had a sloping rear tail-gate window, glass all around, and removable seats. This styling would eventually appear in the production station wagons of Ford, General Motors, and Chrysler during the forties.

The first Packard semi-custom station wagons appeared on the Sixth Series chassis. They were ordered through LeBaron by Packard for promotional purposes. The four that were built that year eventually became the personal transportation of four eastern Packard dealers.

10

The Twelfth Series

The 35th National Automobile Show was sponsored by the Automobile Merchants Association of New York after the Automobile Manufacturers Association decided to wait until November for its show in an effort to help stabilize employment in the automotive industry. The trend to medium-price cars continued. Ford introduced the Lincoln Zephyr and Packard the 120. General Motors would follow shortly with a medium-priced Cadillac. Chrysler, DeSoto, Graham, Hudson, Hupmobile, Pontiac, and Reo, to name a few, had fewer features or less power and all had a new lower price. In an effort to curtail the number of bodies offered, auto manufacturers were pushing two-door and four-door sedans.

Hudson and Terraplane introduced a new "electric hand" fingertip control for gear shifting. The control was mounted on the steering column. General Motors offered the first production all-steel turret tops on their 1935 models. Chevrolet adopted a new type of frame without an X-member. Pontiac produced its one-millionth car. Radios were now installed in three million automobiles, and Alexis de Sakhnoffsky was designing streamlined trucks for White.

The medium-priced non-classic Packard 120 was the sensation of the 35th Show. Never in the history of car merchandising had such a phenomenon taken place. Ten thousand Packard 120's had already been sold sight unseen prior to the introduction date. It was doubly fantastic when you consider the condition of the economy in 1935, the surplus of cars in dealer's inventories, and the hard sell required to convince a customer that he needed a new car. This example, more than any other, brings home the impact of the prestige enjoyed by Packard prior to World War II. Market research specialists estimated that the Packard name was a commodity second only to the Ford title. Packard management carried this asset on the books at the conservative figure of $1.00.

The decision to produce the 120 had been made in 1933. To those familiar with the factory layout, the 120 was to be produced in a separate factory south of the boulevard. The man to head the new project on a temporary basis was Max Gilman. Max Gilman, who had been the Sales Vice-President of Packard's New York Division, was now General Manager of Packard's Detroit Plant.

For low-price production know-how, George Christopher was hired from the bucket mills of G.M.'s Pontiac and Buick Divisions and made Production Manager of the 120 project. George, in turn, hired additional outside personnel who had specific managerial and engineering skills in building down to price, since no one at Packard was trained in the shenanigans of low-cost mass production. George Christopher did such an outstanding job on the 120 product that he was promoted to the position of Assistant Vice-President of Manufacturing on September 4, 1934. A year later, in further recognition, George Christopher was again promoted, this time to Vice-President of Manufacturing. The vacancy was created when E. F. Roberts retired.

Max Gilman started the publicity part of the project in 1934. All commercial media were used to whet the appetite of the American motoring public. The ads explained that

Twelfth Series Eight Model 1201 Coupe Convertible. Price at Detroit $2,580. Although the Twelfth Series reflects a new styling trend, the transition was smoothly made via the Eleventh Series LeBaron customs. Chrome headlight ribs were not used on the Twelfth Series Eight.

Twelfth Series 120 Model 120A Coupe Convertible. Packard's first successful medium-priced car. Packard had 10,000 orders from customers who had yet to see their first 120. At the wheel is Lawrence Tibbett, who announced the new 120 via his radio show.

Twelfth Series Eight Model 1201 Club Sedan. Price at Detroit $2,580. The Twelfth Series Eight did not use the spring loaded bumpers. 700 x 17 tires were used on the Eight and Super Eight and 750 x 17 on the Twelves. Note the re-designed running boards.

Twelfth Series Eight Model 1202 Sport Saloon body by Franay of Paris cost $19,000. Lucas lighting was standard equipment for U. S. automobiles delivered in England, and Marchal lighting if delivered on the Continent.

orders would be taken immediately for future delivery. By January, 1935, Packard had $10,-000,000 cash outright from customers who had yet to see their first 120. On January 6, 1935, on the Lawrence Tibbett radio show, the Packard 120 was announced to the world. Later in the week the cars went on display at the Auto Show and the place was literally jammed. By the end of the model year, 24,995 units were sold and Packard was once again financially flush. The designation "120" stands for the 120″ wheelbase, an identifying technique that had not been employed by Packard since the Eighth Series.

The Twelfth Series was introduced on August 30, 1934, or four months prior to the introduction of the 120. The new styling features gave the car a restrained, streamlined appearance. This styling was destined to be the hallmark of automotive design for the next three years. The sales figures on the Twelfth Series were not as good as on the Eleventh Series. This was due in part to the number of Eleventh Series cars that were sold whose owners would not consider trading for at least three to five years from purchase. The second reason, of course, was the fantastic sales

of the 120, which to a degree reduced the number of sales in the senior series.

Mechanically, the Twelfth Series continued to be the essence of perfection with an extra helping of GO power thrown in for good measure. The Twelves continued to be super checked by the factory and then given a final 250-mile test run on the Packard track at Utica.

The interiors were the epitome of luxuriousness, and quality reigned supreme. The broadcloth wool upholstery was the finest that could be purchased and was more expensive than the finest leather. This broadcloth was made from virgin wool and supplied to Packard by Laidlaw and Company in New York City. When restoring, this material can still be obtained from England. The American importer is Classic Cars, Inc., Morristown, N.J. The bedford cloths, although 50 per cent lighter in weight, can be obtained from domestic manufacturers of light aircraft.

Eighty per cent of the optional paint schemes were metallic in the Twelfth Series. The trim on the Twelfth Series was done in Carpathian elm with American walnut trim. The walnut and Carpathian elm decal material for refinishing the metal pieces can be obtained from station wagon body suppliers. It is unfortunate that more closed cars are not restored, for they embody many of the rare woods, beautiful fabrics, and gracious appointments that would have been impractical in the open classics.

The Eight and Super Eight had their compression ratios boosted and the Twelve had been stroked. It is interesting to note that the advertised horsepower in the Super Eight and Twelve was always on the conservative side. Using the formula that appears at the end of this chapter, it works out that the Super Eight actually delivers 169 h.p. and the Twelve delivers 192 h.p. with a 6.5 compression ratio. With 7-to-1 cylinder heads, the 1935 through 1939 Twelve delivers 202 h.p. When having a Twelve head planed, do not take off more than 7/1000″ or operating difficulties will be encountered. The Eight and Super Eight head can have up to 35/1000″ removed by planing without injurious results. The Eight actually delivers 128 h.p. or two less than advertised.

The Twelfth Series Twelve is equipped with a novel self-cleaning full-flow oil filter. This type of oil filter, slightly modified, would become standard equipment on many World War II aircraft engines. The single coil ignition system replaced the dual coil system of the previous Tenth and Eleventh Series Eight and Super Eight. The Twelve boasted a newly designed distributor which contained one coil for each bank of cylinders.

Among the important mechanical improvements was a copper alloy connecting rod bearing for longer motor life.

The Angleset rear axle fitted with silent hypoid gears allowed lower mounted bodies with headroom maintained.

Fully mounting the mechanism on ball and roller bearings insured a smooth and velvety "feel" at the steering wheel.

Pioneered by Packard, the famous trunnion block absorbed road shocks otherwise passed along to the steering gear.

Twelfth Series Super Eight Model 1204 Coupe. Price at Detroit $3,080. Often called the Opera Coupe. Note front opening doors. Chrome hood louvers identify it as a Super Eight.

Insert bearings made their first appearance in some Eleventh Series engines. However, it was not until the Twelfth Series that all engines had insert bearings. At this time, replacement connecting rod bearings with inserts were made available for Tenth and Eleventh Series engines. This improvement was a natural outgrowth of better metallurgy, which produced the hardened steel crankshaft, the need for higher speed engines to traverse the now high-speed highway systems, and the protection afforded inserts by the development of the new oil filtering system which was incorporated in the Eleventh Series. A by-product of the insert was easier and faster engine overhauling.

The poured bearing used prior to this date was completely adequate for the use intended, and is responsible for saving the engines for today's restorers. The poured connecting rod bearing, being soft and thick, had the ability to absorb foreign matter, close over these minute particles, and thereby protect the shaft from damage. However, with the demand for high speed for sustained periods, the poured

bearing became obsolete. Being thick, it could not dissipate readily the high heat generated by the natural friction of a high-speed engine under load. Fortunately, there are new developments in babbit material, particularly the lead tin variety which will compensate to a degree for the shortcoming of a poured bearing. However, a crankshaft should be metallized and brought back to standard to keep the thickness of the poured bearing to the minimum. The insert bearing is a two-part steel shell onto which is spun molten metal. The type of molten material depends upon the use the engine will be subjected to in its operation.

For the record, there are seven metal alloys that are in general use today in the automotive trade.

1. Cast copper lead with a 1/1000″ tin overlay.
2. Cast copper lead without tin overlay.
3. Centered copper lead.
4. Lead and tin base—22/1000″ thick (BABBITT).
5. Tin base conventional—22/1000″ thick (BABBITT).

Twelfth Series Super Eight Model 1204 Coupe. Price at Detroit $2,880. Sometimes called the gentleman's coupe. Twelfth Series models can be identified by the 90° angle of radiator. Accessory bumper guards.

Super Eight power plant. Note single coil, L-8 filter and oil level gauge outlet.

Twelfth Series Twelve Model 1207 Sedan. Price at Detroit $3,960. The Twelfth Series is the first series that also may be called 1935 Packards.

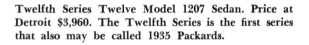

6. Lead base conventional—3/1000″ thick (used for "micro" bearings).

7. Aluminum bearings.

The Twelfth Series used the steel back copper lead alloy bearing (Item 2). If new bearings are being contemplated for restoration, the tin overlay should be requested (Item 1). Tin is an anti-friction metal and is very important in centering the inserts properly during the initial run. With the advent of the inserts, close tolerances are mandatory.

process. The only alternatives to restorers are group participation in having new inserts made, or the machining of oversize stock inserts to fit. The poured bearing as a substitute for the insert is out of the question. The material is too thick and the immediate results are pounding out. This is expedited by the lack of heat dissapation.

The Twelfth Series was also equipped with a heavier generator to insure adequate capacity for the radio, heater, and the many other electrical accessories that were available and

Twelfth Series Twelve Model 1207 Coupe. Price at Detroit $3,280. Double row of hood louvers identify the Twelve.

Too much clearance will result in oil throw-off which can by-pass the piston rings and badly carbon up the engine. It is also suggested that crankshafts that have been ground more than 10/1000″ be metallized and brought back to standard. Inserts that are thicker than 10/1000″ are too thick for good heat dissipation and will cause rapid bearing failure.

The re-babbitting of old shells has met with very poor success. The condition of the shells and the fatigue of the metal shells themselves is responsible for the high failure of this

in high demand. There was much special equipment available for the Twelfth Series. Listed below are a partial list and the cost.

Chromium plated wire wheels	$30.00 each
Chromium plated wheel shields	$ 6.00 each
Chromium plated radiator shell	$10.00 each
Chromium headlights and tail lights	$20.00 each
Trunk rack for cars equipped with five wheels	$35.00 each
Wood wheels (optional equip. of 12's)	$17.00 each
Deluxe equipment which consists of: six wheels, wells in fender, side wheel brackets, and trunk rack. Tires are extra	$65.00

There were no true semi-customs in the Packard sales brochures for the Twelfth Series. Those that carried a Dietrich or Le-Baron body plate were strictly modified stock bodies or stocks made by Murray and Briggs. The true customs still were being ordered through the dealers but were placed with Rollston, Derham, or Brunn direct. Also quite a few Twelfth Series purchasers delivered their own cars to these body shops for special conversion work. Packard also continued to supply extra-long wheelbase chassis to the manufacturers of ambulances and hearses.

A new type distributor and waterproof coil, one for each cylinder block, greatly increased ignition efficiency.

The factory for the first time offered commercial limousines in the Eight and Super Eight to round out this commercial car line.

For the first time in Packard's history, the factory issued a bulletin to the dealers and publicity releases to the press that the Twelfth Series introduced on August 30, 1934, would also be known as 1935 Packards. There was a twofold reason for this change: first, they did this to comply with President Roosevelt's request that automobile announcements be as early in the Fall as possible to help stabilize and reduce unemployment during the winter months; second, Packard was a member of the Automobile Manufacturers Association and, consequently, was a party to holding the new car show in November rather than January.

Packards built prior to the Twelfth Series may not be properly described as a year model car. The earlier series cars, as has been noted,

were introduced at any time during the calendar year and continued to be produced throughout that year and succeeding calendar years. Know your model designation when ordering parts or describing your classic! Only the Packards manufactured after August, 1934, can be referred to by year.

In Chapter 3 we discussed the two basic types of paint, lacquer and enamel. Lacquer has always been used where depth and richness of finish is desired. Synthetic enamel is easier to apply and less expensive because no sanding and compounding is necessary. Both

Oil was conditioned for weather efficiency by a temperature regulator and full-flow filter which was made self-cleaning.

are about the same in durability, but the fact remains that the better paint jobs are done with lacquer.

The depth of lacquer depends on the number of coats and the method of application. The most important point to remember for good results is to keep the lacquer wet. Each coat is blended with the one previously applied so that the final result is like one heavy coat of paint. The secret of good color and richness of tone is getting a good base coat. One well-known car restorer uses a dead black to achieve deep rich-looking tones.

Metallics, which are ground aluminum powders suspended in paint, are much more difficult to apply. They must be applied as wet as possible and be "Fogged in." If this is not done, a spotty effect will result. Home restorers who wish to protect their investment should not do their own painting. Automobile painting is a highly skilled trade and unless you are thoroughly familiar with the techniques it should not be attempted. The use of colors on classics should be carefully considered. Poor planning and the use of wrong color combinations can ruin the finest craftsmanship.

Generally, dark colors tend to make a classic look shorter, dumpier, and hearse-like. Only the most formal of body styles should be repainted in dark colors. Light colors give the appearance of length since they seem to blend the car into the landscape. It is, of course, an

The mighty Twelve. Note heavy duty generator and vacuum booster valve on top of engine manifold. All gas and oil lines and nuts were plated at the factory.

optical illusion but nevertheless very real. Dark colors silhouette an object and the eye stops abruptly at the dividing line between the object and its background. Light colors run or fade into the background and the eye continues past the edge of the object. This, incidently, is the whole basis of the science of camouflage. A dark-colored superstructure or top on a light-colored body should be avoided regardless of body style. The eye is drawn to the top, thus accentuating the height rather than the length. Another technique for giving a classic a low silhouette is by painting all the horizontal surfaces one color and the

vertical surfaces, including the undercarriage, a complimentary color.

There is a serious question as to whether black top material was available for open classics. However, from a color composition viewpoint, a black top on an open classic completely destroys the low silhouette effect and therefore the use of black top material should be avoided.

Early classics were meant to be two-toned to accentuate their long sweeping fenders and hoods and to give them a low silhouette. When streamlining made its appearance, the low silhouette effect was achieved through the metal contour of the body, and this effect is best accentuated through the use of solid light colors.

Striping was also a technique that was not only decorative but added to the optical illusion of lowness and length. Be sure that you do not overlook the color of the striping in obtaining a complimentary color flow.

FORMULA FOR OBTAINING HORSEPOWER

bore $\times$ piston displacement $\times$ rpm $\times$ compression ratio $=$ horsepower

Factors for compression ratio:

6.00 to 1	3.54	7.00 to 1	3.87
6.25	3.62	7.25	3.96
6.50	3.69	7.50	4.03
6.75	3.76	7.75	4.15

Example—Packard Twelve:

3-7/16 bore $\times$ 474 cubic inch displacement $\times$ 3200 rpm $\times$ 6.50 compression ratio = 3.4375 $\times$ 474 = 16294 $\times$ 3200 rpm = 5214 $\times$ 3.63 = 192 h.p.

Twelfth Series instrument panel. Gauges have a brown tint, and the gasoline gauge is also the oil level gauge.

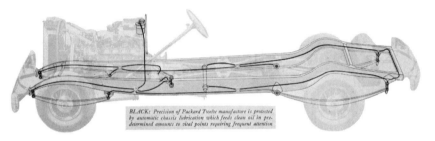

BLACK: Precision of Packard Twelve manufacture is protected by automatic chassis lubrication which feeds clean oil in pre-determined amounts to vital points requiring frequent attention

Chassis showing automatic lubrication system.

11

The Fourteenth Series

Exhibits at the 36th National Automobile Show which was held for the first time in November were not too exciting. Perhaps it was due to the new date and the economic condition of the automobile industry. The A.M.A. reported that 95 per cent of all cars were sold under $750 wholesale. One can see at a glance that not only was the luxury market gone, but those manufacturers in the medium-price field were also in a squeeze. Marmon, Duesenberg, and Stutz were gone, Auburn and Cord were dying despite a temporary stay of execution with the introduction of a beautifully designed compact luxury car called the 810 Cord. Pierce Arrow was going into receivership. In the medium-price field, Reo was discontinuing passenger car production to concentrate on trucks. Reo was the new firm that Ransom E. Olds had built after selling his Oldsmobile operation to General Motors many years before. Nash Motors merged with the Kelvinator Corporation of Detroit to have access to more capital. The by-product of this merger, which would show

up several years later, was diversification, the only key to automotive survival for an independent.

General Motors introduced an inexpensive series of Cadillacs to compete with the Packard 120 and the Lincoln Zephyr and to salvage some form of income to offset the losses being piled up by the Cadillac Division. Hudson introduced a steel torque arm which resulted in easier steering and the elimination of nosing down when the brakes were applied. Also offered was a double automatic emergency braking system with a separate reserve brake system that went into use in the event that the primary brakes failed. All the cars now had the hand brakes on the left of the driver. A feature Packard had incorporated several decades before. Built-in defrosters appeared on many of the new models.

At Packard, the corporate coffers were overflowing with the coin of the realm. The 120 was a tremendous success and it did much to keep the grim reaper from the "Hall of Classics" on Detroit's East Grand Boulevard. Al-

Fourteenth Series Model 120-B Sedan. Price at Detroit $1,075. The luxury market had shrunk to ½ of 1 percent of all automotive production. The 120 would save Packard.

Fourteenth Series Model 120-B Touring Sedan. Price at Detroit, $1,115. The 120-B accounted for 55,042 units for 1936.

Fourteenth Series Eight Model 1401 Sedan. Price at Detroit $2,585. Fourteenth Series cars can be identified by 5° slant of the radiator. The Eight can be identified by the painted hood louvers. Chrome shell, headlights, and taillights were a factory option at a slight additional cost.

though the 120 was not a classic by any stretch of the imagination, nor was it intended to be, it was an honest well-built medium-priced car and in its class it was unsurpassed. It is often said that the 120 was Packard's biggest mistake; this statement couldn't be farther from the truth. A corporation's prime responsibility is to make money for the stockholders, and stockholders want dividends not works of art. Volume production was the economic key to survival in the automotive industry in 1936. Today diversification would seem to be the answer. Packard did not abandon the luxury market to Cadillac, for there was no longer a luxury market. When statistics show that 95 per cent of the cars sold had a wholesale value of $750 or less, the remaining 5 per cent was pretty well taken up by the medium-price market. Packard, as a builder of fine cars, would continue to outsell Cadillac in what was left of the shattered luxury market right up to World War II.

Lincoln, too, was running in the red, but having no public stockholders they did not have to own up to the defunct luxury market although they were well aware of it and had brought out the medium-priced Lincoln Zephyr to offset their losses incurred by Lincoln.

Packard management armed with this information and with the know-how acquired from the 120 decided to introduce an automobile that would fall into the "less than $750 wholesale" market. This automobile would be known as the Packard 110, model 115c. It would be made on the 120 assembly line and would be introduced for the 1937 model year.

The Fourteenth Series continued the same beautiful design which had been introduced in the previous Twelfth Series. Packard management, like many other professional groups of the time, avoided the Thirteenth Series designation. The Packard motor car continued to hold its unique position in the automotive

world. Its purpose was to build a luxury car as nearly perfect as possible, one of long life and enduring style. With the profits from the 120, this high ideal would be continued.

The Eight, Super Eight, and Twelve continued to be built on an individually assembled basis. In the 1936 model year, Packard employed 5100 production workers, 2500 of whom were assigned to the production of 5,985 Senior Packards and the remaining 2600 worked across the street assembling 55,042 Packard 120's. At a glance, these cold figures tell the story most eloquently of the time and money lavished on the Senior Series to insure the hallmark of quality.

The only visual differences between the Fourteenth Series and the Twelfth Series is the 5° slant of the radiator shell and the chrome strips added to the Eight's headlamps. Mechanically, they were identical with one exception; the Twelve oil temperature regulator was now of the conventional design used on the Eight and Super Eight. Had Packard not gone on a year model basis the year before, it can be safely assumed management would have never designated this car as the new Fourteenth Series with these minute changes. The Fourteenth Series was the last series to include a phaeton, dual cowl phaeton, and seven-passenger touring car in the sales brochure. However, these open body styles did appear on later series chassis, but they were on special order from Murray or built by custom coach builders like Derham and Rollston.

The original factory top material on all open models was imported English Burbank material. Later, light tan domestic Haartz cloth material was used. Three ply material is the best weight for folding tops and five ply for non-collapsible sport tops. Snap buttons should always be concealed under a flap of the top material. The use of black top materials or synthetic top materials for replacement should be avoided. Aside from not being au-

Fourteenth Series Super Eight Model 1404 Club Sedan. Price at Detroit $3,170. The Super Eight can be identified by chrome hood louvers. With the exception of the Club Sedan, all Fourteenth Series have fastbacks, and, like the Twelfth Series, front opening doors are standard on all models.

Fourteenth Series Super Eight Model 1404 Coupe Roadster. Price at Detroit $3,070. Wire wheels could be had simply by removing the wheel discs. Bumpers from the Twelve could be had as extra. This was a status option and increased wear on the lighter Super Eight front end components.

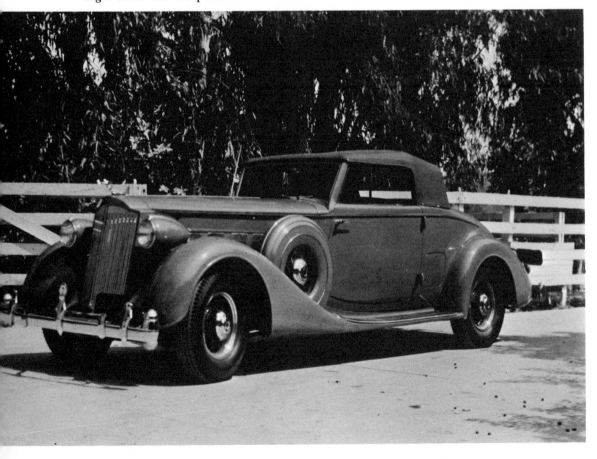

thentic and a deterrent to your investment, the synthetic materials retain the wrinkles that are created from folding the top.

The interchangeability of bodies continued to keep costs down for the luxury manufacturers, and Packard was no exception. The bodies on the Super Eight and Twelves were interchangeable, wheelbase for wheelbase, only the interior appointments being different. The Eight also used the bodies of the Super Eight and Twelve but on the correspondingly shorter chassis. The only exception, which is true of all the previous series, is the smallest wheelbase sedan. It was a high volume model and was not interchangeable with any other sedan body in its series.

These bodies continued to be made of wood and steel. Fine coach builders learned through years of experience that steel is better for some parts and wood is more satisfactory for others, and that in many places a combination of the two is desirable. Wood has a natural lag or hysteresis, which reacts in the body much the same as a crankshaft damper reacts in dampening out annoying vibrations of the crankshaft. Body steel takes a permanent set. It also crystalizes under vibration and cracks. Wood, on the other hand, never takes a permanent set, but lags in returning to its original position. This lag, or hysteresis, absorbs and counteracts any high-pitch vibrations set up by the metal. The railroad industry, since its inception, has never found a more satisfactory combination than wood ties and steel rails for strength, resiliency, durability, and safety.

All-steel bodies, which, of course, are cheaper to produce, have universal appeal to today's automotive manufacturers. This trend definitely started to show up in the mid-Thirties as a cost cutting technique. Madison Avenue had given Detroit the keys to the door of planned obsolescence. Quality was old fashioned, styling was king, and to drive the same model for more than two years was an admis-

sion to your neighbors that you were destitute. In recent years, for those who disagreed with buying a new car every year, the manufacturers have insured your compliance with their theories by building in rapid deterioration of sheet metal, upholstery, plating, and tires.

Custom body building had died by 1936. The small individual shops like Bohman and Schwartz in Pasadena, Durham of Rosemont, Willoughby of Utica, Brunn of Buffalo, and Rollston of New York managed to stay alive because of low overhead. It was to these few custom body plants that the few hundred who still desired something different took their work. The movie colony used Bohman and Schwartz almost exclusively because of their location. The predecessor company of Bohman and Schwartz was the famous Walter M. Murphy Co., which started in 1923. They are probably best remembered today for their beautiful Duesenberg convertible coupe bodies.

Walter Murphy started as a West Coast Leland Lincoln distributor. Walter soon discovered that the high, boxy, and drab-colored Leland Lincoln was about as popular as a dog at the flea circus. Failing to talk Leland into more stylish lines, he purchased the Healey Body Company from Colonel Healey and moved it to Pasadena. He then proceeded to customize and repaint all of the Leland Lincoln cars shipped to California. Within a few years, Ford purchased the Lincoln and restyled it sufficiently to a point where this additional customizing was no longer necessary. It was a natural step to start building special bodies on any chassis for the new rich of the movie world. Later, the wealthy carriage trade from all over the United States were ordering custom built bodies from Murphy. Some of these individuals were the directors of luxury automobile concerns. Soon Murphy was designing and building prototype automobiles for Packard, Duesenberg, Lincoln, Ruxton, Franklin, Au-

Fourteenth Series Super Eight Model 1405 Limousine.
Price at Detroit $3,580. This was the last series that
would offer wood wheels as an option. Fortunately
for restorers, the lustrous wool broadcloths used in
these models can still be duplicated in England.

Fourteenth Series Twelve Model 1407 Sport Phaeton.
Price at Detroit $4,490. The last factory series phae-
ton. The original factory top material on all open
models was imported English Burbank material. Later,
light-tan domestic Haartz cloth material was used.

burn Cord, Rolls Royce, Peerless, Stutz, and for small and medium-price manufacturers.

Murphy Co. is probably best known for their beautiful convertible sedans and coupes. In the mid-twenties, they designed the Auburn convertible sedan and convertible coupe, which remained unchanged for five years. These two body styles accounted for 50 per cent of Auburn's entire production. Because of the quantities needed, the work of building these bodies was sub-contracted to the Limousine Body Company at Kalamazoo. When the Duesenberg J and SJ made its debut, Murphy

to retire and the Walter M. Murphy Co. was dead.

Out of these ashes, two former employees, Christian Bohman and Maurice Schwartz, formed a new company that would continue the traditions of the Murphy Body Co. Maurice became the plant manager and Chris the sales manager.

Maurice Schwartz was born in Austria in 1884 and learned coach building in Europe. The plant in which he worked built many of the royal coaches for the royalty of Europe. In 1910 he came to America and worked for

Fourteenth Series Twelve Model 1408 Town Car by LeBaron. Price at Detroit $6,435. Landau leather is the top material and can still be obtained from Packard's original supplier. The bodies were fabricated at Briggs and shipped to the Packard factory for mounting.

was designated by individual purchasers to build more than 55 per cent of all Duesenberg bodies.

Because of the distance, Packard never purchased semi-customs on the lot basis from Murphy. However, Packard management highly approved of the work done by Walter Murphy. Alvan Macauley and Frederick Alger, President and Chairman of the Board of P.M.C. respectively, both drove Murphy bodied Packards. In 1932, Walter Murphy decided

the Springfield Metal Body Company in Massachusetts. From there he went to work for Willoughby and then the Fisher Brothers. In 1918 he went to California and worked for the Earl Auto Works in Los Angeles. He then joined Walter Murphy in 1923.

Chris Bohman was born in Sweden and came to America in 1912. Like other famous body builders, he started with the "Granddaddy" body builder of them all, Brewster & Co., in New York. He then worked for Holbrook and afterwards went to California to work for Murphy. The Bohman and Schwartz plant was located at 326 West Colorado Avenue in Pasadena.

Fourteenth Series Twelve. Model 1408 Convertible Sedan. Price at Detroit $5,050. The Twelve used a double row of hood louvers. The Fourteenth Series was the last series to have the straight axle, ride control, the bijur system, and the heavy vibration dampening bumpers.

Interior shots of the Fourteenth Series Twelve.

Their most startling creation was the phantom corsair now owned by Herb Shriner. It was designed by Howard Heinz (57 Varieties) for himself. It was a gull winged job built on a 1937 Cord chassis. Some say that if young Howard Heinz had not died, he would have become a leading automotive designer. One of the most beautiful Packards designed and built by Bohman and Schwartz was an Eleventh Series Twelve formal sedan ordered by Jeanette MacDonald. This car is now in a museum at Cape May, New Jersey.

In the late Thirties, and early Forties, many Packard owners turned to Bohman and Schwartz to customize their newly delivered production Packards into exotic one-of-a-kind creations. When the Darrin bodied Packard

by the Packard legal staff, Buick's enthusiasm for the project quickly died. Ranking with the Packard radiator shape was the red hexagon.

Like the radiator contour, the hexagon hubcap first appeared on the 1904 Model L. This hexagon hubcap was designed by Packard's chief engineer, Russel Huff, Jr., for the purpose of providing better leverage for the wrenches. The original hexagons were painted black. This was probably done to cover any scars in the metal left by the wrench. Later the hexagons were painted red as an inspection symbol denoting final inspection. During the classic era, the hexagon on the hubcap was not always red. Between the Twelfth and the Sixteenth Series the Standard Eight and

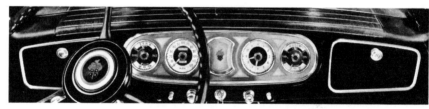

Aside from placement, instrument design and illumination are all-important factors. Packard used big readable figures against translucent dials, indirect lighting controlled by a rheostat, and headlight telltale signals.

came out, demand was so heavy and production so slow that many wealthy Packard *aficionados* turned to Bohman and Schwartz for their own versions of this fabulous body style. In 1944, Bohman and Schwartz closed their doors. Bohman went into the machine shop business, which he stayed in until his death in 1948. Maurice Schwartz continued on as a self-employed coach builder who has helped many antique and classic car restorers put their gleaming jewels back on the road.

Through the years, Packard had distinctive styling characteristics that set it apart from all other automobiles. The most famous was the Packard radiator shape, which started in 1904. Buick in the middle Twenties decided to copy this design for their own product. When the subject of rights was brought to their attention

the Super Eight hubcaps were often the color of the car. The Twelve hubcap could be had with black cloisonné medallions, but most were red.

Through the years, the only written reference to the Packard Motor Company was in small black letters on the hubcap. Modesty was not the reason, but rather an unwritten law among the wealthy that a marque's name plastered all over the vehicle was the rankest form of commercialism. In fact, Packard had an option whereby a wealthy client could have hubcaps and insignia devoid of any written reference to Packard.

By the Fourteenth Series, aluminum heads had become very popular. Packard had been

Closeup of components for Fourteenth Series Twelve.

using aluminum for years, and now that aluminum was becoming less expensive, the whole automobile industry was using it for pistons, crankcases, head, etc. Aluminum heads dissipate heat much more rapidly than cast iron. Its one drawback, which is still very real even in today's automotive manufacturing, is the highly corrosive action that takes place in the presence of permanent type anti-freeze. When permanent type anti-freeze seeps to the pistons, it has a crystallizing effect which eventually destroys the piston. Alcohol with a good rust inhibitor should be used. A rust inhibitor should also be used during the rest of the seasons.

When the Fourteenth Series ended, the big and powerful $3\frac{1}{2} \times 5$ Super Eight was discontinued and the Eight would undergo a metamorphosis. The Fourteenth Series was also the last series to have an option of wire or wood wheels, the straight axle, ride control, the bijur system, and the heavy vibration dampening bumpers.

12

The Fifteenth Series

The 37th National Automobile Show was held during the week of October 27, 1936. The high point of the show was Packard's new six-cylinder car called the 110. It had a 115″ wheelbase, its model designation was 115c, and the engine serial numbers started with T1500. Everybody, it seems, likes a good number! All the Packards shown had the new independent front wheel suspension and hydraulic brakes. Now that there was a Packard for every pocketbook, the Packard display was jammed with potential buyers

Ford introduced a new small 60 h.p., V-8 as a companion to the larger 85 h.p. engine. Oldsmobile and Buick introduced the Automatic Safety Transmission, an automatic gear shift. Cord brought out the model 812, a supercharged version of the 810 which had been introduced a year earlier. It would be Cord's last new model. Chrysler offered an adjustable seat that moved not only back and forth but up and down as well. Studebaker introduced windshield washers as optional equipment. Several manufacturers offered steering column gear shifts and storage batteries under the hood for easy maintenance.

Packard's financial star was at its zenith. Never before and never again would Packard sell as many automobiles or make as much money as it did in 1937. The Fifteenth Series starting line-up featured the highly successful Packard 120 and a new medium-priced six-cylinder car called the 110. The 110 was built to invade the less than $750 wholesale price bracket which accounted for 95 per cent of all cars sold in the United States. The cars were assembled on the 120 production line. Production was closely supervised by George Christopher who was now Vice-President of Manufacturing and had much know-how in low cost volume production. The car was a tremendous success, as was attested by the fact that 65,400 units were sold during 1937. The companion Packard 120 with its eight-cylinder engine added another 50,100 units. Packard was now in fifth place as a volume producer of automobiles. In the backfield, a new Super Eight was introduced which filled

Fifteenth Series Six Model 115C (110) Touring Sedan. Price at Detroit $910. Packard's first six-cylinder car since 1928. The 110 was built to invade the less than $750 wholesale price bracket which accounted for 95 per cent of all cars sold in the United States.

the slot of the previous year's Eight and Super Eight. At fullback, the mighty Twelve.

Packard management, realizing that the luxury car market could no longer support any manufacturer exclusively dedicated to the production of luxury cars, started to phase out the Senior Series over a three-year period. First to go was the big Fourteenth Series Super Eight. The Eight nomenclature was also dropped at the end of the Fourteenth Series. The car that would fill this void was a completely redesigned automobile which would carry on the Super Eight designation. This new Super Eight was just as big, had better roadability, but lacked the tremendous power

of the Fourteenth Series Super Eight. However, this new Super Eight was also scheduled to be phased out at the end of the Sixteenth Series. The mighty Twelve was scheduled for oblivion at the end of the Seventeenth Series. The Eighteenth Series would have a compact luxury car called the Packard 180 as Packard's only luxury classic.

By the end of 1937, the astonishing total of 122,593 Packards had been sold. It is doubly astonishing when you realize that the economy had started on a downswing in 1937. Naturally, the non-classic medium-priced 110 and 120 accounted for 94 per cent of these sales. However, more Twelves were sold in 1937 than in any other year of its production. In

Fifteenth Series Eight Model 120C Touring Sedan. Price at Detroit $1,060. The Packard 110 and 120 accounted for 94 per cent of Packard's 1937 sales.

First Series Eight, Model 143 Touring. Price at Detroit $3,850. Packard's first straight eight. Production started June, 1923. The granddaddy of all Packard eights.

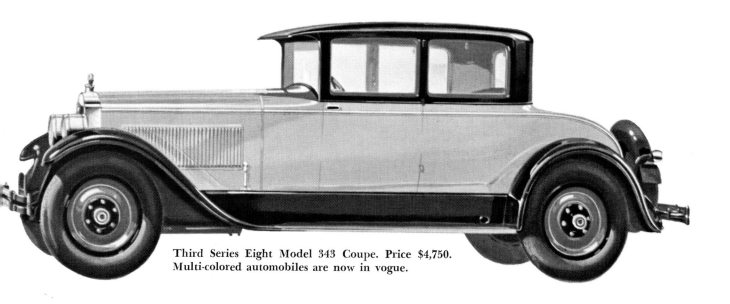

Third Series Eight Model 343 Coupe. Price $4,750. Multi-colored automobiles are now in vogue.

The Author's 443 Custom Phaeton, cost at Detroit $3,875. Standard factory equipment included side mounts and chassis in color.

Sixth Series Eight Model 645 Club Sedan. Cost at Detroit $5,785. An identifying feature of the 645 is the trunk rack with vertical cross bars.

Seventh Series Model 733 Club Sedan. Price at Detroit $2675. Wood spoke wheels were $102.00 extra; fender lamps $20.00 extra. Note right hand taillight which was also available.

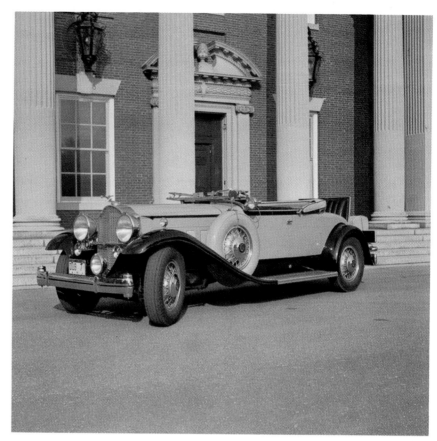

Eighth Series Big Eight Model 840 Roadster. Price at Detroit $3,490. This was Packard's last production roadster. Note the similarity to the Ninth Series automobiles. This effect was achieved by a conversion unit offered to the dealers by the factory to help sell the leftover Eighth Series vehicles at Ninth Series introduction time.

Ninth Series Twin Six Model 906 Sport Phaeton. Price at Detroit $5875. New styling of this model would set the design for the next three years. The pelican and 750 x 18 tires made their appearance on this model.

THE NEW PACKARD EIGHT COLOR COMBINATIONS

PAINT SCHEME A

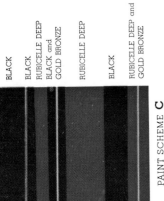
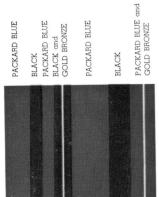
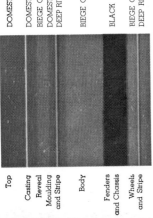

Top	DOMESTIC GRAY
Casting	DOMESTIC GRAY
Reveal	BIEGE GRAY
Moulding and Stripe	DOMESTIC GRAY and DEEP RIVER GREEN
Body	BIEGE GRAY
Fenders and Chassis	BLACK
Wheels and Stripe	BIEGE GRAY and DEEP RIVER GREEN

PAINT SCHEME B

	PACKARD BLUE
	BLACK
	PACKARD BLUE
	BLACK and GOLD BRONZE
	PACKARD BLUE
	BLACK
	PACKARD BLUE and GOLD BRONZE

PAINT SCHEME C

	BLACK
	BLACK
	RUBICELLE DEEP
	BLACK and GOLD BRONZE
	RUBICELLE DEEP
	BLACK
	RUBICELLE DEEP and GOLD BRONZE

PAINT SCHEME D

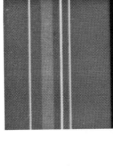

	SHIRVAN GREEN
	BLACK
	SHIRVAN GREEN
	BLACK and GOLD BRONZE
	SHIRVAN GREEN
	BLACK
	SHIRVAN GREEN and GOLD BRONZE

PAINT SCHEME E

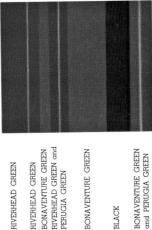

Top	RIVERHEAD GREEN
Casting	RIVERHEAD GREEN
Reveal	BONAVENTURE GREEN
Moulding and Stripe	RIVERHEAD GREEN and PERUGIA GREEN
Body	BONAVENTURE GREEN
Fenders and Chassis	BLACK
Wheels and Stripe	BONAVENTURE GREEN and PERUGIA GREEN

PAINT SCHEME F

	MIDNIGHT BLUE
	MIDNIGHT BLUE
	COUNTESS BLUE
	MIDNIGHT BLUE and LIGHT BLUE
	COUNTESS BLUE
	BLACK
	COUNTESS BLUE and LIGHT BLUE

PAINT SCHEME X

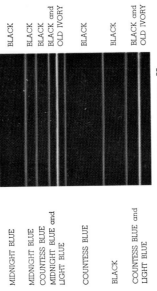

	BLACK
	BLACK
	BLACK
	BLACK and OLD IVORY
	BLACK
	BLACK
	BLACK and OLD IVORY

PAINT SCHEME M

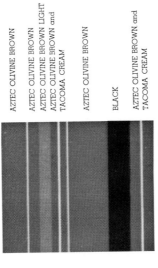

	AZTEC OLIVINE BROWN
	AZTEC OLIVINE BROWN
	AZTEC OLIVINE BROWN LIGHT
	AZTEC OLIVINE BROWN and TACOMA CREAM
	AZTEC OLIVINE BROWN
	BLACK
	AZTEC OLIVINE BROWN and TACOMA CREAM

- TOP
- REVEAL
- MOULDING AND STRIPE
- BODY
- FENDERS AND CHASSIS
- WHEELS AND STRIPE

Sixteenth Series Super Eight Model 1604 Two-Door Sedan by Mayfair of London. Approximate cost $20,000. Delivery was taken in France by a Greek shipping magnet. As a result, it carries a 12 volt Marchal lighting system.

Nineteenth Series 110 Model 1900 Station Wagon. Price at Detroit $1,231. Packard purchased these excellent bodies from the Hercules Body Co. The Nineteenth Series 110 was almost identical to the 120. The only real difference was the eight-cylinder engine in the 120.

teenth Series Twelve Model 1708 Limousine. at Detriot $4,690. Extras included sidemounts uggage rack at $240.00, cormorant at $10.00, rs at $20.00, auxiliary front bumper at $40.00, g lights at $40.00, heater and defroster at . Incidentally, this was George M. Cohan's last sine.

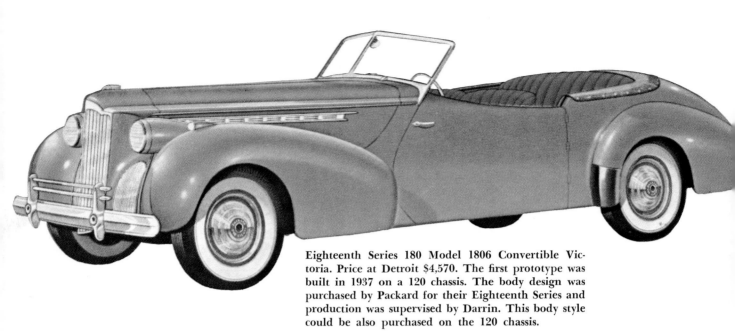

Eighteenth Series 180 Model 1806 Convertible Victoria. Price at Detroit $4,570. The first prototype was built in 1937 on a 120 chassis. The body design was purchased by Packard for their Eighteenth Series and production was supervised by Darrin. This body style could be also purchased on the 120 chassis.

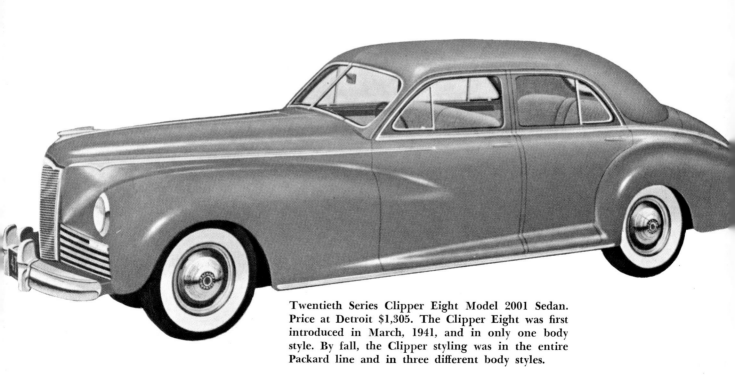

Twentieth Series Clipper Eight Model 2001 Sedan. Price at Detroit $1,305. The Clipper Eight was first introduced in March, 1941, and in only one body style. By fall, the Clipper styling was in the entire Packard line and in three different body styles.

Tenth Series Eight, Model 1002 Phaeton. Price at Detroit $2,370. Chassis in color was $110.00 extra. Yellow-Tan was the most popular color for Packard open cars during the Thirties.

leventh Series Twelve Model 1108 Victoria Con-
ertible by Dietrich. Price at Detroit $6,701. Dietrich
uilt custom bodies can be easily identified by their
ee-type slanting windshields, short cowls, extra long
ood with six ventilators, and the doors are hinged
n the centerpost. It took until 1934 to exhaust the
pply of these bodies which were built in the white
1931.

Twelfth Series Eight Model 1201 Club Sedan. Price at Detroit $2,580. The Twelfth Series Eight did not use the spring loaded bumpers. 700 x 17 tires were used on the Eight and Super Eight and 750 x 17 on the Twelves. Note the re-designed running boards.

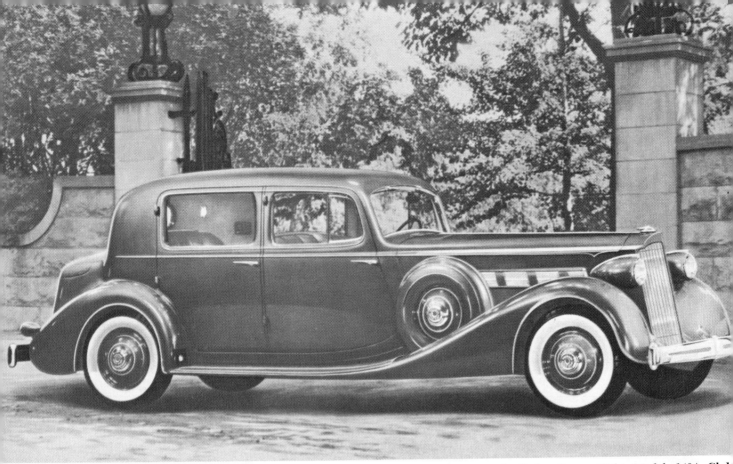

Fourteenth Series Super Eight Model 1404 Club Sedan. Price at Detroit $3,170. The Super Eight can be identified by chrome hood louvers. With the exception of the Club Sedan, all Fourteenth Series have fastbacks, and, like the Twelfth Series, front opening doors are standard on all models.

Fifteenth Series Twelve Model 1507 Club Sedan. Price at Detroit $4,045. Fifteenth Series can be identified by the 30° slant of radiator shell, conventional front opening doors, and chrome bars that carry the side mounts.

Fifteenth Series Eight Model 120C Convertible Sedan. Price at Detroit $1,355. Bodies were built by Murray and were fitted with Dietrich nameplates as a sales promotion.

fact, one-fifth of all Twelves built during the eight years of production were built in 1937.

In the Senior Series, Packard continued to hold to its quality ideals by presenting improved and refined models over those of a year before. The Senior Series was socially "America's First Motor Car." By the end of the year, the Senior Series had accounted for 50.3 per cent of all sales in the all but dead luxury market.

The Fifteenth Series Super Eight and Twelve, which were introduced on September 3, 1936, were completely re-designed automobiles. Chassis-wise, the straight axle had been given up in favor of independent front wheel suspension. This one change alone gave

it a riding quality that has never been surpassed, even in the modern Rolls. The mechanical brakes with booster had been abandoned in favor of a complete hydraulic brake system. The Twelve retained its booster in conjuction with the new hydraulic system, which gave it a power brake system which today is still unsurpassed. The Twelve also had a power-boosted clutch for easy operation. After more than a quarter of a century of operation, it is still rare to find this power system in need of repair.

The Bijur chassis lubrication system was also discontinued in favor of grease fittings. By 1937, the service station industry had reached such proportions that the automatic lubrication system was no longer necessary to protect the chassis. The weight distribution factor had also been changed, making the heavy vibration dampening bumpers unnecessary. Steel disc wheels had replaced the previous year's wire wheels and they had been fitted with 16″ tires. Although the Twelve was fitted with 825 x 16 super cushions, the 750 x 16 six ply gives it better handling qualities and the interchange is recommended.

The Fifteenth Series was the last series to have the 144″ wheelbase and its was used only in conjunction with the Twelve. The Super Eight was now designated 1500, 1501, and 1502, which was the Eight nomenclature of the Fourteenth Series Eight. The Fifteenth Series Super Eight is sometimes referred to as the successor of the Fourteenth Series Eight. This is not accurate, nor it is correct to call it the successor to the Fourteenth Series Super Eight. It is a completely re-designed series using Twelve body components mounted on a lighter chassis and a modified eight-cylinder power plant. Twelve chassis parts are not interchangeable with the Super Eight chassis. They are as different as day and night.

Fifteenth Series Super Eight Model 1501 Convertible Coupe. Price at Detroit $2,830. The Super Eight can be identified by the single strip of four chrome louvers. Fifteenth Series have built-in trunks; chromed headlights, taillights, and shell were still available options.

The Super Eight motor. It bowed to no power plant save the Packard Twelve. Its bore was 3-3/16 inches; its stroke 5 inches; its displacement, 320 cubic inches. It developed more than 135 horsepower at 3200 rpm.

The Super Eight chassis. Completely re-balanced design involved every vital unit and bettered each with a revolutionary engineering newness.

Fifteenth Series Super Eight Model 1500 Touring Sedan. Price at Detroit $2,335. This was Packard's volume classic. It was fitted on 127″ wheelbase and came in only the touring sedan. It had excellent handling qualities and was a real performer.

Fifteenth Series Twelve Model 1507 Club Sedan. Price at Detroit $4,045. Fifteenth Series can be identified by the 30° slant of radiator shell, conventional front opening doors, and chrome bars that carry the sidemounts.

Quick identification points for the Fifteenth Series cars are the chrome bars that hold the fender-mounted spares, the 35° slant to the radiator, the conventional opening front doors, re-designed smaller tail lights, sixteen-inch drop center wheels with large hubcaps and re-designed bumpers. The Super Eight engine now has an externally mounted generator on the left hand forward side of the engine, which, of course, means a re-designed crankcase and gear setup.

There are several major factors responsible for the classic Packard lasting through the dark days of the Depression, the seven-year obsolescent programs, and the scrap drives of World War II. The first and foremost was Packard's ability to build a well-engineered and constructed product. The second was the steadfast devotion of owners to their Packard, whether they were the first owner or the tenth. Lastly, there was a fantastic service organization which took better care of the cars entrusted to them than most people took care of their own bodies.

Fifteenth Series Twelve Model 1507 Convertible Sedan. One-fifth of all Twelves built during the eight years of production were built in 1937. The Twelve was equipped with power assisted brakes and clutch.

When restoring these magnificient classics, be authentic and do the restoration right or don't do it at all. The use of seal beam headlight conversion units, naugahyde upholstery, truck tires, enamel paint, etc., only serve to destroy your investment as well as the beauty of a fine work of art. Don't buy more classics than you can financially restore and maintain. Fortunately, there are only a small segment of so-called enthusiasts who buy potentially fine classics and then promptly park them in their backyards under tarpaulins or in damp poorly constructed shelters where they deteriorate to a point beyond restoration. This is selfishness in its rankest form. These classics should be sold to bonafide enthusiasts at reasonable prices so that they may once again be proud symbols of the golden age of motordom.

The first Packard Darrin was built in 1937. It was a short wheelbased convertible coupe with a tire mounted on the rear. It was not a very pretty car, but it was a forerunner of one of the most graceful body styles that was ever to be seen.

LeBaron a la Briggs was building semi-customs for the Packard factory. These semi-customs consisted of a single-windowed town

Fifteenth Series Twelve Model 1507 Touring Sedan.
Pelican ornament was $20.00 extra and sidemount
mirrors were $20.00 per pair.

Fifteenth Series Twelve interior. This is a conventional touring sedan with a special divider complete with jump seat, compartment, and roll up window. Club sedans could also be ordered on different wheelbases and be equipped with this special partition at extra cost.

car and a two-windowed town car. Both were modified factory formal sedans and touring limousines.

Several Fifteenth Series phaetons and touring cars were ordered from the factory although Packard had dropped these two body styles at the end of the previous series. These bodies were built by Murray, fitted with a Dietrich nameplate, and mounted on a Fifteenth Series chassis. One was delivered to the White House and the balance were purchased by individuals. The most beautiful Fifteenth Series phaeton was designed and built by Kellner of Paris on a 12-cylinder chassis. An unusual touring car body was built by Rollston of New York. One of the unique features about the car was its fixed radiator cap. The radiator filler was located under the hood which was identical to the yet unannounced Sixteenth Series cars. Rollston also built a large unique convertible victoria on a 144"

wheelbase Twelve chassis for Schrafft, the wealthy restaurant owner.

The Rollston Body Company was very busy doing Packard custom work in 1937. In fact, it was their first and last good year since 1931. Rollston, like many other famous custom body builders, started in the early twenties. By 1927, Rollston Body Company was owned by three partners, Julius Veghso, Sam Blotkin, and Harry Lonschein, who was President. The firm was located at 601-603 West 47th Street, New York. In 1929, Sam Blotkin sold out his interest and left. About the same time, the Holbrook Body Company in Hudson, New York, went bankrupt. As a result, Rollston was very fortunate in hiring as their sales manager H. A. Holm, a Holbrook executive.

In addition to body building Rollston also did body remounting on new chassis, repainting, re-chroming the factory nickeled parts, and the customizing of individual luxury cars. (Authenticity of a remounted body on a newer chassis is approved when it was done in the year that the new chassis was manufactured. Naturally, the chassis must be manufactured during the classic era by a luxury car producer and the conversion done by a recognized custom body builder like Rollston.) By April, 1938, Rollston was bankrupt. During the life of the company, 654 bodies had been built. Of these, the last 142 had been built since the fall of 1931. During those lean years, people either did not have the money to purchase custom bodies or, if they did, were afraid to be seen in them. One of Rollston's new cars was stoned by the jobless when it left the premises for delivery.

Rollston, like the majority of other custom body builders, used a single serial system for identification. The first body built carried the digit one, the second body two, etc. There were, of course, builders who used different identification systems, such as Brunn and Co., who would number each individual body style

Fifteenth Series Twelve Model 1507 Cabriolet, All-Weather by LeBaron. Price at Detroit $5,925. Side-mounts and luggage rack were $240 extra.

The Twelve motor. It challenged any power plant on any score. Its bore was 3-7/16 inches; its stroke 4-1/4 inches; its displacement 473 cubic inches. It developed more than 175 horsepower at 3200 rpm.

The Twelve chassis. Completely re-balanced design started with its backbone and swept a beneficial effect throughout its component parts.

for each individual year and for each individual marque. However, the large custom body builders like Dietrich and LeBaron used the same system as Rollston.

In September, 1938, several of the executives of the defunct Rollston Co. just couldn't get body building out of their system. As a result, Rollson, Inc., was founded. Mr. Lonschein was again President; H. A. Holm, Vice-President; Frank Sever, Treasurer; and Rudy Creteur, Secretary. H. A. Holm continued to handle sales, Frank Sever was in charge of the metal shop, and Rudy Creteur was the shop superintendent. He also was Rollson's designer and draftsman. Rudy was no stranger to Rollson. He had been hired by Rollston in 1927; prior to that he had worked for Locke & Company in New York City.

To digress a moment, Locke & Company was started in late 1923 by Mr. Locke in New York City. As was the case with most custom body companies in the early Twenties, business was brisk. Custom bodies were the height of fashion. However, the first big money was the result of the Durant contract given to Locke and Co. for the design of the Durant production cars. The Durant Motor Car Co. at that time was located in Elizabeth, New Jersey, and was second only to Ford in the mass production of automobiles. Later, contracts from Lincoln and Chrysler were received for lot orders. To accommodate this new business, an additional plant was built in Rochester, N. Y. In 1926, in the middle of this new expansion, Mr. Locke died. The company was taken over by Mr. Fleischman, who promptly embarked upon a head-hunting campaign, which completely demoralized management at a time when every hand was needed to make the dual-plant operation a success. As a result, the better employees left the company. When the end came in 1929, Locke's last orders were down to two body

Fifteenth Series instrument panel. Hand throttle and light switch are now mounted in dash. Note windshield defroster outlet.

styles: the convertible club roadster and phaeton for Lincoln.

Rollson, Inc., as one can see, had top talent. Their new offices and plant were at 311 West 66th Street, New York City. They would stay in business until December, 1941. The first Rollson body was No. 655. In the next three years, only 50 bodies were built. Forty-eight of these were on Packard chassis. In addition to the meager body orders, Rollson continued to customize standard factory production models, which helped to keep the firm solvent. When production ended, 705 bodies had been built by Rollston and Rollson over a period of eighteen years.

After the war, Rollson contacted Packard, but unfortunately no one at Packard was interested in custom cars. There were two reasons for this. Packard no longer had a suitable chassis for mounting custom bodies. Secondly, the public was so hungry for new automobiles that anything that had four wheels would sell. As a result, Packard, like all other Detroit manufacturers, was busy turning out medium-priced look-alike cars.

The one exception was Lincoln, who continued to produce the Lincoln Continental.

However, these cars had to be price discounted to sell because the public just wasn't interested in quality cars. The motor car was no longer a symbol of prestige. The prestige symbols were now television, hi-fi, and household gadgets.

Rollson is still in business today making galley and kitchen equipment.

13

The Sixteenth Series

The 38th National Automobile Show held in November, 1937, did not have the sparkle of previous shows. Most of the 38 models were a continuation of the 1937 models with a minor face lifting. The two-year model run for the low- and medium-priced cars was now generally accepted in the industry. With the exception of the Senior Series Packards, the other luxury cars were a continuation of the 1937 offerings. This would be the last show for Pierce Arrow. The last-minute efforts to save it from bankruptcy failed. Due to the lack of mechanical innovations, the emphasis was on the comfort and beauty of the new models.

In 1938 Chrysler introduced fluid coupling for transmissions. It was the opening gun for a raft of new automotive developments that would appear in the 1939 models. Hupp bought the body dies of the now defunct Cord. The dies were later resold to Graham for their 1940 and 1941 Skylark and Hollywood models in a last ditch effort to spark new life into that make. Both companies

finally discontinued automotive production in 1941. In 1938 a new Senior Packard was added to the Russian fleet, Josef Stalin bought a new Super Eight convertible sedan.

The Packard Motor Car Company was now one of the biggest and the richest of the independent automotive producers. This was a real accomplishment when you consider that Packard did not make a low-priced car, and that it was in this low-priced market that the American consumer spent 95 per cent of his new-car dollars. Naturally, Packard's success was due to well-built automobiles and the prestige bestowed upon the medium-priced Packard by the Senior luxury line of past years. It can't be repeated too often that Packard did not leave the luxury market, but that the luxury market evaporated, leaving Cadillac, Lincoln, and Packard as "the last of the Mohicans."

Packard's engine business was still good, but volume had been abandoned due to the need for very inch of space for the production of the medium-priced cars. During these years,

Sixteenth Series Six Model 1600 Club Coupe and
Convertible Coupe. Price at Detroit $1,120 and $1,235
respectively. The all-steel body with one piece steel
top and steel floor were used on the Six and Eight.

Sixteenth Series Eight Model 1601 Two-Door Sedan
and Business Coupe. Price at Detroit $1,295, and
$1,225 respectively. The Eight for 1938 would become
the 1939 Super Eight.

Sixteenth Series Eight Model 1601 All-Weather panel Brougham by Rollston. Price at New York City $5,100. The Packard Eight when fitted with meritorious coachwork can achieve full classic status.

Packard had developed and added to their engine line a new pancake 12 engine which was highly successful in the omnibus industry. Soon the famous 12-cylinder marine engine would go to war. Research and development continued to get a large share of the yearly budget to improve the breed. A new high speed eight-cylinder engine with hydraulic valve lifts was under development for the Eighteenth Series.

On September 30, 1937, the new Sixteenth Series automobiles by Packard were introduced. In the medium-price line, the cars had been completely re-designed, re-styled, and renamed. The 110 and 120 nomenclature had been temporarily abandoned in favor of two time-honored names that management felt would add additional prestige to the medium-price line and help smooth the way to any public resentment at the discontinuance of the really big Senior Packards. The 110 would now be known as the Packard Six and the 120 was now the Packard Eight. The sales pitch for the year would be "The Six and Eight for Thirty Eight." Internally, the Packard Six was now designated as model 1600 and the Packard Eight was model 1601, 1601D, and 1602. The cars had also grown in size. The Six now had a 122" wheelbase and the Eight had a 127" wheelbase, 139" wheelbase, and 148" wheelbase. This car was to become the Seventeenth Series Super Eight with only slight modifications. Both models were completely re-designed and the knowledgeable knew that they were seeing a fleeting glimpse of Packard's future thinking. It should be mentioned again that this planning was by choice and based on good market research. Packard countered by reducing the prices on the Six up to $105 on all models. No reduction was offered on the Eight for it would destroy the well-laid plans of upgrading the Eight in the Seventeenth Series.

By March, the stock market had hit bottom and by May so had business. The adjusted Index of Industrial Production had sunk to

76. In nine short months it had lost just about two-thirds of the ground gained during all the painful years of the New Deal. Automotive production dropped 40 per cent. As a result of these economic conditions, the year closed out showing 30,050 Sixes had been sold and 22,624 Eights had been sold. This was a drop of 62,826 units over the previous series.

The Sixteenth Senior Series, which now was comprised of the Super Eight and Twelve, introduced many new styling changes which were well accepted by the dwindling "Carriage Trade." Although basic body construction was identical to the Fifteenth Series, a new veed windshield, an attractive new instrument panel, which incidentally was the only Senior Series not wood grained, and new body hardware made its appearance. The outside body hardware such as door handles and running board rub strips were stainless steel. Unfortunately for Packard historians, the Sixteenth Series was the only series to use a decal vehicle plate that soon chipped and fell away to dust.

Less conspicious innovations were the ivory-like deluxe steering wheel, built-in dual defrosters, and a four-position lighting system (Park, City, Drive, Drive Pass). An extra lighting accessory were fender lights, miniature reproductions of the headlights which were fitted to the top crown of the fenders. On the wiring diagrams they are only identified as courtesy lights. These courtesy lights were first made available in the Twelfth Series and were discontinued at the end of the Seventeeth Series. The Eighteenth Series was the first series to use seal beam headlights and white-frosted fender-mounted parking lights. New massive front fenders with a re-designed grill and hood were also incorporated in the Sixteenth Series.

The 144″ wheelbase was dropped and each corresponding wheelbase was reduced by five inches. This reduction in length of wheelbase resulted in a re-designed weight distribution

A typical Packard dealership in 1938. Note the complete absence of Super Eights and Twelves. Most Super Eights and all Twelves were made on the basis of specific orders.

and a new steering geometry which gave these Senior Series Packards fantastic handling qualities. The Sixteenth Series was definitely the epitome of maneuverability among the classic Packards. All body components including hood and fenders were now interchangeable with the Super Eight.

Minor changes had taken place in the power plants. Water flow through the Super Eight blocks had been increased by 29 per cent and the valve clearances made wider. The oil dip stick and oil filler location on the Twelve had been changed to allow easier accessibility with the larger fenders. Naturally, this required a new block casting, and the interchange of a Fifteenth Series Twelve with a Sixteenth Series Twelve is easily recognizable even to an amateur, and should be avoided for the sake of authenticity.

The Super Eight is easily identified by the five narrow chrome louvers on each side of the hood. The Super Eights also have thin stainless steel strips on the luggage rack. The

Sixteenth Series Eight Model 1602 Town Car by
Franay of Paris. Approximate cost $9,000. This car re-
ceived first prize in the *concours d'élégance* at Bois
de Boulogne. The Packard Eight had a complete line
of semi-customs.

Sixteenth Series Super Eight Model 1604 Victoria.
Price at Detroit $3,670. Super Eight Series can be
identified by the row of five chrome louvers on each
side of hood. The Sixteenth Series had a re-designed
front end, veed windshield, and a beautiful new instrument panel.

upholstery has wide vertical pleats and the carpeting is wool broadloom. The Sixteenth Series Super Eight was the last of Packard's really big Super Eight motor cars.

The Twelves can quickly be identified by the distinctive red cloisonné medallion on the hubcaps, which is the hallmark of all Twelves. The Twelves also have cast strips on the luggage rack plus a cloisonné medallion with a gold crest. Interiors have a large box pleat in the upholstery and wood window moldings. The exceptions to this rule are the Twelve limousines purchased for commercial livery; their interiors are like the Super Eight. The Sixteenth Series Twelve can be identified by the single row of three adjustable louvers on each side of the hood. The Sixteenth Series Senior cars were the first Series to have beefed up fenders, painted metallic gray instrument panel, stationery hood ornament, and the radiator filler under the hood.

The Sixteenth Series Super Eight and Twelve were truly magnificent classics in every

The Packard Mayfair instrument panel in the English tradition.

sense of the word. It is often heard that this or that year classic Packard was the best, followed by a long dissertation on the virtues of this or that particular model and why it was the last "real" classic. Often these statements can be analyzed to what model the owner-orator is driving at that particular time. Fortunately there is no best year, every Packard Series has its own group of delightful characteristics which are different from its predecessors and its successors.

Some semi-customs were still being ordered from the factory. Most were of the modified formal car variety by Briggs with a LeBaron body plate. The individual customs listed in the Sixteenth Series catalogue were by Brunn and Rollson. Most of the Rollsons were of the razor-edge town-car type mounted on the "Eight" chassis. The trend toward the small wheelbase town car had become popular. Other examples of this trend could be seen in the Brewster-bodied Fords and the Brunn-bodied Lincoln Zephyrs. Some of these chassis, when fitted with meritorious coachwork, can achieve full classic status upon application.

Sixteenth Series Super Eight Model 1604 Two-Door Sedan by Mayfair of London. Approximate cost $20,000. Delivery was taken in France by a Greek shipping magnate. As a result, it carries a 12 volt Marchal lighting system.

Sixteenth Series Twelve Model 1607 Coupe Roadster. Price at Detroit $4,375. Sixteenth Series used much stainless steel hardware on body. Only series to have lacquered pearl-gray instrument panel.

Packard had also commissioned Brunn to build their famous cabriolet touring and cabriolet all-weather for the Super Eight and Twelve chassis. In order to keep the price of the bodies within reason, Packard had Brunn and Co. incorporate factory components like convertible sedan doors in the construction. The bodies were undoubtedly the finest of the late semi-custom formal bodies. They also have the honor of being the most expensive to ever grace a Packard chassis. These semi-customs were carried in the Packard catalogue during the Sixteenth and Seventeenth Series. Unfortunately, the economic conditions could not support the cost of these models. As a result, 17 Brunn-bodied Packards were sold in 1938 and 18 in 1939. For those who have these rare gems, the body number is under the right front seat. Brunn body numbers started with the digit one for each new model year.

The production of Rollson semi-customs

amounted to ten, and approximately five more were full customs that were ordered direct by individual customers who had purchased chassis.

Out in California, Darrin was negotiating with the Packard Motor Car Company on a possible future body contract. The talks, however, were bogged down due to the distance from Detroit and the uncertain economic climate. However, Packard's interest was kept alive by the ten orders from individual customers for his special convertible bodies. The trend toward the small chassis for custom work was definitely here.

Brunn and Co. was established in Buffalo, New York, in 1908 by Herman A. Brunn. The Brunn family had been in the carriage business for more than 50 years prior to 1908. Before the classic era, Brunn and Co. received world-wide acclaim for the custom bodies they had built on foreign chassis that were con-

Sixteenth Series Twelve Model 1608 Sedan for seven passengers. Price at Detroit $4,485. The Twelve can be identified by the row of three adjustable louvers on each side of the hood. Sixteenth Series radiator filler is located under the hood.

stantly being shown at the custom salons in New York and San Francisco. Hermann Brunn was that rare combination of the stylist and engineer. As a result, Brunn developed many body innovations that were adopted by the industry as a whole, such as the double entry door, the metal boot to conceal not only the top but also a tonneau windshield, and the pillarless two-door coupe. Brunn and Co. built

As was shown earlier with Murphy of Pasadena, if ever a motor car company needed help in the design and construction of their bodies, it was the Lincoln by Leland.

A short time later, Ford acquired the Leland Lincoln and the styling and engineering contracts with Brunn were continued. The new Lincoln division of the Ford Motor Company was, of course, headed by Edsel Ford. If any

Sixteenth Series Twelve Model 1608 All-Weather Cabriolet by Brunn. Price at Buffalo $8,510. Seventeen Sixteenth Series Brunn Cabriolets were built. The bodies were also available on the Super Eight chassis.

more bodies for the Lincoln chassis than for all other makes combined, and they were also Edsel Ford's favorite personal choice. It was probably because of the large number of Lincoln semi-custom body orders that the facilities could not be stretched to handle heavy additional semi-custom business from Packard. In 1921, the Leland Lincoln people approached Brunn to help re-design and re-style the monstrosities that were called bodies.

one person should ever be selected and honored as the mentor the custom body, the honor should go to Edsel Ford without question. It was through his devoted interest that firms like Brunn, Dietrich, Judkins, Willoughby, and even Fleetwood bloomed to full maturity during the "Golden Age of Motordom." If Edsel had been allowed a free hand by his father in the mechanical end of the production, Packard would have had a tough and worthy adversary in the luxury car field. Edsel Ford and Alvan Macauley were the partners and the chief planners of the classic era. Edsel put the custom body builders in busi-

Sixteenth Series Twelve Model 1608 Convertible Victoria by Derham. Approximate cost $8,500 at Rosemont, Pennsylvania. Note windshield and top treatment. Sixteenth Series used molded rubber running boards.

Sixteenth Series Twelve Model 1608 Phaeton by Derham. Approximate cost $9,500 at Rosemont, Pennsylvania. Note windshield treatment and tonneau windshield.

ness, and Alvan supplied the volume orders to keep them in business.

Prior to the classic era, most of the good custom body builders were headed for bankruptcy. The public demand for low-cost closed cars made it financially impossible for them to compete with volume producers. This also caused many of their automotive customers, who produced assembled cars, to go under. It was during this time that Edsel Ford came to the rescue of the better body builders and stayed with them to the end.

The last Packard chassis to use a large number of Brunn built bodies was the 443. It was not until late 1937 that Packard again gave Brunn a contract for bodies. Had the recession not hit so hard, it might have been the beginning of a renewed association. Unfortunately, when the contract with Brunn expired, production had amounted to only thirty-five bodies. Brunn continued to build custom bodies right up to World War II and then they went into war work, never again returning to building custom bodies.

Cadillac never fully realized the value of the custom body as a powerful sales tool. Most of the true custom bodied Cadillacs were commissioned by private owners who had purchased chassis. The Fisher brothers, seven in number, had done such a good selling job of their own wares to the directors of General Motors that the need for a variety of semi-custom bodies on Cadillacs and LaSalles was overlooked. It was a miserly consolation to say that they owned Fleetwood. Buying a custom body company, ripping it up by the roots in Pennsylvania, and consolidating it into a production division in Detroit hardly provides the atmosphere for creative thinking. Their sales figures during the classic era stand as moot evidence to this approach.

The year 1938 saw the end of Willoughby & Co., builders of fine custom bodies. Packard had used Willoughby bodies in their semi-

custom catologues in the late Twenties. Like the Brunn body, there were large orders for Willoughby bodies on the 443 chassis. The Willoughby Custom Body Co. was established in 1914 in Utica, New York. Between the years 1914 and 1921 they were production body maufacturers for such makes as Cole, Locomobile, Marmon, and Studebaker. In those days, most independent automobile manufacturers did not own their own body plants. When the squeeze hit, Willoughby still had Locomobile and Rolls Royce at Springfield. When these firms started on the downgrade, Edsel Ford again came to the rescue. The resulting Lincoln orders put Willoughby back in a good financial condition. Packard also helped through the good offices of Mr. Parvis, Packard's New York sales head. Later, Duesenberg chassis purchasers filled the Willoughby coffers. Franklin was also a heavy user of Willoughby bodies.

Willoughby bodies were made of hard ash reinforced with forged iron. The outside was made of sheet aluminum from the belt line down. The windshield pillars, rear quarters, and door frames were made of aluminum castings. One by one, Willoughby's customers went bankrupt and only Lincoln was left; unfortunately there just weren't enough Lincoln cars being sold to support Willoughby.

For the future car collector of the Fifties and Sixties 1938 was a bad year. Auto dealers were so jammed with used cars that automobile manufacturers set up a program by which each dealer was paid $25 for every used car engine they destroyed with a crowbar. That, they felt, would help new-car sales. Many classics were destroyed during this purge.

Economic conditions were such that the classics were slowly disappearing. Auburn, Cord, Duesenberg, and Pierce Arrow were now orphans. General Motors was taking a long look at Cadillac—the losses had to stop. Packard was still financially healthy, but it was

Typical of the Packard Twelve interior was the deep-pile carpet's sponge rubber backing to seal out stray wet or weather. Overstuffed like a household divan, the armchair upholstered rear seat invited the passenger to enjoy true repose. The mouldings were of genuine burled walnut.

the year for decision. The Senior Series Super Eight would be discontinued with the end of the model year. The Twelve would continue one more year. In the meantime, the Senior Series would remain masterpieces in limited editions, symbols of a gracious way of life. It was once said, "There is an art to living that not all master. There are a certain few who know the life abundant and live it in its fullest. To them, time rightfully unfolds a host of comfortable pleasures. For the world creates for them, and them alone, its limited editions of masterpieces." Was it to end?

14

The Seventeenth Series

In early November of 1938, the 39th National Automobile Show at Grand Central Palace in New York City was packed. On view were approximately 200 cars and chassis, 50 exhibits of accessories, exhibits of science and safety, and action displays. The passenger cars shown were Bantam, Buick, Cadillac, Chevrolet, Chrysler, DeSoto, Dodge, Graham, Hudson, Hupmobile, LaSalle, Nash, Oldsmobile, Overland, Packard, Plymouth, Pontiac, and Studebaker.

Ford Motor Company was on an independent kick again and had its own show at 1710 Broadway, corner of 54th Street. For the record, the new Mercury was displayed, and in 1939 the first three Lincoln Continentals were built for Edsel and his two sons.

The new 1939 models displayed had styling as well as numerous engineering changes. It can safely be assumed that this unusual amount and combination of changes resulted from the 1938 slump and the need to tempt potential new-car customers. It is a sad commentary that bad economic conditions make for better products at a time when few can afford them.

Front-end styling had changed drastically. The narrower, sloping hood and massive box fenders were now in style with straighter profiles and brilliant chrome "cat walk" grilles. Headlights and tail lights were now being molded into the fenders. Running boards were now optional equipment on many models. Buick introduced built-in direction signals, which are now legally required in fifty States on new cars. Chrysler products had a speedometer with a lit needle which changed colors with the speed of the car. Plymouth also introduced a vacuum operated convertible top.

It was also the year that many manufacturers were just getting around to adopting the hypoid differential so that they could have a lower body silhouette. Packard had first introduced this type of differential in 1925.

Most cars shown had more horsepower, longer wheelbases, and lighter frames and bodies. The cost accountant was becoming

149

Seventeenth Series Six Model 1700 Touring Sedan. Price at Detroit $1,065. The Packard Six was the best buy in the industry. The Six shared the same body shell with the Seventeenth Series 120 and Super Eight. Packard introduces No Rol, which keeps the car from rolling backward when stopped on an incline.

Seventeenth Series 120 Model 1702 Limousine. Price at Detroit $1,955. The 120 nomenclature was back now that the promotional plan to upgrade the Sixteenth Series Eight to the Seventeenth Series Super Eight was complete.

more important than the chief engineer. Nash introduced "conditioned air" heating which heated and filtered fresh air from the outside, and then circulated it inside the car with a fan, a system which now has been adopted by every American manufacturer. Most manufacturers now had a column shift as optional equipment and Chevrolet had it vacuum operated. Several manufacturers offered coil spring rear suspension in place of leaf springs. Packard offered "Econo-drive," an overdrive transmission on their six- and eight-cylinder cars. Also a shock was added to the rear sway bar.

Packard's fortieth anniversary was in 1939, and, as far as management was concerned, it was just another year for implementing the plans for the new Eighteenth Series which would be introduced in the Fall. The press thought otherwise. Packard was the most respected automotive manufacturer in the business. Their record had never been blemished by shady deals, cut-throat supplier operations, and tyrannical management. Packard's relations with its employees were the best in the industry. They had never been shut down by a strike and the labor turnover was the lowest in the industry.

Packard's President Alvan Macauley was referred to by all other automobile company executives as the "gentleman of the industry."

Macauley had studied law and engineering and had been hired by Henry Joy in 1910 as General Manager. In 1913, he became Vice President, and in 1916 he became President. Henry Joy, Macauley's predecessor, had resigned when the board of directors refused to sell the company to Charles W. Nash and James J. Storrow, who were former General Motor executives. The capital for the transaction was to be supplied by Lee Higginson and Co. When the Packard deal fell through, Nash and his backers purchased Rambler in Kenosha, Wisconsin.

Macauley preserved the basic concept of the Packard brothers for forty years. Packard was "a gentlemen's car built by gentlemen." He was a dynamic executive and he concerned himself with every phase of the company operation. He dealt on a first-name basis with all of the custom body builders, and made many trips to Europe to keep well-informed on European styling. He attended all of the Packard sales conventions and was an inspiration to the sales force. Management was basically engineering-oriented, and he was equally at home with the engineers. Alvan Macauley became Chairman of the Board in 1942. During World War II he was President of the Automotive Council for War Production. In 1948, he retired.

For forty years, Packard had also worked

Seventeenth Series Super Eight Model 1703 Formal Town Car by Rollson. Rollson was the successor to Rollston Company which was reorganized in September 1938. Town car bodies were built by many firms including Larkin of San Francisco and Derham of Rosemont.

Seventeenth Series Super Eight Model 1705 Touring Limousine. Price at Detroit $2,294. Only this model and the 1705 Touring Sedan are considered classics. The other models used the Six and 120 bodies and were of medium price, which excludes them from being classics. The Super Eight would be the last to have the famous Packard aluminum crankcase with detachable block.

tirelessly for the betterment of the industry. In the early years, Henry Joy headed a group of manufacturers who negotiated the reduction of the Selden patent royalties. This group later became the Automobile Manufacturers Association. Coincidental to this, Joy was one of the driving forces behind the Lincoln Highway project. Alvan Macauley carried on this interest and was President of the Automobile Manufacturers Association for seventeen years. As a result of this outstanding record, many unsolicited news releases and congratulations of the industry were received by Packard via the press and radio on their fortieth anniversary.

At Packard, 1939 was strictly to be a transitional year. The model 120 was back in the lineup to fill the gap left by the Sixteenth Series Eight for 1938. The Eight of the Sixteenth Series, as mentioned in the last chapter, became the Super Eight of the Seventeenth Series. Its only claim to the golden past was its Sixteenth Series Super Eight engine. The firewall of its all-steel body was hollowed out to accommodate the longer Super Eight engine. As a motor car, it was well constructed, mechanically excellent, and, with the addition of an optional overdrive, had a much higher cruising speed at lower engine

Seventeenth Series Twelve Model 1707 Coupe Roadster. Price at Detroit $4,375. The Super Eight and Twelve can be identified by alternately painted grill bars.

revolutions than its Sixteenth Series predecessor.

Unfortunately, the Seventeenth Series Super Eight lacked the refinements and attention to detail that its Senior Series predecessor possessed, and well it should, when you consider that the most expensive Seventeenth Series Super Eight was $336 cheaper than the least expensive Sixteenth Series Super Eight. It is for this reason, that only the most expensive Super Eight Series fall under the definition of a classic. The exception to this rule is when the model 1703 and 1704 are fitted with meritorious coachwork. Classic or not, the Super Eight was every inch an automobile and the best in the price class in which it competed. It sold well, and if this was what the customers wanted, Packard planned to accommodate them. This, however, was small consolation, for the luxury market for the large powerful cars was gone.

The mighty Seventeenth Series Twelve was all that was left of the once proud triumvirate of the Senior Series Packard. This was to be its last year of production and only 446 would be sold. In construction, it was identical to the Sixteenth Series Twelve. It was often said that the 1937 to 1939 Twelve was the nearest thing to steam. It could accelerate

from 3 to 30 miles an hour in high gear in 8½ seconds. When you consider the average weight of a Twelve was over 2½ tons, this was fabulous performance. The 1939 Twelve was also a gas miser; it was not uncommon for owners to get 12 miles to a gallon.

The Seventeenth Series can be identified by the alternately painted grille bars, an optional column shift ($240 extra), burled walnut grained instrument panel, re-designed instrument gauge faces, a pushbutton radio mounted in the center of the dash, and a Twelve medallion mounted on each side of the hood.

The Twelve was continued on the 134" and 139" wheelbase and had ten different body styles. Although classed as factory production bodies, all Seventeenth Series Twelves were made up on individual order only.

When August came, the Twelve was gone but not to be forgotten. It would take its place in the Hall of Classics alongside Packard's flying *Gray Wolf* and the "Boss of the Road." In the eight years that the Twelve was produced, 5,744 units were built and sold. Never again would there be built in America a car of true elegance and supreme quality.

The people who purchased Twelves in 1939 read like "Who's Who." The late King Gustaf V of Sweden bought a seven-passenger limousine. The last famous Packard at the White House was a 1939 V-12 seven-passenger touring. Its body and windows were bullet-

Seventeenth Series Twelve Coupe Roadster interior. Column shift was a $240.00 extra.

proof. A V-12 Lincoln was also purchased at the same time. Both cars were equipped to withstand a direct hit from a 50-caliber machine gun. The fabric tops were hydraulically operated from actuating buttons placed in three different interior locations. The tops were reinforced to repel a hand grenade dropped from a height of 250 feet. The Lincoln is now in the Henry Ford Museum and the Packard is residing in the Lars Anderson Museum in Brookline, Mass. George M. Cohan bought a seven-passenger limousine. The Packard Motor Car Company stamped the vehicle plate on the car's firewall with the following legend, "George M. Cohan, N.Y.C. 1939." Nathan Orhbach bought a Brunn bodied Twelve. The movie colony also bought their usual quota of Twelves.

Packard received its first defense contract in 1939. It was negotiated with the Navy in 1938, and production started in early 1939 for the famous twelve-cylinder PT boat engine. This engine was again the brainchild of Jesse Vincent, Packard's engineering Vice-President. Jesse Vincent joined the Packard Motor Car Co. in 1912. He had quit school at the eighth grade and had gained his engineering background working in machine shops and through correspondence courses. He designed the famous Twin Six engine which was discussed in an earlier chapter. Prior to

America's entry into World War I, Vincent was summoned to Washington to help develop an engine which would be rugged, powerful, and practical, and could be given to several manufacturers for production. Using the Twin Six as a basic starting point, the famous Liberty engine was evolved.

After World War I, Vincent's engine was further developed by him for peacetime military use and for marine racing competition. In fact, Colonel Vincent piloted one of his own boats to a gold cup in 1922. Through the years, he and his staff designed and developed sixes, V-eights, straight eights, V-twelves, inverted V-twelves, horizontal twelves and 24-cylinder W engines. It is little wonder that Packard was not only mechanically superior to all other marques, but was always ahead of its time in engineering. When you add to this Alvan Macauley's interest in styling, it is little wonder that Packard dominated the luxury car field on a world-wide basis for forty-odd years.

The semi-customs for the Seventeenth Series were by Brunn and Rollston and were listed for the Twelves only. Brunn would receive orders for a handful and Rollson

Seventeenth Series Twelve Model 1707 Coupe. Price at Detroit $4,185. The Twelve would be discontinued with this Series. Cadillac and Lincoln would drop their large classics in 1940.

Seventeenth Series Twelve Coupe interior. This car is equipped with the standard steering wheel. A deluxe wheel was $20.00.

Seventeenth Series Twelve Model 1707 Formal Sedan. Price at Detroit $4,865. This model had a leather top, vanity cases, and divider window as standard equipment.

would receive even fewer. Most of the true customs still being built were executed by Derham of Rosemont, Pa. Although Derham's production was not what it once had been, they were still healthy financially. Since Derham had an outstanding reputation, a loyal clientele, had never "gone Detroit," and was within easy access of Boston, New York, Philadelphia, and Washington, his business continued to flourish. However, for added insurance, Derham took on a new Chrysler agency. This association with Chrysler resulted in a few beautifully designed custom-bodied Chryslers in the early Forties.

Derham was also doing a brisk business in the refitting of custom bodies to new chassis. Many of the bodies had been built by Dietrich, LeBaron, etc., who, of course, were no longer in business, and Derham was the only one locally available to handle this work. Also, the money just wasn't around anymore for the new custom bodies designed from scratch. Derham also customized factory production cars for the *cognoscenti* who wanted something different but no longer had the funds.

It was the era of change in America, the wealthy industrialists of the late nineteenth century and early twentieth century were a disappearing breed. Their estates could no longer be maintained by their heirs and were being broken up for housing developments. Soon income taxes would reach a level that would prohibit a new generation of self-made wealth. What little money was left in the East for luxury cars, Derham got.

Derham was the last body builder to produce beautiful phaetons on the Seventeenth Series Twelve. He also produced a beautiful and unusual victoria on this same chassis. However, most of the work done on Packards was the conversion of seven-passenger limousines to long wheelbase formal sedans, and the conversion of three-window sedans to formal sedans by the addition of a divider window, a padded leather top, and a different interior.

The Derham Body Co. was started in 1887 by Joseph J. Derham. Like many carriage builders of the late nineteenth century, they successfully made the technological transition to the automobile body business. As with Brewster, the reputation gained in the carriage business stood Derham in good stead for building custom bodies for automobiles. By 1916, Derham opened a second plant in Philadelphia and was supplying semi-custom lot body orders to Philadelphia Packard, New York Packard, and Hudson of Philadelphia. New York Packard was the birthplace of Packard's interest in the custom body. It was first started by Grover Forrest who conceived the Packard custom body department for New York. His successor Mr. Parvis sold the

Seventeenth Series Twelve Model 1708 Limousine. Price at Detriot $4,690. Extras included sidemounts and luggage rack at $240.00, cormorant at $10.00, mirrors at $20.00, auxillary front bumper at $40.00, driving lights at $40.00, heater and defroster at $40.00. Incidentally, this was George M. Cohan's last limousine.

need for custom bodies to Alvan Macauley in the late teens.

Joseph Derham had four sons, all of whom, fortunately, followed in his footsteps and joined the business. Joseph Jr. took over body design. Phillip coordinated production and sales, and James worked in sales and administration. When Joseph Jr. died suddenly, Enos, the youngest son, left college and also joined the family business. Enos still runs the business today.

By 1926 business was booming. The Packard Motor Car Company was Derham's largest customer for semi-custom bodies. Individual custom bodies on other luxury American chassis were pouring in. At the peak of this volume business, Joseph J. Derham died. The year was 1928. This adjustment period would have been difficult enough, but to add insult to injury, Phillip had a falling out with his three brothers over body design and production. As a result, Phillip left the company and formed the Floyd-Derham Body Co. Floyd was a Bryn Mawr automobile dealer. This venture lasted a little over a year and it was a financial fiasco. Unfortunately, the pirating

of personnel from Derham, the poorer quality of coachwork, and the damage to the parent company's good will due to the confusion of names had its effect on Derham at a time when the economic conditions of the country would soon destroy many famous body builders.

Soon the Philadelphia plant would be closed down and the operation consolidated in Rosemont. During the depression Thirties, Derham made out better than most of the custom body builders. In 1929, Edsel Ford gave Derham an order for ten of Derham's special convertible roadsters that were the talk of the industry. The body style was first shown on a Packard chassis at the custom salon. Later the body was placed on several Stutz chassis. The orders from Lincoln and Packard kept Derham going during this time of crisis in 1930 and 1931.

In addition to maintenance, restoration, and body conversion mentioned earlier in the chapter, Derham turned their hand to

Seventeenth Series Twelve Model 1708 Club Sedan by Bohman and Schwartz. Approximate price at Pasadena, Calif. $9,000. One of the most elegant bodies ever to appear on a Packard chassis. Freight charges and dealer make-ready ran approximately 6 per cent on all Seventeenth Series classics.

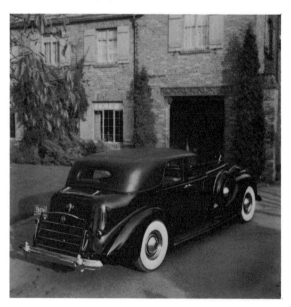

Seventeenth Series Twelve identification marks.

town cars on Plymouth and Ford chassis. This was rather profitable and it gave them an opportunity to keep some of their old customers who could no longer afford to purchase the luxury car chassis and have them fitted with town car bodies. The Brewster Body Co. in Long Island was also building small town cars on a V-8 chassis and calling them Brewster Fords. They differed from Derham's efforts in that they were completely disguised and did not look like a Ford.

After the war, Derham was still in business building custom bodies for a handful of world citizens. In 1946, Derham designed and built two custom town and country Chryslers. In 1953, Packard commissioned Derham to build several formal sedans that were to be included in the 1954 sales brochure. In 1957, Derham built a Mark II Continental convertible coupe for the Ford people. Today Derham is still building custom bodied cars, customizing today's luxury cars, and doing some restoration work on the classic cars that made them famous.

Seventeenth Series Twelve Model 1708 Touring Cabriolet by Brunn. Price at Buffalo $8,355. Leather for roof and rear quarters and a leather interior could be ordered at slight additional cost.

15

The Eighteenth Series

The 40th National Automobile Show was held for the first time in early October, 1939, which was twenty-seven days earlier than the previous year's show. This was done at the request of the Automobile manufacturers who wished to tie in the announcement of their new models with the show. New mechanical innovations and the resurrection of two-tone paint jobs were the keynote of the show. The show was well attended and there was money with which to buy. Defense contracts were being given out at an ever-increasing rate and unemployment was dropping. Sealed beam headlights made their appearance on most models as did pushbutton radios. Automatic overdrives became available on most makes and running boards were becoming passé. Heaters and defrosters were now standard equipment on most models with many makes switching to the under-the-seat heater installation.

Hudson introduced "Air Foam" cushions and a hood lock release under the dash. Oldsmobile introduced Hydra-Matic Drive. They equipped all their models with all-coil spring suspension, four-way stabilization, and knee action front wheel suspension. Olds was now popularly known as G.M.'s experimental car. Powell Crosley, Jr., introduced the Crosley compact car. It was way ahead of its time, and sales, therefore, were very marginal. The surprise package at the show was the air-conditioning optional equipment for all Packard cars. This was truly a product of the future and it did much to keep up the prestige of Packard in advanced engineering.

Nearly every make now had a station wagon in their line. Ford had started the trend in the Model A more than a decade ago. However, they had still not caught the public's fancy, for station wagon sales accounted for less than 1 per cent of the total motor vehicles in the country. The four-door sedan still led in sales with the two-door sedan a close second. In 1939 the 75th million motor car was produced in the United States. Ford produced its 27th million vehicle and Chevrolet its 15th million.

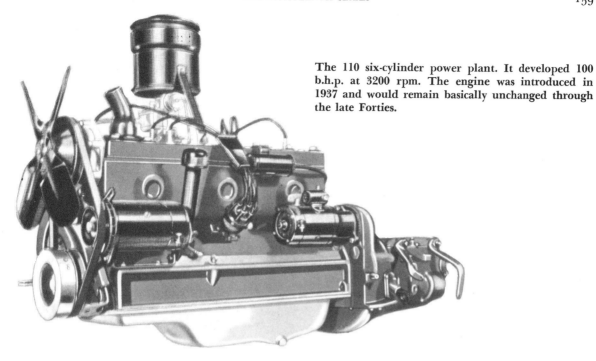

The 110 six-cylinder power plant. It developed 100 b.h.p. at 3200 rpm. The engine was introduced in 1937 and would remain basically unchanged through the late Forties.

Eighteenth Series 110 Model 1800 Touring Sedan. Price at Detroit $975. 110 nomenclature now designated the Packard Six. 62,300 units were sold during the model year proving the popularity of the Six.

Packard was well received at the show. There was a model for just about every pocket-book plus a line of custom cars by Darrin and Rollson. This year, 1940, saw the culmination of Packard's four-year plan to concentrate its efforts in the medium-price field. It had been a hard decision to make, but one that was based on the cold fact that the luxury market was dead—1940 would see the discontinuance of the big twelve-cylinder Lincoln and the Cadillac Sixteen. Based on the times and the general corporate philosophy throughout the industry, it was the right decision, but Packard

of floor space would represent the ultimate in manufacturing efficiency. The former 120 and Six plants were converted to body building and the production of stampings. A wide bridge was built across Grand Boulevard to carry the bodies from the South to the North Plant. New chassis conveyor lines were set up in the main plant. There was now a grand total of four miles of major conveyor systems on which all four series would be built.

The engine plant was now running on two shifts, producing three different passenger car engines, pancake bus engines, and PT

Eighteenth Series 120 Model 1801 Convertible Sedan. Price at Detroit $1,550. Eighteenth Series can be quickly identified by the individual headlights with sealbeam units. This was the first year that Packard as well as the automobile industry as a whole adapted the sealbeam unit.

would never again regain the prestige it had gained in the first three decades of the century.

To those familiar with the Packard factory layout it will be recalled that the 120 and Six were produced in a separate factory south of the Boulevard. Increased demand for the medium-priced cars had taxed this facility to the utmost. Thus, the Senior Series Packards, which were built in the big part of the factory, were taking up valuable space and machinery. Experts were brought in to rearrange the vast plant completely so that the entire 89 acres

boat engines. In a few short months they would also be producing the famous but complicated 12-cylinder Rolls Royce Merlin engine. The Ford Motor Company had originally accepted this contract and then refused it because of the financial losses that would be incurred under the complicated and naive defense contract.

The Government then turned to Packard, the master engine builders. First, the Defense Plant Corporation contract system was studied and then rewritten by Packard's General Counsel, Henry E. Bodman. This contract was called Plancor No. 1 and it was so well done that it became the standard form contract for the Defense Plant Corporation.

The second part of the operation was handled by Jesse Vincent and his engineering

Eighteenth Series 160 Model 1803 Club Coupe. Price at Detroit $1,524. The 160 has been primarily rejected as a classic because of its low cost and, in comparison to its predecessors, its austere appointments.

staff. By carefully re-engineering the Rolls Merlin engine, they not only simplified it for volume production but increased the horsepower by a considerable amount. By the end of World War II, Packard had produced more Rolls Merlin engines than the total production of the five United Kingdom plants.

The new Eighteenth Series consisted of the 110 and 120, which were the volume production cars of the Packard line, and two brand new models designated the 160 and 180. The 160 nomenclature had been derived from the also brand-new straight eight power plant that was rated at 160 horsepower. The 180 designation for the new luxury line was strictly

arbitrary since both models used the same engine and chassis.

In general appearance they were similar. The grill was now long and narrow with the typical catwalk grills, which were now in vogue, between the grill and fenders. The styling was still of the evolutionary concept. Tire covers for the fender mounted spares were one piece and completely enclosed the spares. This would be the last series to have the headlights as a separate unit mounted on top of the fenders. These headlights were the first to use the sealed beam light units with matching parking lights which had frosted white bullet shaped lenses. The Sales Promotion Department became so enthralled over the sealed beam unit that they set up a dealer

Eighteenth Series 180 Model 1806 Club Sedan. $2,243 at Detroit. The new narrow radiator with catwalk side grills will set the trend right into the Fifties for Packard.

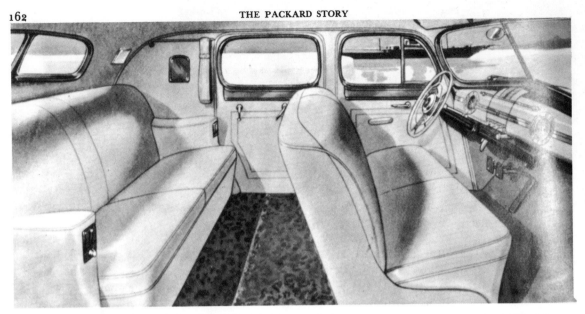

Eighteenth Series 180 production interior. Note gauge arrangement and plastic instrument panel. "Woodwork" was simulated Carpathian elm. Air conditioning is introduced—another Packard first.

promotion to sell their customers the idea of converting their Twelfth through Seventeenth Series Packard headlights to seal beams. This conversion consisted of installing two sealed beam units, screwing up the original headlight wiring system, and placing two Eighteenth Series parking lights on the fenders, all for $35.00.

All major historic automobile clubs frown on such conversions, and cars judged in open competition that have sealed beam conversions are severely docked in points. As of 1963, no state in the Union requires a show car to have sealed beam units. It should also be pointed out that sealed beams are no panacea. In many foreign countries, sealed beam units are outlawed as inadequate. The use of good polished reflectors, 50-32 bulbs, and new wiring will give more light than a sealed beam unit. In lieu of new wiring, the installation of lighting relays may be used provided they are installed in a tasteful and workman-like manner without losing points under the Authenticity category.

The Eighteenth Series 160 was the line successor to the Seventeenth Series Super Eight although completely re-designed with a new chassis and body components. It has been primarily rejected as a classic because of its low cost and, by comparison to its predecessors, its austere appointments. However, a 160 chassis fitted with custom coachwork can gain classic status upon the owner's application to the Classic Car Club of America. The 180, although using the same engine and chassis components as the 160, was the deluxe series created for those who still remembered and wanted the gracious automotive luxury of the earlier decade.

The 160-horsepower big eight engine was brand new. This basic engine with refinements would be used by Packard through 1954. These engines were the first Packard automobile engines to use hydraulic valve lifters. The previous series Twelve used hydraulic valve silencers; there is a difference. It was an excellent modern engine even by today's standards and in some respects superior to the Eights of the Classic era.

The use of plastics, particularly in the instrument panels, was a bad decision but a common one with most automobile manu-

Eighteenth Series 180 Model 1808, All-Weather Town car by Rollson. $4,574 at New York City. Body is a modified touring. The design of the parking light is an Eighteen Series identification mark.

facturers in 1940. It cracked, it warped, and it changed colors, particularly under sunlight and the accompanying heat. The purchase of a good dash from a parts car is about the only remedy when restoring.

The 110 and 120 were beautifully designed and constructed. There was no better buy for the money. The 160 and 180 accounted for 7,562 units. The year 1940 proved to be Packard's second biggest sales year in its history; 98,000 units on the nose were sold to the eager public. The gamble to move into the medium-price field had paid rich dividends. Would it continue? Everybody longed for a Packard and now just about everyone could buy one. Time would tell.

Custom coachwork, like the old soldier, never died, it just faded away. Of the little coachwork being done in 1940, 90 per cent of the output found its way to the Packard chassis. The last custom body builder to be mentioned in this book is Howard "Dutch" Darrin. He is last only because it was the Eighteenth Series Packard that made his name a household word.

Since 1937, Packard management had watched the beautifully designed convertible bodies mounted on the 120 and Super Eight chassis coming from his shop in Hollywood. Naturally, the movie stars and the low, racy Packards that they had purchased were constantly in the news, and this whet the appetite of the wealthy car-owning citizens all over the country. Packard had negotiated with Darrin for several years, but distance was always the fly in the ointment. Finally, they convinced him to come to Detroit and design semi-custom bodies for them. The first fifteen bodies were constructed in the Hollywood shop during 1937, 1938, and 1939.

So great was the demand for the Eighteenth Series victoria, convertible sedan, and sport sedan that there was a six-month delivery wait. In many cases, the potential customer was not about to wait six months for the car of his choice. To circumvent this problem, customers would buy a Packard chassis and then, if they lived on the West Coast, have Bohman and Schwartz build for them a replica of the Darrin-designed body. If they lived in the East, they would commission Rollson or Derham. This was, in a sense, an ideal situation because it meant additional business for the other body builders who also needed work.

Interior view of the Bohman & Schwartz Model 1808 Five-Passenger Sedan.

Eighteen Series 180 Model 1808 Sedan by Bohman and Schwartz. Approximately $7,500 at Pasadena. Car is equipped with retractable running board steps, Honduras mahogany interior cabinets and trim, and Persian lamb's wool carpeting.

Dutch Darrin's life story also reads much like that "old gang of mine." In 1922, he was in Paris representing the new LeBaron Co. of New York, which was owned by Ray Dietrich, Ralph Roberts, and Tom Hibbard. When Tom Hibbard went to Paris later in the year, it was with Darrin that the two flew the coop and established Hibbard and Darrin of Paris. Their first coup was to sweet talk Minerva out of chassis at $600 each, design beautifully bodied formal cars, and peddle them to wealthy Americans touring Europe at $9,000 each.

Within a year, the new firm of Hibbard and Darrin had found the money tree and were now financially in a position to experiment with their first love—radical body styles. One radical body design was complete with sliding doors.

In 1926, Rolls Royce of Springfield ordered two different convertible sedan body styles. Rolls was so pleased with the results that they ordered fifty bodies more of each design.

Next came General Motors, who wished to incorporate the Hibbard and Darrin hood and fender treatment into their 1927-28 Cadillac and LaSalle cars. For this styling, G.M.

Eighteenth Series 180 Model 1807 Sport Sedan by Darrin. $6,100 at Detroit. Darrins can be identified by the low hood silhouette and narrow louver strip. Body is a true semi-custom and has no body components in common with production bodies.

paid Hibbard and Darrin a $25,000 consulting fee plus a $1,000 a month retainer for the duration of the model run. It is because of this continental touch that General Motors is often and unjustly accused of stealing their design from Isotta Fraschini and Hispano-Suiza.

In 1928, at the height of their success, Hibbard and Darrin called it a day and went their separate ways. Darrin decided to remain in France and soon he formed a new partnership with a French banker by the name of Fernandez. By this time, the custom body industry in America and Europe was in full bloom. This partnership is responsible for some of the most eloquent body styles to ever grace a luxury chassis. In addition to their custom work, they had consulting contracts with most of the luxury European marques plus General Motors and several large production manufacturers like Dodge and Studebaker. As pointed out in earlier chapters, many of our mass production makes used the consulting services of our best custom body designers. As a result every make had its own personality. When these creative and independent designers went out of business, the era of the look-alike cars began, which was approximately in the year 1939.

Custom interior for Darrin bodied Packards. Notice the re-designed and pleated instrument panel. These interiors would spark the post World War II boom in pleated upholstery and in the rolled padded dash. It would be copied by auto manufacturers and hot rodder alike.

Darrin received in 1930 the French Brevet d'Invention award for introducing the under cowl steering, which was soon adopted by the custom industry here and abroad. Although the award mentioned safety, the prime effect was to give the car a longer hood line by dropping the steering wheel below the cowl.

The most elegant Packard designed by Fernandez and Darrin was a Tenth Series

Twelve convertible sedan. It was long and low with a three-position top. The three-position top is best explained by saying top up and top down are positions one and two. The third position is when the top folds halfway back to form an open chauffeur's compartment for formal use. Unfortunately, this beautiful 12-cylinder convertible sedan is now decaying in a damp garage and is unavailable to the real enthusiasts.

The Fernandez and Darrin partnership

Eighteenth Series 180 Model 1807 Convertible Sedan by Darrin. Price at Detroit $6,300. Approximately ten units were built. Six are known to exist today.

continued until 1937, at which time the French economy died. Darrin reluctantly packed his bag and returned to America. When he arrived in America, he went to Hollywood and established Darrin of Paris on the Sunset Strip. From the beginning, business was excellent, doing one-of-a-kind customs for Hollywood stars. The first car that he designed and built in Hollywood was neither a luxury car nor for a star. It was a 1937 Ford V-8 four-place victoria with a rear mounted spare. It was for an army colonel, who incidently still owns the car and lives on Sunset Strip. This same year also saw the first Darrin Packard victoria on a 120 chassis and a rear mounted spare. For the next two years, Darrin built some of the most fabulous and unique custom cars in America. Rudy Stoessel and Burt Chalmers were in charge of construction and sales. Eventually, these two men became partners in Coachcraft, Ltd., of Hollywood.

In 1939, Darrin closed his business and went to work with Packard designing production cars and, of course, the Packard Darrin Series. When World War II came, Howard Darrin was a field commander in an army contract flying school. After the war he went to work for Kaiser. The first four years were sheer frustration because management felt they knew more about styling than the stylists. It wasn't until 1951 that Kaiser produced a car that was left unchanged after leaving Darrin's drawing board. Concurrent with this, he designed a beautiful Kaiser Darrin sports car with sliding doors and a fiberglas body. Unfortunately, it was all in vain; Kaiser had taken such a licking in the automobile business that he transferred his passenger car operation to Brazil.

The new Eighteenth Series 160–180 power plant. This engine would remain virtually unchanged through 1954.

16

The Nineteenth Series

The war clouds were gathering as the public jammed into Grand Central Palace in New York City. It was the week of October 12, 1940, and the event was the 41st National Automobile Show. Few knew that it would be the last of a series of auto shows that had begun in 1900.

The General Motors Exhibit was large and well attended. Several G.M. dream cars were on display and would become the production cars of the late Forties. The LaSalle was conspicuous by its absence. With the Cadillac Model 61 and 62, the Buick 90, and the Olds 98 all in the same price range, there was no place for LaSalle. In addition to this, the public was well aware that the LaSalle was a Cadillac with a different grill and a much lower price. As a result, LaSalle actually hurt Cadillac sales. The Cadillac Sixteen was also discontinued. The era of the large luxury cars was dead. The new Cadillac models were smaller, lower priced, and extremely attractive. They would be the style leader for the balance of the decade. The Hydra-Matic Drive that was first offered in the Oldsmobile was

now available in the Cadillac. Oldsmobile and Pontiac had interchangeable six- and eight-cylinder engines on a basic frame. The only way that you could tell a six from an eight was the small print on the hood and trunk. Buick offered twin carburetors and tiny spark-plugs which in combination gave the new owners gray hair trying to keep the cars running properly.

The Ford Motor Company had re-buried the hatchet and was once again participating in the Auto Show. The big Lincoln Twelve was gone. Both Ford and G.M. had tried to get an extra year's production (1940) out of their Twelve and Sixteen, respectively, to use up the surplus of parts. Ford's counterpart of the now compact luxury car was the Lincoln Continental.

Chrysler was now offering the Fluid Drive transmissions on their Dodge, DeSoto, and Chrysler products. Chrysler introduced a two-speed electric windshield wiper and a safety rim which kept the tire on the rim when a blowout occurred. Also displayed was a complete line of Plymouth trucks. Plymouth trucks

Nineteenth Series 110 Model 1900 Station Wagon. Price at Detroit $1,231. Packard purchased these excellent bodies from the Hercules Body Co. The Nineteenth Series 110 was almost identical to the 120. The only real difference was the eight-cylinder engine in the 120.

had been in production since 1937 and ended in 1942.

Packard's exhibit was packed as usual. The new 1941 Nineteenth Series line-up completely encompassed the medium- and high-priced field. The six-cylinder Packard had a Special and Deluxe Series. The eight-cylinder cars started with the medium-priced 120, the upper medium-priced 160 Super Eight, and the high-priced 180 Custom Super Eight. The exhibit was also sprinkled with several Darrin and LeBaron styled bodies which were real crowd pleasers.

Later in the year (March 4, 1941) Packard introduced their first "Clipper." It was an eight-cylinder car on a 127″ wheelbase. Although strictly a medium-priced car ($1,420 at Detroit), it was an immediate success, with 16,600 units being sold during its six-month model run. Price-wise it was in competition with the Cadillac 61 and 62, which had prices of $1,445 and $1,495 respectively.

The Nineteenth Series can be identified by its headlights, which were now incorporated into the re-designed fenders. The vertical grill remained unchanged, but wide vertical side grill sections were added. The bumpers were also re-designed. The instrument panel was re-designed and came in several colors to harmonize with the interior. Unfortunately for the collector, it was mostly constructed of plastic, the miracle product of the Forties, which warped, cracked, and faded. All instrument gauges had a common single rectangular plastic faceplate. Along with air-conditioning (a $1,080 extra) there was an electromatic clutch and automatic windows as optional equipment. Running boards were now optional also. There were some changes in the body panels, but the basic dies constructed for the Eighteenth Series were still being used. The Nineteenth Series 160 and 180 continued to share the same engine and chassis which was introduced in the Eighteenth Series.

The 180 Custom Super Eight continued to be Packard's prestige car and it was on this chassis that 99 per cent of all custom bodies built in 1941 were placed. The Darrin de-

2

Nineteenth Series 160 Model 1905 Limousine Touring. Price at Detroit $2,161. All Nineteenth Series cars can be identified by the new headlight location, re-designed bumpers and taillights. Many beautiful two-tone metallic colors were introduced.

Nineteenth Series 180 Model 1907 Touring Sedan. Price at Detroit $2,632. The first year of optional running boards. Several body styles were reserved for the 180. The balance was shared by the entire line.

signed victorias were the most popular because of their beautiful design and because, being semi-custom, production was now in a position to meet demand. The four-door Darrin convertible was on special order only and not listed as a semi-custom. Therefore, only six were built on the Nineteenth Series chassis. LeBaron was runner-up in the production of semi-custom bodies. LeBaron, which was now a Briggs Body Company product, produced extremely well-designed and graceful bodies. The Sport Brougham was the most desired, but the limousine and sedan received the bulk of the orders. Rollson was third in production of semi-customs and first in the production of true customs. However, this was small consolation, since the total number of orders did not support the Rollson operation. Bohman and Schwartz in California continued to produce many unique customs for the 180 chassis, particularly in the convertible coupe body style.

In production cars, engineering and design research was still Packard's backbone to insure fine automobiles regardless of price class. In fact, by 1941 nearly all the motor cars on the road in one way or another were beneficiaries of Packard pioneering in engineering and manufacturing. Listed below are but a few of the contributions made by Packard to the motor car world in the past forty years.

First to develop thermostatic control of water circulation in a motor car.

First to locate the hand brake at driver's left.

First to use the selective gear shift with "H" movement.

First to use a steering wheel instead of a tiller handle.

First to hook up the accelerator pedal and hand throttle.

First to patent automobile wheels interchangeable at hub.

First to offer ribbed jacket water-cooled cylinders.

First to obtain patent on radiator with top and bottom reservoirs with tubes.

First to offer hypoid gears in rear axle.

First to use the central automatic chassis lubricator system.

First to introduce in America the "trunnion block" which, in its day, added to driving safety by eliminating wheel "shimmy."

First to offer "ride control"—a mechanism for controlling shock absorber activity.

First to provide a package compartment in instrument panel.

First to provide sun visors.

First to use aluminum pistons.

First to use constant action windshield wipers by employing a vacuum pump.

First to use lateral stabilizer.

First to use built-in under-fender cooling tunnels.

First to introduce complete air-conditioning in production cars.

First to use electrically controlled overdrive.

First to use automatic radiator shutters as standard equipment.

First to include front and rear bumpers as standard equipment.

First to equip cars with balloon tires as standard equipment.

First American company to offer a V-type twelve-cylinder engine.

At the factory, experimental Packards continued to be built. Some were prototypes of cars that would go into production five to eight years later. G.M. is often given the credit for the dream car approach to marketing but nothing could be further from the truth. Typical examples to the contrary were the front end drive twelve-cylinder car produced in 1931, the Chicago World's Fair golden "Car of the Dome," the 1934 LeBaron

Nineteenth Series instrument panel, plastic was color harmonized in gray or beige with Carpathian elm simulated trim. The radio was a $63.50 option.

Nineteenth Series 180 Model 1908 Limousine by LeBaron. Price at Detroit $5,595. These particular bodies were modified standard factory units being supplied by Briggs.

Nineteenth Series 180 Model 1906 Coupe de Ville by Darrin. Although primarily an exhibition dream car, several were built including an Eighteenth Series model for select customers.

fastback coupes designed by Edward Macauley, the son of Alvan Macauley. (By 1941, Edward Macauley was one of Packard's chief stylists and a rising young executive. His designs were radical for their time but time always proved him right.)

The 1941 experimental car was called the *Phantom;* body and fenders were integral and had clean flowing lines devoid of chrome. Kaiser-Frazer and Studebaker generally share the credit in the late Forties for this type of streamlining. The Phantom had wrap-around bumpers, dual headlights, and a "mouth organ" grill. This prototype, which unfortunately was slightly modified, was to become the 1948 to 1950 production cars by a combination of factors that were yet unknown to Packard. It will be remembered that throughout Packard's history, Russians, Red or White, were the biggest Packard fanciers in the world and their interest today has not abated in the slightest. It has always been assumed that the Russians had a little Japanese in them and that they copied the 160 and 180

Packard for their official state cars. It wasn't until recently that the true story came out.

During World War II, Russia and the United States became unholy partners in the war against the Axis. To keep this alliance in good working order, F. D. R. embarked upon a giveaway program that would jeopardize the free world for many generations to come. As part of the giveaway program, F. D. R. squeezed Packard management in the interest of patriotism to sell to Russia at nominal cost the dies of the 160 and 180 Packard. As a result of this agreement, Packard only had the Clipper Series dies with which to produce a new car at the cessation of hostilities, and, of course, this chassis was not suited to custom body work nor could this medium-priced car be upgraded to a true luxury car.

Naturally, management had mixed emotions on the sale of the dies. Some felt that the medium-priced field was all that was necessary to survive. Some of the older members of management felt that a prestige car was needed, regardless of the amount sold, to add luster to the medium-priced cars. However, all agreed it was the patriotic thing to do. After the deed was done, it was rather academic, since in the intermediate years following the war, cars were bought on the basis of availability, not quality, and there was no way to gauge the merits of either side of the argument.

In the meantime, the Russian love affair with the Packard automobile continued. The Russian version of the 180 was built right through 1959. However, the construction of the car was much cruder. The sedans built by the Russians weighed close to 7500 lbs. and had six-cylinder motors that made them completely underpowered. The four-door convertible sedan was extremely attractive,

In 1941, turn signal lights became standard equipment on the 180 series and optional equipment on the other series. The installation of turn signals as a safety factor on earlier Packards and for that matter on any other classic is approved by the Classic Car Club of America and no points will be deducted under Authenticity, provided the installation is done in an esthetically pleasing manner. This means double-filament bulbs being installed within the existing fender parking lights or in a pair of driving lights mounted on the front bumpers. Naturally,

incorporating some of the Russian's own ideas, but was also under-powered. The entire production of these cars was for state consumption only. In 1960, the Russians brought out their version of the 1955-1956 Packard styling. Evidently the Russians, like the American public, did not like the post-war styling through 1954. The Russian-Caribbean models are almost identical to the American product. Even the instrument panel was identical. However, attention to quality is crude. The sedan bodies differed considerably from their American counterpart. To the casual observer, they look like a cross between a 1955 Packard body and a Checker Cab body. As late as 1963, new Russian versions of the 1955-1956 Packard Caribbeans could be seen leading the May Day parade across Red Square in Moscow.

Nineteenth Series 180 Model 1906 Convertible Victoria by Darrin. Price at Detroit $4,595. This styling was a design milestone in automotive history.

the driving lights must be of the proper era. For the classics that do not have twin tail lights, the solution can be obtained by the installation of an identical twin tail light and the brake light sockets fitted with double filament bulbs. Ninety-nine per cent of the American makes had a twin tail light as optional equipment as far back as 1925. The driver's turn indicator switch should be a double-throw single-pole switch mounted under the instrumental panel. European makes have the additional option of electric arm direction signals. Failure to observe these rules of installation will result in serious point losses under the category of Authenticity.

It is often said that one should go the

Nineteenth Series 180 Model 1907 Sport Brougham by LeBaron. Price at Detroit $3,545. Air conditioning was $1,080 extra. These models were semi-customs.

whole way and equip all cars with hydraulic brakes, too. Hydraulic brakes, like sealed beam headlights, are no panacea. Properly adjusted mechanical brakes, new woven linings, and stainless·steel replacement brake cables are more than adequate to handle the car's needs. The one drawback of hydraulic brakes from a collector's viewpoint is their rapid deterioration. Disk brakes will soon replace hydraulic shoe brakes, and since mechanical brakes were designed for the needs of the motor car at that point of its development, the constant mechanical updating of a classic is destroying the very reason for preserving a classic, which is the story of transportation at a particular point in our automotive history.

The year 1941 was Packard's forty-second year in the automobile business. In these forty-two years, 908 marques had made their appearance in the United States and now Packard was one of twenty-two that still remained. Since 1899, Packard had weathered two depressions, changing markets, and the fickle public. Packard's financial position was sheer ecstacy to any stockholder. There was

plenty of working capital, no outstanding bank loans, no bonded indebtedness, and no preferred stock. Rights, privileges, franchises, inventions (and goodwill) were carried on the company books at $1.00.

Packard's plant was one of the most modern in the world. It provided Packard with its own engines, transmissions, rear axles, front suspension systems, steering gears, and bodies. The proving grounds, which were completed in 1928, were fabulous. They cost over a million dollars to build, and extended over 500 acres.

Here, under greatly aggravated driving conditions, engineering theory and manufacturing practice had to meet the acid test. On the fastest 2½ mile concrete oval track in America, Packard cars were driven day after day to prove endurance and speed. A sand pit, "Death Valley," provided the severest test that could be devised for proving the stamina of engine, clutch, transmission, and differential. A twelve-mile system of dirt roads complete with railroad ties, water holes, and hills

Nineteenth Series 180 Model 1907 Convertible Victoria by Bohman and Schwartz. Approximate cost at Pasadena was $6,000. Note front fender treatment that would soon reappear on General Motors cars.

presented in exaggerated form every conceivable test for proving an automobile. It was a true story of quality, and Packard knew how to tell it.

When 1941 had ended, Packard had sold another 72,855 automobiles. This was only 25,145 units less than the Eighteenth Series, which was Packard's second best year. However, this decrease was directly due to the influx of defense contracts which tied up a good portion of the production facilities.

Experimental Packard "Phantom" was built in 1941 by designer Edward Macauley (at wheel). Note wraparound bumpers and "mouth organ" grille which would appear many years later in production.

17

The Twentieth Series

The Twentieth Series was to be the last chapter in the story of the classic Packard. Construction of the Twentieth Series was begun on August 25, 1941, under a limited production order issued by the government, and ended on February 9, 1942, by government decree. In these five months of production, 33,776 units were produced.

In the Senior Series, Packard added a two-door and four-door Clipper to both the Custom Super Eight (180) and the Super Eight (160) lines. These Senior Clippers can be identified by their narrow vertical grille with small horizontal bars, and their side grilles which consist of wide horizontal bars that wrap completely around the front fenders. The inexpensive Clippers do not have the grille bars that wrap around the fenders.

The Custom Super Eight 180 that had the conventionally styled bodies remained virtually unchanged from the previous year. The last of the custom and semi-custom bodies appeared on this 180 chassis. The customer was offered from the catalogue a LeBaron Touring Limousine or Touring Sedan which, of course, was built by the Briggs Body Company. Incidentally, Briggs was now building most of Packard's all-steel bodies. Also available from the catalogue was a Convertible victoria by Darrin, which was now a production body style which was built in the Packard plant under the supervision of Howard Darrin. The only true semi-custom bodies offered by Packard were by Rollson of New York City, who contributed a town car and an all-weather cabriolet. The least expensive of these custom bodies started at $4,783, which was the convertible victoria by Darrin on a 127" wheelbase. Production on the Twentieth Series 180 lasted a little over five months and in that time only 672 cars were produced and this figure included the 180 Clippers.

The Super Eight 160, with a motor and chassis identical to the 180, was fitted with more austere furnishings and sold in the medium-priced class. With the exception of the two Clipper models, which had also been added to the 160 line, the balance of the body styles were identical to the Nineteenth Series 160's. Total 160 production for the Twentieth Series amounted to 2,580 units. Very few of these units were the Clipper model.

The Twentieth Series was the last series to use the 160 and 180 nomenclature. As we saw in an earlier chapter, these were the dies that would soon be given to the Russians. These Twentieth Series Senior automobiles can be identified by their horizontal grill bars, which are located under the headlights, and the large dish hubcaps. The 110 and 120 Models of the previous year had been dis-

cator speedometer needles that changed colors as the car increased speed. In other words, the needle would be green from zero to 30, yellow from 30 to 50, and red after 50. It was on the Clipper Series that Packard would gamble its post-war fortunes.

In 1942 America was at war. The past year had seen the nation's fighting machine grow to gigantic proportions and dispatched to every corner on the globe. Dim-out was a new word in our language and also a complete failure. Headlight lenses had the upper half painted black and all six-wheeled automobiles

Twentieth Series Clipper Eight Model 2001 Sedan. Price at Detroit $1,305. The Clipper Eight was first introduced in March, 1941, and in only one body style. By fall, the Clipper styling was in the entire Packard line and in three different body styles.

continued. In their place appeared a full Clipper line to be known as the Clipper Special and the Clipper Custom. A six-or-eight-cylinder engine was available in either model. Because of its advanced design and low-medium price tag, it was a solid sales item. These cars can be identified by their long vertical grill with small horizontal bars, but they do not have the wrap-around horizontal grilles of the Senior Series Clippers. These models could be had with direction signals, overdrive, and electromatic clutch, but only at extra cost. They also used the color indi-

lost their sixth wheel and tire to the scrap drive by government order. The standard gas ration for civilians was four gallons, signified by an "A" sticker on the rear window.

Packard was now fully committed to the war effort. In less than a year, huge new buildings were erected and millions of dollars were spent for machinery and tools. Their wartime products were, of course, the Rolls Royce twelve-cylinder aircraft engine and the Packard twelve-cylinder marine engine. These marine engines were installed in the Patrol torpedo boats of the U. S., British, and Canadian navies. Three twelve-cylinder engines were installed in each PT boat. When World War II had ended, Packard had produced 55,523 Rolls Royce aircraft engines and 13,000 marine engines. No greater tribute could be

Twentieth Series Clipper Six Model 2000 Club Sedan. Price at Detroit $1,215. This series was available in Special or Custom models. The difference between the Special and Custom was in horsepower and radiator capacity only.

Twentienth Series Clipper 160 Model 2003 Touring Sedan. Price at Detroit $1,635. The 180 Clipper cost $480 more and differed from the 160 in interior appointments only.

Interior view of the Clipper Series. This instrument
panel would be a Packard trademark for many years
to come.

Twentieth Series 160 Model 2023 Coupe Convertible.
Price at Detroit $1,795. Packard would not have an-
other convertible in their line until the 1948 model
year.

paid to the inherently balanced twelve-cylinder engine than World War II. Almost 90 per cent of the in-line aircraft engines ordered by the government were of the twelve-cylinder variety. The biggest producers of these engines were Allison, Packard, and Rolls Royce.

In 1942 there was the largest number of management promotions since 1916. This was basically due to two factors. First, several of the board of directors retired. Most of these men had been directors since 1910. They had been millionaires when they had become directors and when they retired, they were multimillionaires. Dexter Mason Ferry, Jr., who had built a successful pocket seed business for the home gardener, had originally

invested $5,000 and reaped over a million dollars in dividends over the years. Second, the almost overnight expansion meant that all hands were required to staff the key spots. Alvan Macauley was elected Chairman of the Board of Directors. In this key spot, he would oversee the entire management complex.

George Christopher became President. His production skills would now be used to supervise Packard's war production. George Christopher was a relative newcomer to Packard but a seasoned and mature executive. As stated earlier in the book, he was a General Motors production genius who had come to Packard in early 1934 to mastermind the Packard 120 production. He was promoted to Assistant Vice-President of Manufacturing in

Interior shot of the convertible coupe showing the traditional dash of the prewar line. Packard auto production was suspended on February 7, 1942.

September, 1934. In 1937, he was again pro-moted to Vice-President of Manufacturing. He held this position until 1942, when he became the President.

Hugh Ferry became Vice-President. Like Macauley, he had been hired by Packard in the year 1910. His first job was as a payroll clerk. In 1919 he became the Assistant Treasurer. Later he became Treasurer and then Vice-President. In 1949, he would succeed George Christopher as President of Packard. Ferry, like all Packard executives, took part in community as well as national affairs. In the early Thirties, he headed a committee of Detroit industrialists who put the closed Detroit banks on their feet. In 1952 Hugh Ferry became Chairman of the Board. Shortly after his elevation to Chairman, he hired James Nance as President in 1952. James Nance was the super stove salesman from Hotpoint.

The Packard vehicle number system through 1942 has been of untold value to the car restorer. With this system the vehicle number can be found on a rectangular plate which is usually mounted on the firewall. It is more than just a serial system for insurance and registration purposes to the restorer, for it identifies for him the series, the model, the body style, the production number, and the approximate age of his automobile. Prior to the Eighth Series (August, 1930) the vehicle numbers were basically the same numbers that appeared on the engine and other chassis components. This system identifies the series and approximate age only.

With the advent of the Eighth Series, which was discussed in Chapter 6, a more sophisticated vehicle numbering system came into being. This serial system consisted of a *Body Type* code *Plus* the *Production Number* (BTPPN). The *Body Type* numbers consisted of two or more digits and were used by Packard in their internal record-keeping from the very beginning. Now they would also be used

on the car and be the first group of digits on the vehicle plate. The next digit or digits represented the *Production Number* of the body style. For example, a classic is located with a vehicle number of 471-23 stamped on the firewall. The owner by consulting the appendix ascertains that 471 is the numerical code assigned to an Eighth Series phaeton with a 140″ wheelbase. The second digits of the vehicle number tell him that it is the 23rd production phaeton assembled in the 840 Series. The year, of course, is unimportant, since Packard did not build year model cars until 1935.

The next question most car owners ask is how many cars of their own particular body style were made, and if their car is rare. This is where knowledge of Packard's history comes in. The Packard historian knows that the factory records are fairly complete except in the area of how many bodies were made for each Series. The factory did not feel that this information was of historical significance or of market research value at the time, since Packard production was based on firm orders from the dealers, and the building of cars on price speculation was unheard of. As a result, this information was not kept. However, when the cars were current, this body information was readily available by checking the last vehicle numbers assigned in a particular Series and adding them up. The Packard historian uses basically the same technique, but the difference being that he must write to each vehicle owner of a particular series rather than just turn a page at the factory to obtain the information needed (see Chapter 6, 840 body analysis).

The above system remained unchanged through the Eleventh Series. Starting with the Twelfth Series (August, 1934) the production number of each body style started with a 200 base. For example, a Twelfth Series Super Eight production club sedan has a body style code of 856. If it were the twenty-third

Twentieth Series 160 Model 2004 Touring Sedan. Price at Detroit $1,905. During World War II, F. D. R. persuaded Packard to sell all their body dies to Russia. This left only the Clipper Series for post-war competition.

Twentieth Series 180 Model 2008 Sedan Touring. Price at Detroit $2,817. Twentieth Series can be identified by the horizontal grille bars and large dish hub caps.

club sedan built, its production number would be 223 and the entire vehicle number would be 856-223. Starting with the Sixteenth Series (August, 1937), the production number of each body style started with a 2000 base. In other words, twenty-third Sixteenth Series Twelve club sedan produced would have a vehicle number of 1136-2023. This system carried through to World War II and the discontinuance of automotive production. (Custom built cars have a different series system for vehicle numbers.) Since Packard did not know what kind of a body would be on the chassis, the vehicle number is composed of the model plus the production number of the chassis, i.e., 840-23 1205-23 or 1607-23, depending upon the year it was produced. Fortunately, custom cars usually have an additional custom body serial number which is located elsewhere in the body to identify its builder. Custom cars built prior to the Eighth Series have a vehicle number identical to production cars and up until now only the custom body serial number located on another part of the chassis can identify them.

Twentieth Series 180 Model 2008 Limousine by LeBaron. Price at Detroit $5,795. This would be the last series to have coachwork by LeBaron and Darrin.

18

The Postwar Packards

From 1942 to V-J Day, Packard concerned itself with war production. So efficient was production and so carefully were costs controlled that Packard entered the postwar world as one of two automobile companies with no debt, and in the strongest financial position in its history. When World War II ended, Packard tackled the many problems associated with converting a plant from war work to civilian goods. Personnel had to be retrained, a sales organization rebuilt, and a production line set up.

Packard's roughest problem was obtaining steel. Three of Packard's pre-war suppliers had changed hands, forcing Packard to purchase odd lot steel at premium prices. The parts suppliers not only had steel shortages but strikes to contend with. The combined total of their problems caused the company to operate in the red through 1948. Fortunately, the loss of $4,959,808 on plant operation was offset by $3,454,999 profits from sales and a federal tax refund of $2,600,000.

From October, 1945, through September,

1947, Packard produced the Twenty-first Series. As planned, it was a continuation of the 1942 model run. In 1945 production consisted of 2,722 Packard Eight sedans only. In 1946, 42,102 Packards were built, consisting of the Packard Six, Packard Super Eight, and the Packard Custom Super. In 1947 production topped 55,477.

While these models were in production, Packard started ordering the dies for the production of the dream car designed by Ed Macauley in 1940. Because of the various postwar material shortages and the need for a Packard convertible, it was decided to concentrate on the convertible and introduce the other models a short time later. This was Packard's first convertible in six years. The car was introduced as the first of the Twenty-second Series in August of 1947. The car was an immediate success primarily because of the public's hunger for new models and because many prospective buyers were waiting for a Packard convertible. Several months later the balance of the Twenty-second Series was introduced. The Twenty-second Series Six was set aside for taxi use only and a new small eight was added to the line. There were now three different eight-cylinder engines which Packard designated as the Eight, Super Eight, and Custom Eight. These new Twenty-second Series models were developed at a cost of $15,000,000. The net result was 98,897 cars sold, which gave the company one of its best profit years.

Through the years, the body design of the Twenty-second Series took a real beating from the independent self-styled automotive writers. They nicknamed it the "inverted bath tub" and the "pregnant elephant." However, for the record, the 1948 Packard won top honors in seven automobile design contests. It was awarded the Fashion Car of the Year gold medal of the New York Fashion Academy. The Super Eight won a Grand Prix at Rome and the convertible won the title of the "finest and most beautiful car in the Show" at Cucuta, Colombia. The Twenty-

second Series was also awarded the *concours d'élégance* at Caracas, Monte Carlo, Sofar, Lebanon, and Lucerne.

The Twenty-third Series (1949) and the Twenty-fourth Series (1950) continued the same styling. This was the three-year model run which was the accepted practice in the automobile industry at that time. In 1949, Packard celebrated its 50th anniversary by introducing a new automatic transmission called Ultramatic. The public helped celebrate by buying 104,593 units, which was 5,000 fewer than their 1937 all-time high. Unfortunately, many of these sales were to lower income groups who had surplus dollars after World War II and who would never again be in a position to purchase an expensive car. The remainder of the "carriage trade" and the new-wealth class were switching their allegiance to Cadillac. As a result, Packard's repeat business, which is the main-stay of any sales organization, was gone.

In March of 1951, the Twenty-fourth

Twenty-First Series Clipper Eight Model 2101 Sedan. Price at Detroit $1,570. Twenty-First Series can be identified by wide horizontal grille bars that match the wrap-around fender grilles. This series was started October 19, 1945, and ended September, 1947.

Twenty-Second Series Golden Anniversary Packards. The new lines consisted of three Eights and three body styles. The six-cylinder engine was available for taxi service only. This new styling concept was spearheaded by Ed Macauley in 1941. This styling carried through to September, 1950 although those cars produced in 1950 were designated the Twenty-Third Series.

Twenty-Second Series Eight Model 2293 Station Wagon. Price at Detroit $3,425. This was the first all-steel station wagon in the industry.

Series was introduced. It was completely re-designed style-wise, but mechanically it was still the same rugged car. The Ultramatic transmission which had been introduced on the Twenty-third Series was still available, as was overdrive. The appointments were austere and the body lines bulbous. As a result, sales continued to drop although Packard was still as financially sound as it was in 1946. Hugh Ferry, now 64, started looking for a replacement. The replacement was James Nance, the hot-shot appliance salesman who had made business history in bringing Hotpoint from tenth to third place in the durable white goods industry in a few short years. In 1952 the Packard board of directors officially elected Jim Nance as President, and Hugh Ferry became Chairman of the Board.

Under Nance's leadership, management was given a complete shake-up and youth was accented in all departments. For the first time a retirement program was initiated for the executive staff. Quite a few ex-Hotpoint executives were hired to replace many of Packard's key executives who were forced into retirement. Historical files, which were probably the most complete industrial history of any U. S. firm, were ordered to be destroyed. Obsolete parts which kept early Packards in good repair were also ordered to be

destroyed. Packard, like Rolls Royce, took pride in being able to supply parts for its earliest models. In fact, this department started to show a profit as the first surges of interest in classic Packards were felt. The manager of the department was a Classic Car Club member but, unfortunately, this gentleman contracted polio at the precise moment that the destruction order was given. As a result, the parts were scrapped without any warning.

Concurrently with the program of destroying the past, Nance gave orders for a completely re-designed car with advanced mechanical innovations, and it was to be ready for the 1954 model year which was less than eighteen months away. Under normal circumstances, this would have been a tall order, but with a new management team plagued with internal friction, low morale, and new job responsibilities, it was out of the question.

In the meantime, the Twenty-fifth Series (1952) and the Twenty-sixth Series would continue as scheduled. To add prestige to the line, a Derham-bodied formal sedan was

Jim Nance elected President of Packard Motor Car Company in 1952. Diversification began immediately.

added and the limousine line was highlighted. Starting with the Twenty-fourth, Packard introduced a new model designation based on body styles rather than power plants. The idea behind this was to further reduce the number of power plants offered and give the impression of a full line of cars. This concept was successfully used by Cadillac and Lincoln. The lower-priced Packard Eights were now called Model 200's. The middle-priced hardtop and convertible were designated Model 250. The middle-priced sedan was Model 300 and the expensive custom sedan was designated as the Model 400 Patrician. The highly stylized convertible in this high-priced luxury line was called the Packard Caribbean. The Caribbean was the production version of the hand-made Packard Pan American dream cars. The Packard Caribbean, which was produced through 1956, has already become a collector's item.

In the Twenty-sixth Series (1953) Model 200 became the Clipper and Clipper Deluxe. This, of course, was an advertising technique to give the public an impression of a medium-priced line and a luxury line. The Model 300

Twenty-Fourth Series 250 Model 2467 Mayfair Coupe. Price at Detroit $3,234. "Contour styling" was introduced, plus the 250, 300, and 400 model nomenclature. The Twenty-Fourth Series was introduced in March, 1951.

designation became the Cavalier Series and the Model 400 became the Patrician Series.

Back on executive row, Nance's deadline for the all-new 1954 Packard was drawing near and it was becoming apparent that the time schedule laid down was entirely too ambitious. As a result, the body style introduced in 1951 was extended to a four-year model run. The 1954 models were designated as the Fifty-fourth Series, a nomenclature which is a dead giveaway that it was a stop-gap measure. Nance had now been President for two years and had embarked upon an expansion program that would have taxed even the U. S. Mint. In addition to his revolutionary new car concept, which was costing millions, he built a new multi-million dollar engine plant in Utica, Michigan. This was part of his plan to automate and update Packard facilities. In addition, his plan also called for the making of as many Packard parts as possible and buying as few parts as possible from other automobile manufacturers and suppliers. This plan boomeranged. American Motors, as an example, purchased engines from Packard on a reciprocal purchase program. When Packard stopped buying parts from American Motors, American

Twenty-Fifth Series (1952) Pan American Convertible. These were built primarily as show cars. They were the forerunners of the Caribbean series.

Twenty-Sixth Series (1953) Model 2653 Formal Sedan by Derham. Price at Detroit $6,531. Packard's first custom since 1942. Under Nance, the limousine and executive sedan are back in the line and air conditioning is again made a company option.

Motors cancelled their engine contract with Packard. Not only did this kill additional income, but it also reduced regular income since the engine plant output had to be reduced.

Nance also at this time merged with Studebaker. The idea behind this was to have a complete line of cars with dual dealerships like Chrysler and General Motors. Unfortunately, Studebaker was the worst company that could have been picked for a merger. Outright purchase using a stock swap would have been a far better choice, as we will see later. Studebaker had weak management and was in deep financial trouble. This was no secret in the automotive trade, since Studebaker's suppliers knew of the firm's financial problems. When the ill-fated merger was ap-

proved by the stockholders in 1954, Nance was merely President, the Chairman of the Board being Studebaker's top executive. This unholy alliance resulted in two autonomous automobile companies operating on Packard's capital. The last part of the Nance plan was to diversify into other industries. A space research firm and a small tractor outfit were acquired. The idea was extremely sound, but the financial timing was wrong. He was overtaxing his diminishing capital.

In the middle of this financial chaos, the all-new and not too thoroughly tested 1955 Packard was introduced. The new model was designated First Series. First Series nomenclature had not been used since 1923 when Pack-

Fifty-Fourth Series (1954) Custom Limousine. Price at Detroit $6,800. Series designation was changed primarily as a stopgap measure. Merger with Studebaker is now in the cards.

ard introduced the Big Eight. Nance's new Packard was indeed an advanced automotive product. It had a revolutionary torsion bar suspension system which did away with coil and leaf springs. It had an electrically actuated leveling device that automatically corrected for different weight loads, a new electric push-button transmission and a new high speed V-8 engine plus a beautiful new body shell. The new First Series had a high-priced Packard Caribbean convertible as the top car. In

The jubilation, however, was short lived. The cars soon developed bugs with all of the new innovations. The new engines developed valve troubles as a result of soft lifters. The load leveling device developed short circuits in the actuating switch mounted on the frame because there was no cover to protect it from the elements. The electric console which operated the transmission also developed trouble when the contacts would shear off. However, sales for 1955 soared over the previ-

First Series (1955) Patrician Sedan. Price at Detroit $4,800. The all new V-8 Packard. Introduced torsion bar suspension, load levelizer, electronic pushbutton Ultramatic and stabilizer bars. New engine plant in Utica now complete.

descending order, there was a Patrician four-door sedan and a 400 hardtop. The Clipper series was continued as a medium-priced car. Unfortunately, the limousine, which is not only a good prestige item but also a good non-discounting item, was dropped from the line. However, Packard was now back in the luxury car class for the first time since 1942.

ous year. Unfortunately, Packard would pay dearly for these bugs and the public's loss of confidence would show up in the sales of the 1956 models.

With the introduction of the 1956 models, Packard was in financial trouble as the result of over-expansion. Nance went on the road in search of capital. The bank refused to extend any more credit. Studebaker was a millstone, the new engine plant was running in the red for lack of orders, and Studebaker-Packard was the only firm without government

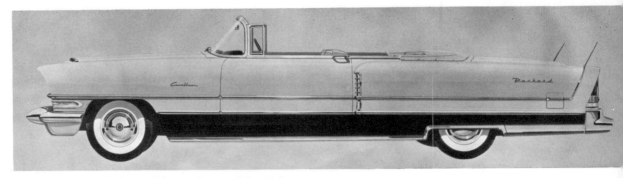

Second Series (1956) Caribbean Convertible. Price at Detroit $6,200. There was also a two-door hardtop Caribbean in this series. Within a year all automotive operations would be consolidated in South Bend, Indiana.

The Balboa, Packard's 1953 Dream Car. This model features a sharply different roof styling. The rear window is flat and has a reverse slope. The gentlemen are William H. Graves (left), V. P. of Engineering, and Edward Macauley, Chief Styling Engineer.

orders. The government soon became aware of Packard's situation and a Senate investigating committee was set up to study the problem particularly in the area of possible government contracts. During the course of the testimony, it was learned by innuendo that one of the top corporate officials, who also held a minor honorary government post, had steered contracts away from Studebaker-Packard for fear of any charges of conflict of interest. By the time the Senate recommended to the Defense Department that government contracts be given to Packard, time had run out. Nance quit under fire and Studebaker management took over. Their first act was to sign a three-year management contract with Curtiss Wright. This unholy alliance was a result of Curtiss Wright's need for a company with heavy tax losses as a write-off against their heavy profits in the aircraft industry. Studebaker received operating capital to concentrate on compact cars in South Bend. When the contract was signed, Curtiss Wright systematically plundered Packard to insure heavy tax losses.

After the management contract was signed, Curtiss Wright's conduct in dismantling the Packard holdings in Detroit is highly questionable. First, they put up for sale the Detroit plant and equipment. Second, they took over the Utica engine plant for one of their own manufacturing facilities. The proving grounds were sold to Ford. This all happened in 1956. It is little wonder that only 13,193 Packards were produced under these circumstances.

On the human side, this was a rough blow for thousands of Packard factory workers who had never known any other type of employment. Twenty-five per cent of the work force had been employed by Packard since 1925. Forty-five per cent had worked for Packard since 1930 and the balance since 1950. Now they were all jobless. The dealer organization was demoralized and soon most would close

down or take on a new franchise. David Sol, a professional stockholder's attorney and a Packard stockholder himself, tried to make the government see what was taking place, but his fight was uphill all the way.

During these final years, Packard continued to develop new designs using the traditional radiator. These dream cars represented Packard's plan for the future. The designing of these cars was under the direction of the company stylist, Richard A. Teague. Unfortunately, these were the years of limited budgets and the cars were the products of crash programs. As we have read, even the new 1955 First Series came about under these conditions.

In 1953, the Balboa was introduced. This design incorporated the reverse rear window which would be used with terrific success in the late Fifties and early Sixties by the Ford Motor Car Company. Also in 1953, the Pan American came into being, which was actually the pilot model of the Caribbean. In 1954, Gray Wolf III was introduced. It was officially christened Panther Daytona. About six of the Fiberglas-bodied personal cars were built and then Nance killed it. In 1955, the Packard Request was built. It was the result of the thousands of letters received by the factory to return to Packard's traditional radiator. The car was introduced at the Chicago Show, promised to the Classic Car Club of America, and then scrapped before the promise was fulfilled. In 1956, Packard built the Predictor for the Chicago Show in just ninety days. The body was built by Ghia on a standard 122″ Clipper chassis. Many of its features have become standard styling features of the cars of the early Sixties. It should also be mentioned that during this period, the styling and engineering departments were working jointly on a new twelve-cylinder car complete with the famous hood and radiator.

In 1957, all automotive operations were consolidated in Studebaker's South Bend,

The Packard Request (1955). This design was a result
of thousands of letters requesting the return to the
traditional radiator of the Thirties. A new twelve-
cylinder car was also on the drawing boards but time
was running out.

The Predictor (1956). Packard's last dream car. The
body was by Ghia on a standard 122″ Clipper chassis.
It portended dual headlights, predated Edsel's horse
collar, Lincoln-Mercury's breezeway rear window, and
the clean sculptured body treatment of the Sixties.
Time had run out.

The Packard Panther. Three were built as show cars.
It was powered by a 212-horsepower straight eight
with a McCollough blower and was fully instru-
mented. The body is constructed of Fiberglass.

The Packard Hawk (1958). During the years of 1957 and 1958 the Studebaker Packard Corporation of South Bend, Indiana, built a line of Studebakers with minor hardware changes and called them the Packard Clipper (1957) and the Packard (1958). Production finally ended in 1958. In 1964, the name Packard was dropped from the corporate name.

Indiana, plant. Curtiss Wright's parting shot was to negotiate a sales contract with the North American Benz Corporation for Studebaker dealers to sell Mercedes Benz automobiles. In return for this contract, Curtiss Wright received certain German diesel engine patents owned by Mercedes Benz. Packard was dead, but Studebaker was not planning on giving it a decent burial. They manufactured a regular line of Studebakers, grafted on Packard clipper tail lights, and called it a Packard. Needless to say, sales fell—to

5,543. In 1958, they named their most expensive Hawk series car Packard, and sales again dropped—to 1,745.

Although rumors persisted, it was generally known in automobile circles that there would never again be a luxury Packard: little clues like the narrow assembly tracks at the Studebaker plant that could never accommodate a large chassis made this clear. Also, late in 1958 Studebaker sent a communique to all company personnel to dispose of all company-owned Packards and suggested the use of Studebaker cars and trucks in all operations. In 1962, Studebaker officially dropped Packard from their title. In 1964 Studebaker stopped producing Studebaker automobiles in the United States.

The Packard that was never to be. This Executive Sedan was scheduled for the 1957 model run but was never produced. THE LAST PACKARD!

Appendix

1899—Model A.

Model — A	Cylinders — 1	Price — $1,250
Produced — 1899	Bore & Stroke — 5 1/2 x 6	W.B. — 71"
Cars produced — 1	Brake H.P. — 12	Body Style — Buggy Type

The first Packard car appeared on the streets of Warren, Ohio, November 6, 1899. It was a one-seater model of the buggy type equipped with wire wheels. The power unit was a single cylinder horizontal motor with a single chain drive to the rear wheels. The motor was rated a 12 brake horsepower. It was a product of the genius of James W. Packard and William D. Packard, who together with G. L. Weiss and W. A. Hatcher organized the partnership of Packard and Weiss in July 1899.

1900—Model B.

Model — B	Cylinders — 1	Price — $1,750
Produced — 1900	Bore & Stroke — 5 1/2 x 6	W.B. — 76"
Cars produced — 3	Brake H.P. — 12	Body Style — Buggy Type

1901—Model C.

Model — C	Cylinders — 1	Price — $2,000
Produced — 1901	Bore & Stroke — 6 x 6 1/2	W.B. — 75"
Cars Produced — 5	Brake H.P. — 12	Body Style — Runabout

Model — F (Old Pacific)	Cylinder — 1	Price — $3,000
Produced — 1902	Bore & Stroke — 6 x 6 1/2	W.B. — 75"
Cars produced — 1	Brake H.P. — 12	Body Style — Runabout

Three experimental two cylinder 24 hp engines were also built in this model.

1902—Model F.

1903—Model K.

Model — K	Cylinders — 4	Price — $7,500
Produced — 1903	Bore & Stroke — 6 x 6 1/2	W.B. — 91"
Cars produced — 34	Brake H.P. — 24	Body Style — Touring

1904—Model L.

Model — L	Cylinders — 4	Price — $4,850
Produced — 1904	Bore & Stroke — NA	W.B. — 91"
Cars produced — 250	Brake H.P. — 26	Body Style — Touring

Model — N	Cylinder — 4	Price — $3,500
Produced — 1905	Bore & Stroke — NA	W.B. — 106"
Cars produced — 481	Brake H.P. — 28	Body Style — Touring

1905—Model N.

Series — None	Bore & Stroke — 4 1/2 x 5 1/2
Name — Four	H.P. AMA — 24
Produced — 1905-1906	Brake — 70
Cars produced — 728	Motor # — 2000-2729
Models — S	Vehicle # — None

Body Type		Passenger	Shipping	Factory List &
Number	Style	Capacity	Weight	Date Effective
Model S	(119" wheelbase)			1905-1906
	Touring	4	2600	$4150

1906—Model S.

1907—Model 30.

Series — None	Bore & Stroke — 5 x 5 1/2
Name — Four	H.P. AMA — 30
Produced — 1906-1907	Brake — 85
Cars produced — 1,128	Motor # — 3000-4134
Models — U	Vehicle # — None

Body Type		Passenger	Shipping	Factory List &
Number	Style	Capacity	Weight	Date Effective
Model U	(121" wheelbase)			1906-1907
	Touring	4	2600	$4200

1908—Model 30.

Series — None	Bore & Stroke — 5 x 5 1/2		
Name — Four	H.P. AMA — 30		
Produced — 1907-1908	Brake — 85		
Cars produced — 1303	Motor # — 5000-6311		
Models — UA	Vehicle # — None		

Body Type		Passenger Capacity	Shipping Weight	Factory List & Date Effective
Number	Style			
Model UA	(123" wheelbase)			1907-1908
	Touring	4	2600	$4200

Series — None	Bore & Stroke — UB, UBS 5 x 5 1/2 NA 4 1/16 x 5 1/8		
Name — Four	H.P. AMA — UB, UBS 30 NA 18		
Produced — 1908-1909	Brake — UB, UBS 85 NA 53		
Cars produced — UB - UBS 1,501 NA 802	Motor # — UB 6480-7086 UBS 7500-8999 NA 9000-9802		
Models — UB, UBS, NA	Vehicle # — None		

Body Type			Passenger Capacity	Shipping Weight	Factory List & Date Effective
Number	Style				
Model		(Wheelbase)			1908-1909
UB	Touring	123"	4	2600	$4200
UBS	Runabout	108"	4	2600	4200
NA	Touring	112"	4	2900	3200

1909—Model 30.

1909—Model 18.

Series — None	Bore & Stroke — UC, UCS 5 x 5 1/2 NB 4 1/16 x 5 1/8
Name — Four	H.P. AMA — UC, UCS 30 NB 18
Produced — 1909-1910	Brake — UC, UCS 85 NB 53
Cars produced — UC, UCS 2,493 NB 766	Motor # — UC 10,000-11,999 UCS 13,000-13,518 NB 12,000-12,837
Models — UC, UCS, NB	Vehicle # — None

Number	Body Type Style	(Wheelbase)	Passenger Capacity	Shipping Weight	Factory List & Date Effective
Model					1909-1910
UC	Touring	123"	4	3600	$4200
UCS	Runabout	108"	4	3600	4200
NB	Touring	112"	4	3000	3200

1910—Model 30.

Series — None	Bore & Stroke — UD, UDS 5 x 5 1/2
	NC 4 1/16 x 5 1/8
Name — Four	H.P. AMA — UD, UDS 30
	NC 18
Produced — 1910-1911	Brake — UD, UDS 85
	NC 53
Cars produced — UD-UDS	Motor — UD 15,000-15,999
1,865	UDS 16,000-16,884
NC 360	NC 18,800-19,176
Models — UD, UDS, NC	Vehicle # — None

| Body Type | | Passenger | Shipping | Factory List & |
Number	Style	Capacity	Weight	Date Effective
Model	(Wheelbase)			1910-1911
UD	Touring	123"	4	3800	$4200
UDS	Runabout	108"	4	3800	4200
NC	Touring	112"	4	3100	3200

Series — None	Bore & Stroke — 4 1/16 x 5 1/8
Name — Four	H.P. AMA — 18
Produced — 1911-1912	Brake — 53
Cars produced — 350	Motor # — 26,000 - 27,000
Models — NE	Vehicle # — None

| Body Type | | Passenger | Shipping | Factory List & |
Number	Style	Capacity	Weight	Date Effective
Model NE	(Wheelbase)			1911-1912
NESQ	Coupe	112"	2	3000	$3900
NEFR	Limousine	112"	5	3300	4400
NEFQ	Limousine, Imperial	112"	5	3300	4600
NESJ	Runabout	108"	2	3800	3200
NEFJ	Touring	112"	5	3400	3200

1911—Model 18.

1912—Model 18.

1911—Model 30.

Series — None	Bore & Stroke — 5 x 5 1/2
Name — Four	H.P. AMA — 30
Produced — 1911-1912	Brake — 85
Cars Produced — 1,250	Motor # — 20,000-22,999
Models — UE	Vehicle # — None

| Body Type | | Passenger | Shipping | Factory List & |
Number	Style	Capacity	Weight	Date Effective
Model UE	(Wheelbase)			1911-1912
UEPQ	Brougham	123"	4	3900	$5500
UESQ	Coupe	123"	2	3500	4900
UEFR	Limousine	129"	5-7	3900	5450
UEFQ	Limousine, Imperial	129"	5-7	4000	5650
UEPJ	Phaeton	129"	5	3600	4200
UEST	Runabout	114"	2	3300	4200
UEC	Touring	123"	5-7	3700	4200

1912—Model 30.

Series — None	Bore & Stroke — 4 1/8 x 5 1/2
Name — Six	H.P. AMA — 48
Produced — 1911-1913	Brake — 105
Cars Produced — 1,349	Motor # — 23,000-25,999
Models — 1248	Vehicle # — None

| Body Type | | Passenger | Shipping | Factory List & |
Number	Style	Capacity	Weight	Date Effective
Model 1248	(Wheelbase)			1911-1913
PY—PB	Brougham	132"	4	4100	$6300
PC	Coupe	132"	2	3700	5700
TM	Limousine	138"	5-7	4100	6250
TQ	Limousine, Imperial	138"	5-7	4200	6450
PJ	Phaeton	132"	5	3800	5000
RJ	Runabout	121"	2	3300	5000
TR—TJ	Touring	132"	5-7	3900	5000

1912—Model 48.

Series — None	Bore & Stroke — 4 1/2 x 5 1/2
Name — Six	H.P. AMA — 48
Produced — 1912-1913	Brake — 105
Cars produced — 1,000	Motor # — 35,000 - 37,999
Models — 1348	Vehicle # — None

Body Type		Passenger	Shipping	Factory List &
Number	Style	Capacity	Weight	Date Effective
Model 1348	(Wheelbase)			1912-1913
TE	Touring 138"	5	4500	$4850

1913—Model 48.

Series — None	Bore & Stroke — 4 x 5 1/2
Name — Six	H.P. AMA — 38
Produced — 1912-1914	Brake — 80
Cars Produced — 1,618	Motor # — 38,000-42,000
Models — 138	Vehicle # — None

	Body Type		Passenger	Shipping	Factory List &
Number	Style		Capacity	Weight	Date Effective
Model 138		(Wheelbase)			1912-1914
PB, PY	Brougham	134"	4	4375	$5200
RC	Coupe	134"	2	4070	4500
RY	Coupe, Imperial	134"	4	4175	4900
TG	Landaulet	138"	5	4430	5300
TK	Landaulet, Imperial	138"	5	4495	5500
TR	Limousine	138"	5	4400	5200
TQ	Limousine, Imperial	138"	5	4510	5400
PH	Phaeton	134"	4	4070	4150
PJ	Phaeton	134"	5	4110	4150
RJ	Runabout	115"	2	3820	4050
TE, TB, TJ	Touring	134"	5	4070	4150

1913-Model 38.

1914—Model 238.

		Bore & Stroke — 4 x 5 1/2
Series — None		
Name — Six		H.P. AMA — 38
Produced — 1913-1914		Brake — 80
Cars Produced — 1,501		Motor # — 53,000-56,000
Models — 238		Vehicle # — None

Body Type		Passenger	Shipping	Factory List &
Number	Style	Capacity	Weight	Date Effective
Model 238	(Wheelbase)			1913-1914
36	Brougham	140"	6	4735	$5000
37	Brougham, Salon	140"	4	4685	4950
38	Coupe	140"	3	4382	4450
43	Landaulet	140"	6	4660	4900
41	Landaulet	140"	5-7	4700	4950
34	Landaulet, Cabriolet	140"	5-7	4747	5000
42	Limousine	140"	6	4677	4900
40	Limousine	140"	5-7	4712	4950
44	Limousine, Cabriolet	140"	5-7	4757	5000
50	Limousine, Imperial	140"	6	4785	5100
31	Limousine, Imperial	140"	5-7	4818	5150
33	Limousine, Salon	140"	5-7	4763	5100
51	Phaeton	140"	5	4360	3750
28	Phaeton	140"	4	4293	3750
29	Runabout	140"	2	4113	3750
27	Touring, Salon	140"	5-7	4426	3850
30	Touring, Salon	140"	6	4376	3850
46	Touring, Special	140"	6	4395	3350

Series — None	Bore & Stroke — 4 x 5 1/2
Name — Six	H.P. AMA — 38
Produced — 1914-1915	Brake — 80
Cars Produced — 1,801	Motor # — 75,000-77,000
Models — 338	Vehicle # — None

| Body Type | | Passenger | Shipping | Factory List & |
Number	Style	Capacity	Weight	Date Effective
Model 338	**(140" wheelbase)**			**1914-1915**
79	Brougham	6	4785	$5000
80	Brougham, Salon	4	4735	4950
59	Coupe	3	4432	4450
76	Landaulet	6	4710	4900
75	Landaulet	5-7	4750	4950
77	Landaulet, Cabriolet	5-7	4797	5000
71	Limousine	6	4727	4900
72	Limousine	5-7	4762	4950
74	Limousine, Cabriolet	6	4769	4950
73	Limousine, Cabriolet	5-7	4807	5000
69	Limousine, Imperial	6	4835	5100
68	Limousine, Imperial	5-7	4868	5150
70	Limousine, Salon	5-7	4813	5100
65	Phaeton	5	4410	3750
66	Phaeton	4	4343	3750
67	Runabout	2	4163	3750
63	Touring	5-7	4476	3850
60	Touring, Salon	6	4426	3850
61	Touring, Special	6	4445	3850

1915-Model 338.

1914—Model 48.

Series — None	Bore & Stroke — 4 1/2 x 5 1/2
Name — Six	H.P. AMA — 48
Produced — 1913-1915	Brake — 105
Cars produced — 1,499	Motor # — 50,000 - 52,000
Models — 448	Vehicle # — None

| Body Type | | Passenger | Shipping | Factory List & |
Number	Style	Capacity	Weight	Date Effective
Model 1448	(Wheelbase)			1913-1915
30	Touring	143"	5	4700	$4850

Series — None	Bore & Stroke — 4 1/2 x 5 1/2
Name — Six	H.P. AMA — 48
Produced — 1914	Brake — 105
Cars Produced — 441	Motor # — 63,000–66,000
Models — 448	Vehicle # — None

Body Type		Passenger	Shipping	Factory List &
Number	Style	Capacity	Weight	Date Effective

Model 448   (143" wheelbase)

Number	Style	Passenger Capacity	Shipping Weight	Factory List
79	Brougham	6	4932	$6000
80	Brougham, Salon	4	4882	5950
59	Coupe	3	4577	5450
76	Landaulet	6	4857	5900
75	Landaulet	5-7	4897	5950
77	Landaulet, Cabriolet	5-7	4944	6000
71	Limousine	5-7	4909	5950
72	Limousine	6	4874	5900
74	Limousine, Cabriolet	6	4916	5950
73	Limousine, Cabriolet	5-7	4954	6000
69	Limousine, Imperial	6	4982	6100
68	Limousine, Imperial	5-7	5015	6150
70	Limousine, Salon	5-7	4960	6100
65	Phaeton	5	4557	4750
66	Phaeton	4	4490	4750
67	Runabout	2	4310	4750
63	Touring	5-7	4623	4850
60	Touring, Salon	6	4573	4850

1914—Model 448.

Series — None	Bore & Stroke — 4 1/2 x 5 1/2
Name — Six	H.P. AMA — AMA 48
Produced — 1914-1915	Brake — 105
Cars Produced — 360	Motor # — 78,000-78,586
Models — 548	Vehicle # — None

Body Type		Passenger	Shipping	Factory List &
Number	Style	Capacity	Weight	Date Effective
Model 548	(143" wheelbase)			
79	Brougham	6	4932	$6000
80	Brougham, Salon	6	4882	5950
59	Coupe	4	4577	5450
76	Landaulet	6	4857	5900
75	Landaulet	5-7	4897	5950
77	Landaulet, Cabriolet	5-7	4944	6000
71	Limousine	6	4874	5900
72	Limousine	5-7	4909	5950
74	Limousine, Cabriolet	6	4913	5950
73	Limousine, Cabriolet	5-7	4954	6000
69	Limousine, Imperial	6	4982	6100
68	Limousine, Imperial	5-7	5015	6150
70	Limousine, Salon	5-7	4960	6100
65	Phaeton	4	4490	4750
66	Phaeton	5	4557	4750
67	Runabout	2	4310	4750
63	Touring	5-7	4623	4850
60	Touring, Salon	6	4573	4850

Series — None	Bore & Stroke — 3 x 5
Name — Twin Six	H.P. AMA — 43.2
Produced — 1915-1916	Brake — 85
Cars produced — 3606	Motor # — 80,000 - 87,787
Models — 125	Vehicle # — None

Body Type		Passenger Capacity	Shipping Weight	Factory List & Date Effective	
Number	Style				
Model 125	(125" wheelbase)			6-1-15	9-17-15
83	Brougham, Salon	4	4365	$5050	$4200
84	Coupe	3	4175	3550	3700
115	Landaulet	6	4395	4000	4150
114	Limousine	6	4415	4000	4150
81	Phaeton	5	4130	2600	2750
117	Phaeton, Salon	5	4120	2600	2750
82	Runabout	2	3910	2600	2750
118	Touring	5-7	4190	2600	2750
119	Touring, Salon	5-7	4180	2600	2750

Twin Six—First Series.

Series — None   Bore & Stroke — 3 x 5

Name — Twin Six   H.P. AMA — 43.2

Produced — 1915-1916   Brake — 85

Cars produced — 4140   Motor # — 80,000 - 87,787

Models — 135   Vehicle # — None

| Body Type | | Passenger | Shipping | Factory List & | |
Number	Style	Capacity	Weight	Date Effective	
Model 135 (135" wheelbase)				6-1-15	9-17-15
111	Brougham, Salon	4	4475	$4400	$4600
102	Landaulet	6	4540	4350	4550
107	Landaulet	5-7	4680	4400	4600
103	Landaulet, Cabriolet	5-7	4620	4450	4650
100	Limousine	6	4550	4350	4550
105	Limousine	5-7	4585	4400	4600
101	Limousine, Cabriolet	5-7	4630	4450	4650
98	Limousine, Imperial	5-7	4715	4600	4800
99	Limousine, Salon	5-7	4660	4550	4750
94	Phaeton	5	4220	2950	3150
95	Phaeton, Salon	5	4210	2950	3150
90	Touring	5-7	4285	2950	3150
91	Touring, Salon	5-7	4275	2950	3150

Twin Six—Second Series.

Series — None	Bore & Stroke — 3 x 5
Name — Twin Six	H.P. AMA — 43.2
Produced — 1916-1917	Brake — 85
Cars produced — 4950	Motor # — 125,000 - 149,999
Models — 225	Vehicle # — None

Body Type		Passenger	Shipping	Factory List &	
Number	Style	Capacity	Weight	Date Effective	
Model 225 (126" wheelbase)				7-1-16	11-9-16
150	Brougham	4	4550	$3965	$4500
151	Coupe	3	4425	4265	4150
153	Landaulet	6	4680	3265	4500
152	Limousine	6	4700	4315	4450
146	Phaeton	5	4375	2865	3050
147	Phaeton, Salon	5	4365	2865	3050
149	Runabout	2	4150	2865	3050
167	Runabout	4	4250	2865	3050
145	Touring	5-7	4460	2865	3050

Series — None | Bore & Stroke — 3 x 5
Name — Twin Six | H.P. AMA — 43.2
Produced — 1916-1917 | Brake — 85
Cars produced — 4049 | Motor # — 125,050 - 149,999
Models — 235 | Vehicle # — None

Body Type		Passenger	Shipping	Factory List &	
Number	Style	Capacity	Weight	Date Effective	
Model 235	(135" wheelbase)			7-1-16	11-9-16
166	Brougham, Salon	4	4740	$4715	$4950
162	Landaulet	6	4790	4715	4950
163	Landaulet	7	4800	4765	5000
165	Landaulet, Cabriolet	7	4850	4815	5050
160	Limousine	6	4800	4665	4900
161	Limousine	7	4850	4715	4950
164	Limousine, Cabriolet	7	4900	4765	5000
158	Limousine, Imperial	7	4970	4915	5150
159	Limousine, Salon	7	4910	4865	5100
156	Phaeton	5	4450	3265	3500
157	Phaeton, Salon	5	4440	3265	3500
154	Touring	7	4562	3265	3500
155	Touring, Salon	7	4552	3265	3500

Series — None	Bore & Stroke — 3 x 5
Name — Twin Six	H.P. AMA — 43.2
Produced — Begun 1917-19	Brake — 90
Cars produced — 4181	Motor # — 150,000 - 160,129
Models — 325	Vehicle # — S-20000 - 168433

| Body Type | | Passenger | Shipping | Factory List & | |
Number	Style	Capacity	Weight	Date Effective	
Model 325	(128" wheelbase)			6-1-17	7-25-19
184	Brougham	6	4372	$5050	$
185	Brougham	7	4755	5150	6950
174	Coupe	4	4326	4800	6600
173	Landaulet	7	4745	5050	6850
172	Limousine	7	4710	5000	6800
175	Limousine, Imperial	7	4860	5200	
181	Phaeton	5	4280	3450	5200
183	Phaeton, Salon	5	4250	3450	
171	Runabout	4	4210	3450	5200
168	Touring	7	4435	3450	5200
169	Touring, Salon	7	4400	3450	

Series — None   Bore & Stroke — 3 x 5

Name — Twin Six   H.P. AMA — 43.2

Produced — Begun 1917–   Brake — 90
            1919

Cars produced — 5406   Motor # — 150,000 - 160,129

Models — 335   Vehicle # — S-20000-168433

Body Type		Passenger Capacity	Shipping Weight	Factory List & Date Effective	
Number	Style				
Model 335	(136" wheelbase)			6-1-17	7-24-19
185	Brougham	7	4845	$5500	$7300
180	Landaulet	7	4825	5450	7200
207	Limousine	7	4780	5400	7150
194	Touring	7	4490	3850	5550
177	Touring, Salon	7	4465	3850	5550
178	Limousine, Imperial	7	4920	5600	7350

Twin Six—Third Series.

The Single Six—116.

Series — First	Bore & Stroke — 3 3/8 x 4 1/2
Name — Single Six	H.P. AMA — 27.3
Produced — Begun 1920-22	Brake — 54
Cars produced — 8800	Motor # — 1 - 8999
Models — 116	Vehicle # — Same as motor

Body Type		Passenger	Shipping	Factory List &	
Number	Style	Capacity	Weight	Date Effective	
Model 116 (116" wheelbase)				9-1-20	9-24-21
193	Coupe	4	2990	$4835	$3350
191	Runabout	2	2790	3640	2350
192	Sedan	5	3170	4950	3350
190	Touring	5	2920	3640	2350

Series — None Bore & Stroke — 3 x 5

Name — Twin Six H.P. AMA — 43.2

Produced — Begun 1920-24 Brake — 90

Cars Produced — 8770 Motor # — 160,130 - 169,000

Models — 335 Vehicle # — S-20000-168433

| Body Type | | Passenger | Shipping | Factory List & | |
Number	Style	Capacity	Weight	Date Effective	
Model 335	(136" wheelbase)			4-14-20	2-13-22
185	Coupe	4-5	4430	$	$5240
209-227	Coupe, Duplex	4-5	4580	7750	5240
178,179-207	Limousine	7	4595	7900	5275
195	Phaeton	4-5	4300	5550	3850
196	Runabout	4	4245	5500	3850
177	Sedan	7	4520	—	5400
208-226	Sedan, Duplex	7	4670	8000	5400
176-194	Touring	7	4470	5550	3850

Series — First	Bore & Stroke — 3 3/8 x 5
Name — Six	H.P. AMA — 27.34
Produced — Begun 1922-24	Brake — 54
Cars produced — 126 18192 133 4004	Motor # — 9,000 - 36,000
Models — 126-133	Vehicle # — Same as motor

Body Type Number	Style	Passenger Capacity	Shipping Weight	Factory List & Date Effective	
Model 126	(126" wheelbase)			4-20-22	6-14-23
222	Coupe	4	3305	$3175	
230	Coupe	5	3360	3350	
231	Limousine, Sedan	5	3525	3325	
223	Runabout	2-4	3030	2485	
221	Sedan	5	3455	3275	
232	Sedan, Touring	5	3360		$2750
224	Sport	4	3165	2650	
220	Touring	5	3225	2485	
Model 133	(133" wheelbase)				
229	Limousine	7	3680	3575	
228	Sedan	7	3555	3525	
225	Touring	7	3355	2685	

The Single Six—126.

Series — First   Bore & Stroke — 3 3/8 x 5

Name — Eight   H.P. AMA — 36.4

Produced — 6-14-23 to   Brake — 84
         2-2-25

Cars produced — 136 7871   Motor # — 200,000 - 208,399
             143 4894

Models — 136-143   Vehicle # — Same as motor

| Body Type | | Passenger | Shipping | Factory List & | |
Number	Style	Capacity	Weight	Date Effective	
Model 136 (136" wheelbase)				6-14-23	12-27-23
239	Coupe	4	4125	$4550	
242	Coupe	5	4204	4725	
234	Runabout	2-4	3879	3850	
237	Sedan	5	4260	4650	
243	Sedan,				
	Limousine	5	4275	4700	
246	Sport	4	3810		$3800
244	Touring	5	3990	3650	
Model 143 (143" wheelbase)					
240	Sedan	5-7	4379	4900	
241	Sedan,				
	Limousine	5-7	4434	4950	
245	Touring	5-7	4074	3850	

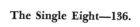
The Single Eight—136.

Series — Second	Bore & Stroke — 3 3/8 x 5
Name — Six	H.P. AMA — 27.34
Produced — 12-27-23 to 2-2-25	Brake — 54
Cars produced — 9611	Motor # — 37,000 - 49,499
Models — 226-233	Vehicle # — Same as motor

Body Type		Passenger Capacity	Shipping Weight	Factory List & Date Effective	
Number	Style				
Model 226 (126" wheelbase)				12-27-23	1-2-25
222	Coupe	4	3438	$3275	$2585
230	Coupe	5	3537	3450	2685
223	Runabout	2-4	3317	2785	2785
221	Sedan	5	3582	3375	2585
231	Sedan, Limousine	5	3682	3425	2785
232	Sedan, Touring	5	3360	2850	
224	Sport	4	3323	2750	2750
220	Touring	5	3317	2585	2585
Model 233 (133" wheelbase)					
228	Sedan	5-7	3715	3625	2785
229	Sedan, Limousine	5-7	3817	3675	2885
225	Touring	5-7	3432	2785	

The Packard Six—226.

Series — Second

Name — Eight

Produced — 2-2-25 to
            8-2-26

Cars produced — 5680

Models — 236 - 243

Bore & Stroke — 3 3/8 x 5

H.P. AMA — 36.4

Brake — 84

Motor # — 209,000 - 219,999

Vehicle # — Same as motor

Body Type		Passenger	Shipping	Factory List &	
Number	Style	Capacity	Weight	Date Effective	
Model 236 (136" wheelbase)				2-2-25	4-1-25
239	Coupe	4	4147	$4650	
242	Coupe	5	4337	4825	
281	Holbrook	2	4178		$3750
234	Runabout	4	3965	3950	
253	Sedan	5	4433	4750	
257	Sedan, Limousine	5	4535	4850	
246	Sport	4	4023	3900	
244	Touring	5	4090	3750	
Model 243					
254	Sedan	5-7	4560	5000	
255	Sedan, Club	5	4573		4890
256	Sedan, Limousine	5-7	4615	5100	
245	Touring	5-7	4104	3950	

Series — Third	Bore & Stroke — 3 1/2 x 5
Name — Six	H.P. AMA — 29.40
Produced — 2-2-25 to 8-2-26	Brake — 61
Cars produced — 40,358	Motor # — 49,500 - 94,900
Models — 326-333	Vehicle # — Same as motor

Body Type Number	Style	Passenger Capacity	Shipping Weight	Factory List & Date Effective	
Model 326	(126" wheelbase)			2-2-25	3-10-26
268	Coupe	2	3590	$2660	
222	Coupe	4	3658	2585	
230	Coupe	5	3876	2685	
226	Phaeton	5	3558	2585	
223	Runabout	4	3458	2785	
221	Sedan	5	3842	2585	
231	Sedan, Limousine	5	3974	2785	
224	Sport	4	3595	2750	
220	Touring	5	3653	3585	
Model 333	(133" wheelbase)				
266	Sedan	5-7	3948	2785	
265	Sedan, Club	5	4080		$2725
267	Sedan, Limousine	5-7	4038	2885	
225	Touring	5-7	3698	2785	

Series — Third   Bore & Stroke — 3 1/2 x 5

Name — Eight   H.P. AMA — 39.2

Produced — 8-2-26 to 7-1-27   Brake — 106

Cars produced — 4096   Motor # — 220,000 to 224,999

Models — 336, 343   Vehicle # — Same as motor

| Body Type | | Passenger | Shipping | Factory List & |
Number	Style	Capacity	Weight	Date Effective
Model 336	(136" wheelbase)			8-2-26
291	Phaeton	5	4130	3750
292	Runabout	4	4110	3850
293	Sedan	5	4430	4750
Model 343	(143" wheelbase)			
290	Touring	5-7	4250	3950
294	Sedan	5-7	4660	5000
295	Sedan, Limousine	5-7	4700	5100
296	Sedan, Club	5	4550	4890
297	Coupe	4	4475	4750

Series — Fourth	Bore & Stroke — 3 1/2 x 5
Name — Single Six	H.P. AMA — 29.4
Produced — 8-2-26 to 7-1-27	Brake — 82
Cars produced — 25,335	Motor # — 95,000 to 124,999
Models — 426,433	Vehicle # — Same as motor

Body Type Number	Style	Passenger Capacity	Shipping Weight	Factory List & Date Effective 8-2-26	3-1-27
Model 426 (126" wheelbase)					
301	Phaeton	5	3590	$2585	$2250
302	Roadster	4	3545	2685	2350
303	Sedan	5	3925	2585	2250
Model 433 (133" wheelbase)					
300	Touring	5-7	3790	2785	
304	Sedan	5-7	4070	2785	
305	Sedan, Limousine	5-7	4130	2885	
306	Sedan, Club	5	4015	2725	
307	Coupe	4	3925	2685	

Series — Fourth	Bore & Stroke — 3 1/2 x 5
Name — Single Eight	H.P. AMA — 39.2
Produced — 7-1-27 to 8-1-28	Brake — 106
Cars produced — 10,568	Motor # — 220,000 to 232,999
Models — 443	Vehicle # — Same as motor

Body Type Number	Style	Passenger Capacity	Shipping Weight	Factory List & Date Effective 7-1-27	1-3-28	3-1-28
Model 443 Standard	(143" wheelbase)					
380	Touring	5-7	4200	$4050	$3975	$3975
381	Phaeton	5	4130	3975	3875	3875
382	Runabout	4	4110	3975	3875	3875
384	Sedan	5-7	4550	5150	4450	4450
385	Sedan Limousine	5-7	4710	5250	4550	4550
386	Sedan, Club	5	4360	4950	4450	4450
387	Coupe	4	4400	4950	4450	4250
388	Coupe	2-4	4400	—	4150	3950
389	Coupe, Convertible	2	4345	—	4250	4050
Model 443 Custom	(143" wheelbase)					
310	Touring	5-7	4395	—	3975	3975
311	Phaeton	5	4295	—	3875	3875
312	Runabout	4	4290	—	3875	3875
314	Sedan	5-7	4825	—	4450	4450
315	Sedan, Limousine	5-7	4900	—	4550	4550
316	Sedan, Club	5	4585	—	4450	4450
317	Coupe	4	4510	—	4450	4250
318	Coupe	2-4	4626	—	4150	3950
319	Coupe, Convertible	2	4380	—	4250	4050

Series — Fifth	Bore & Stroke — 3 1/2 x 5
Name — Single Six	H.P. AMA — 29.4
Produced — 7-1-27 to 8-1-28	Brake — 82
Cars produced — 41,750	Motor # — 125,000 to 166,941
Models — 526,533	Vehicle # — Same as motor

Body Type		Passenger	Shipping	Factory List &	
Number	Style	Capacity	Weight	Date Effective	
Model 526 (126" wheelbase)				7-1-27	7-9-28
301	Phaeton	5	3665	$2275	$1975
302	Runabout	4	3620	2275	1975
303	Sedan	5	4000	2280	1985
308	Coupe	2-4	3950	2350	2050
309	Coupe, Convertible	2-4	3875	2425	2125
Model 533 (133" wheelbase)					
300	Touring	5-7	3865	2485	2185
304	Sedan	5-7	4145	2685	2385
305	Sedan, Limousine	5-7	4205	2785	2485
306	Sedan, Club	5	4085	2685	2385
307	Coupe	4	4000	2685	2385
321	Phaeton	5	3745	2385	2085
322	Runabout	4	3700	2385	2085

Series — Sixth   Bore & Stroke — 3 3/16 x 5

Name — Standard Eight   H.P. AMA — 32.5

Produced — 8-1-28 to   Brake — 90
              8-20-29

Cars produced — 43,130   Motor # — 233,000 to 276,208

Models — 626-633   Vehicle # — Same as motor

Body Type		Passenger	Shipping	Factory List &	
Number	Style	Capacity	Weight	Date Effective	
Model 626	(126" wheelbase)			8-1-28	3-4-29
333	Sedan	5	4185	$2,435	$2,275
338	Coupe	2-4	4100	2,510	2,350
339	Coupe,				
	Convertible	2-4	4020	2,585	2,425
Model 633	(133" wheelbase)				
330	Touring	5-7	3950	2,635	2,475
334	Sedan	5-7	4440	2,735	2,575
335	Sedan,				
	Limousine	5-7	4475	2,835	2,675
336	Sedan, Club	5	4240	2,735	2,575
337	Coupe	4	4180	2,735	2,575
351	Phaeton	5	3905	2,535	2,375
352	Roadster	4	3805	2,535	2,375

Series — Sixth   Bore & Stroke — 3 1/2 x 5

Name — Speedster Eight   H.P. AMA — 39.2

Produced — 8-1-28 to   Brake — 106
            8-20-29

Cars produced — 70   Motor # — 166,942 to 167,012

Models — 626   Vehicle # — Same as motor

Body Type		Passenger	Shipping	Factory List &
Number	Style	Capacity	Weight	Date Effective
Model 626 Speedster	(126 1/2" wheelbase)			8-1-28
391	Phaeton	4	4065	$5,000
392	Roadster	2-4	4165	5,000

Series — Sixth		Bore & Stroke — 3 1/2 x 5	
Name — Custom and DeLuxe Eight		H.P. AMA — 39.2	
Produced — 8-1-28 to 8-20-29		Brake — 106	
Cars produced — 11,862		Motor # — 167,013 to 178,999	
Models — 640-645		Vehicle # — Same as motor	

Body Type Number	Style	Passenger Capacity	Shipping Weight	Factory List & Date Effective	
Model 640 Custom	(140" wheelbase)			8-1-28	9-1-28
340	Touring	5-7	4390	$3,275	
341	Phaeton	5	4370	3,175	
342	Roadster	4	4285	3,175	
344	Sedan	5-7	4835	3,750	
345	Sedan, Limousine	5-7	4910	3,850	
346	Sedan, Club	5	4655	3,750	
347	Coupe, Club	4	4535	3,750	
348	Coupe	2-4	4560	3,250	
349	Coupe, Convertible	2-4	4475	3,350	
Model 645 DeLuxe	(145" wheelbase)				
370	Touring	5-7	4890		$4,585
371	Phaeton	5	4870		4,585
372	Roadster	2-4	4785		4,585
373	Sport, Phaeton	5	4890		4,935
374	Sedan	5-7	5335		5,785
375	Sedan, Limousine	5-7	5410		5,985
376	Sedan, Club	5	5155		5,785
377	Coupe	5	5125		5,735
378	Coupe	2-4	5060		5,385

Series — Seventh	Bore & Stroke — 3 3/16 x 5
Name — Standard Eight	H.P. AMA — 32.5
Produced — 8-20-29 to 8-14-30	Brake — 90
Cars produced — 28,262	Motor # — 277,000 to 319,999
Models — 726 - 733	Vehicle # — Same as motor

Body Type		Passenger	Shipping	Factory List &	
Number	Style	Capacity	Weight	Date Effective	
Model 726 (127 1/2" wheelbase)				8-20-29	1-13-30
403	Sedan	5	4265	$2375	$2485
Model 733 (134 1/2" wheelbase)					
400	Touring	5-7	4055	2525	
401	Phaeton	4	3935	2425	
402	Roadster	2-4	3945	2425	
404	Sedan	5-7	4500	2675	2785
405	Sedan, Limousine	5-7	4555	2775	2885
406	Sedan, Club	5	4325	2675	
407	Coupe	5	4255	2675	
408	Coupe	2-4	4180	2525	
409	Coupe, Convertible	2-4	4100	2550	
431	Phaeton, Sport	4	4130	2725	

Series — Seventh			Bore & Stroke — 3 1/2 x 5	
Name — Speedster Eight			H.P. AMA — 39.2	
Produced — 9-29-29 to 8-14-30			Brake — 145	
Cars produced — 150			Motor # — 184,000 to 184,500	
Models — 734			Vehicle # — Same as motor	

Body Type		Passenger	Shipping	Factory List &
Number	Style	Capacity	Weight	Date Effective
Model 734 (134" wheelbase)				9-29-29
422	Roadster (Boattail)	2	4295	$5210
443	Sedan	5	4660	6000
445	Phaeton	4	4300	5200
447	Coupe Victoria	5	4525	6000
452	Roadster	2-4	4435	5200

Series — Seventh	Bore & Stroke — 3 1/2 x 5
Name — Custom & DeLuxe Eight	H.P. AMA — 39.2
Produced — 8-20-29 to 8-14-30	Brake — 106
Cars produced — 8,102	Motor # — 179,000 to 187,999
Models — 740 to 745	Vehicle # — Same as motor

Body Type Number	Style	Passenger Capacity	Shipping Weight	Factory List & Date Effective	
Model 740 Custom	(140 1/2" wheelbase)			8-20-29	8-15-30
410	Touring	5-7	4345	$3325	$2825
411	Phaeton	4	4250	3190	2690
412	Roadster	2-4	4245	3190	2690
413	Sedan	5	4560	3585	3085
414	Sedan	5-7	4765	3785	3285
415	Sedan, Limousine	5-7	4810	3885	3385
416	Sedan, Club	5	4580	3750	3250
417	Coupe	5	4555	3650	3150
418	Coupe	2-4	4500	3295	2795
419	Coupe, Convertible	2-4	4425	3350	2850
441	Phaeton, Sport	4	4450	3490	2990
Model 745 DeLuxe	(145 1/2" wheelbase)				
420	Touring	5-7	4745	4585	
421	Phaeton	4	4645	4585	
422	Roadster	2-4	4695	4585	
423	Sedan	5	4805	4985	
424	Sedan	5-7	5095	5185	
425	Sedan, Limousine	5-7	5140	5350	
426	Sedan, Club	5	5000	5150	
427	Coupe	5	4995	5100	
428	Coupe	2-4	4875	4785	
429	Coupe, Convertible	2-4	4665	4885	
451	Phaeton, Sport	4	4845	4885	

Series — Eighth

Name — Standard Eight

Produced — 8-14-30 to
  6-23-31

Cars Produced — 12,105

Models — 826-833

Bore & Stroke — 3 3/16 x 5

H.P. AMA — 32.5

Brake — 100 at 3200 RPM

Motor # — 320,000 to 339,999

Vehicle # — Same as motor

Body Type		Passenger	Shipping	Factory List &
Number	Style	Capacity	Weight	Date Effective
Model 826 Standard	(127 1/2" wheelbase)			8-14-30
463	Sedan	5	4479	$2385
Model 833 Standard	(134 1/2" wheelbase)			
460	Touring	5-7	4256	2525
461	Phaeton	4	4185	2425
462	Roadster	2-4	4140	2425
464	Sedan	7	4665	2785
465	Sedan, Limousine	5-7	4695	2885
466	Sedan, Club	5	4488	2675
467	Coupe	5	4308	2675
468	Coupe	2-4	4360	2525
469	Coupe, Convertible	2-4	4290	2550
481	Phaeton, Sport	4	4285	2725
483	Sedan, Convertible	5	4555	3465
Model 833 Individual Custom	(134 1/2" wheelbase)			
1881	Sedan, Convertible Dietrich	4	4442	4375
1879	Vict. Convertible, Dietrich	4	4186	4275
3000	Cabriolet, All-weather	5-7	4684	4850
3001	Landaulet, All-weather	5-7	4684	5050
3002	Town Car, All-weather	5-7	4744	4975
3003	Town Car, Landaulet, All-weather	5-7	4744	5175
3004	Sedan, Cabriolet, Limousine	5-6	4485	4490
3008	Cabriolet Sport, All-weather	5-7	4614	4850
3009	Landaulet, Sport, All-weather	5-7	4614	5050

Series — Eighth	Bore & Stroke — 3 1/2 x 5
Name — Custom & DeLuxe Eight	H.P. AMA — 39.2
Produced — 8-14-30 to 6-23-31	Brake — 120 at 3200 RPM
Cars produced — 3345	Motor # — 188,000 to 192,999
Models — 840-845	Vehicle # — Same as motor

Body Type		Passenger	Shipping	Factory List &	
Number	Style	Capacity	Weight	Date Effective	
Model 840 Custom	(140 1/2" wheelbase)			8-14-30	8-20-30
470	Touring	5-7	4507	$3595	
471	Phaeton	4	4439	3490	
472	Roadster	2-4	4383	3490	
473	Sedan	5	4955	3795	
476	Sedan, Club	5	4720	3950	
477	Coupe	5	4673	3850	
478	Coupe	2-4	4592	3545	
479	Coupe, Convertible	2-4	3595	3595	
491	Phaeton, Sport	4	4535	3790	
Model 840 Individual Custom	(140 1/2" wheelbase)				
1881	Sedan, Convertible, Dietrich	4	4674	$5275	
1879	Victoria, Convertible	4	4418	5175	
3000	Cabriolet, All-weather	5-7	4916	5750	
3001	Landaulet, All-weather	5-7	4976	5950	
3002	Town Car, All-weather	5-7	4976	5875	
3003	Town Car, Landaulet	5-6	4976	6075	
3008	Cabriolet, Sport, All-weather	5-7	4846	5750	

| 3009 | Landaulet,
Sport,
All-weather | 5-7 | 4846 | | 5950 |

Model 845 DeLuxe   (145 1/2" wheelbase)

| 474 | Sedan | 5-7 | 5010 | 4150 |
| 475 | Sedan,
Limousine | 5-7 | 5080 | 4285 |

Series — Ninth
Name — Light Eight
Produced — 1-9-32 to 1-5-33
Cars produced — 6750
Models — 900

Bore & Stroke — 3 3/16 x 5
H.P. AMA — 32.5
Brake — 110
Motor # — 360,000 to 369,999
Vehicle # — BTPPN

Body Type Number	Style	Passenger Capacity	Shipping Weight	Factory List & Date Effective
Model 900 (127" wheelbase)				1-9-32
558	Coupe	2-4	3990	$1795
559	Coupe, Roadster	2-4	3930	1795
563	Coupe, Sedan	5	4060	1795
553	Sedan	5	4115	1750

Series — Ninth	Bore & Stroke — 3 3/16 x 5
Name — Standard Eight	H.P. AMA — 32.5
Produced — 6-23-31 to 1-5-33	Brake — 110 at 3200
Cars produced — 7,659	Motor # — 340,000 to 359,999
Models — 901-2	Vehicle # — Body type plus production number (BTPPN)

Body Type		Passenger	Shipping	Factory List &	
Number	Style	Capacity	Weight	Date Effective	
Model 901 (129 1/2" wheelbase)				6-23-31	6-1-32
503	Sedan	5	4570	$2485	$2350
Model 902 (136 1/2" wheelbase)					
500	Touring	5-7	4345	2775	2700
501	Phaeton	4	4300	2650	2850
504	Sedan	5-7	4735	2885	3035
505	Sedan, Limousine	5-7	4770	2985	3185
506	Sedan, Club	5	4555	2775	2975
507	Coupe	5	4505	2795	2945
508	Coupe	2-4	4475	2675	2795
509	Coupe, Roadster	2-4	4420	2650	2850
521	Phaeton, Sport	5	4400	2950	3150
523	Sedan, Convertible	5	4573	3445	3450
527	Victoria, Convertible	5	4317	3395	3395
543	Sedan	5	4590	2685	2885

Series — Ninth	Bore & Stroke — 3 1/2 x 5
Name — Eight Deluxe	H.P. AMA — 39.2
Produced — 6-17-31 to 1-5-33	Brake — 135 at 3200
Cars produced — 1,655	Motor # — 193,000 to 199,999
Models — 903-4	Vehicle # — BTPPN

| Body Type | | Passenger | Shipping | Factory List & Date Effective | | |
Number	Style	Capacity	Weight	6-17-31	6-23-31	6-1-32
Model 903	(142 1/2" wheelbase)					
510	Touring	5-7	4760		$3795	$3595
511	Phaeton	4	4715		3690	3490
513	Sedan	5	5045		3845	3445
516	Sedan, Club	5	5000		3890	3595
517	Coupe	5	4985		3850	3550
518	Coupe	2-4	4890		3725	3350
519	Coupe, Roadster	2-4	4825		3750	3450
531	Phaeton, Sport	4	4795		3990	3790
533	Sedan, Convertible	5	4985		4550	4095
537	Victoria, Convertible	5	4727		4495	4025
Model 904	(147 1/2" wheelbase)					
514	Sedan	5-7	5195		4150	3695
515	Sedan Limousine	5-7	5240		4285	3895

| Body Type | | Passenger | Shipping | Factory List & |
Number	Style	Capacity	Weight	Date Effective
Model 904 (147 1/2" wheelbase)				6-17-31 6-23-31 6-1-32
Individual Custom				
2068	Coupe, Stationary, Dietrich	2-4	5000	$5900
2069	Phaeton, Sport, Dietrich	4	4800	5800
2070	Sedan, Convertible, Dietrich	5	5100	6250
2071	Coupe, Convertible, Dietrich	2-4	4965	6050
2070	Victoria, Convertible Dietrich	4	4815	6150
4000	Cabriolet, All-weather	5-7	5250	6850
4001	Landaulet, All-weather	5-7	5250	7250
4002	Town Car, All-weather	5-7	5310	6850
4003	Landaulet-Town Car, All-weather	5-7	5310	7250
4004	Limousine, Sedan, Cabriolet	6	5050	6850
4005	Sedan, Sport	5	5030	6850
4006	Brougham, All-weather	5-7	5293	6850
4007	Limousine, Sedan, Dietrich	6	5075	6850
4008	Cabriolet, Sport, All-weather	5-7	5180	6850
4009	Landaulet, Sport, All-weather	5-7	5180	7250

Series — Ninth	Bore & Stroke — 3 7/16 x 4
Name — Twin Six	H.P. AMA — 56.7
Produced — 6-17-31 to 1-7-33	Brake — 160 at 3200
Cars produced — 549	Motor # — 900,000 to 900,999
Models — 905-6	Vehicle # — BTPPN

Body Type Number	Style	Passenger Capacity	Shipping Weight	Factory List & Date Effective		
				6-17-31	1-9-32	6-1-32
Model 905	(142 1/2" wheelbase)					
570	Touring	5-7	5315		$3895	$4395
571	Phaeton	4	5275		3790	4290
573	Sedan	5	5635		3745	4245
576	Sedan, Club	5	5585		3895	4395
577	Coupe	5	5485		3850	4350
578	Coupe	2-4	5425		3650	4150
579	Coupe Roadster	2-4	5350		3750	4250
581	Phaeton, Sport	4	5375		4090	4590
583	Sedan, Convertible	5	5255		4395	4895
587	Victoria, Convertible	5	5180		4325	4825
Model 906	(147 1/2" wheelbase)					
574	Sedan	5-7	5765		3995	4495
575	Sedan, Limousine	5-7	5830		4195	4695
Model 906 Individual Custom	(147" wheelbase)					
2068	Coupe, Dietrich	2-4	5180	$6600		
2069	Phaeton, Sport Dietrich	4	4980	6500		
2070	Sedan, Convertible, Dietrich	5	5280	6950		
2071	Coupe, Convertible, Dietrich	2-4	5145	6750		
2072	Victoria, Convertible, Dietrich	4	4995	6850		

4000	Cabriolet, All-weather	5-7	5430	7550
4001	Landaulet, All-weather	5-7	5430	7950
4002	Town Car, All-weather	5-7	5490	7550
4003	Landaulet, Town Car, All-weather	5-7	5490	7950

Series — Tenth	Bore & Stroke — 3 3/16 x 5
Name — Eight	H.P. AMA — 32.5
Produced — 1-5-33 to 8-21-33	Brake — 120 at 3200 RPM
Cars produced — 2980	Motor # — 370,000 to 373,999
Models — 1001-2	Vehicle # — Body type plus body number

Body Type		Passenger Capacity	Shipping Weight	Factory List & Date Effective	
Number	Style				
Model 1001	(127 1/2" wheelbase)			1-5-33	2-9-33
602	Coupe, Sedan	5	4245	$2190	
603	Sedan	5	4335	2150	
608	Coupe	2-4	4200	2160	
609	Coupe, Roadster	2-4	4150	2250	
Model 1002	(136" wheelbase)				
610	Touring	5-7	4275	2390	
611	Phaeton	5	4270	2370	
613	Sedan	5	4590	2385	
614	Sedan	7	4640	2455	
615	Limousine	5-7	4725	2550	
616	Sedan, Club	5	4545	2390	
617	Coupe	5	4500	2440	
618	Coupe	2-4	4455	2350	
623	Sedan, Convertible	5	4515	2890	
627	Convertible, Victoria	5	4540	2780	
5633	Sedan, Formal	5	4900	$3085	

Series — Tenth   Bore & Stroke — 3 1/2 x 5

Name — Super Eight   H.P. AMA — 39.2

Produced — 1-5-33 to   Brake — 145 at 3200 RPM
           8-21-33

Cars produced — 1300   Motor # — 750,000 to 751,999

Models — 1003-4   Vehicle # — BTPPN

Body Type		Passenger	Shipping	Factory List &	
Number	Style	Capacity	Weight	Date Effective	
Model 1003 (135" wheelbase)				1-5-33	2-9-33
653	Sedan	5	4815	$2750	
Model 1004 (142" wheelbase)					
650	Touring	5-7	4610	2980	
651	Phaeton	5	4490	2890	
654	Sedan	5-7	4965	3090	
655	Limousine	5-7	5025	3280	
656	Sedan, Club	5	4795	2975	
657	Coupe	5	4780	2980	
658	Coupe	2-4	4670	2780	
659	Coupe, Roadster	2-4	4625	2870	
661	Phaeton, Sport	2-4	4690	3150	
663	Sedan, Convertible	5	4840	3590	
667	Convertible, Victoria	5	4795	3440	
673	Sedan, Formal	5	5155	$3600	

Series — Tenth	Bore & Stroke — 3 7/16 x 4
Name — Twelve	H.P. AMA — 56.7
Produced — 1-5-33 to 8-21-33	Brake — 160 at 3200 RPM
Cars produced — 520	Motor # — 901,000 to 901,599
Models — 1005-6	Vehicle # — BTPPN

Body Type		Passenger	Shipping	Factory List &
Number	Style	Capacity	Weight	Date Effective
Model 1005 (142" wheelbase) Standard				1-5-33 1-7-33 2-10-33
631	Phaeton	5	5095	$3790
633	Sedan	5	5385	3860
636	Sedan, Club	5	5400	3880
637	Coupe	5	5300	3890
638	Coupe	2-4	5255	3720
639	Coupe, Roadster	2-4	5160	3850
641	Phaeton, Sport	5	5175	4090
643	Sedan, Con-vertible	5	5405	4650
647	Victoria, Con-vertible	5	5225	4490
5633	Sedan, Formal	5	5690	$4560
Model 1006 (147" wheelbase) Standard				
634	Sedan	5-7	5600	4085
635	Limousine	5-7	5650	4285

| Body Type | | Passenger | Shipping | Factory List & |
Number	Style	Capacity	Weight	Date Effective
Model 1006 (147" wheelbase)				1-5-33 1-7-33 2-10-33
Dietrich Custom				
3068	Coupe,			
	Stationary	2-4	5360	$6000
3069	Phaeton,			
	Sport	4	5160	5875
3070	Sedan,			
	Convertible	5	5460	6570
3071	Runabout,			
	Convertible	2-4	5325	6085
3072	Victoria,			
	Convertible	4	5175	6070
3182	Sedan,			
	Formal	5-7	5735	7000
Model 1006 (147" wheelbase)				
LeBaron Custom				
758	Cabriolet,			
	All-weather	5-7	5610	7000
759	Town Car,			
	All-weather	5-7	5670	7000
Model 1006 (147" wheelbase)				
Packard Custom				
4000	Cabriolet,			
	All-weather	5-7	5650	$6030
4001	Landaulet,			
	All-weather	5-7	5650	6250
4002	Town Car,			
	All-weather	5-7	5610	6080
4003	Town Car,			
	Landaulet	5-7	5610	6250
4004	Limousine,			
	Landaulet	5-7	5650	6000
4005	Sedan, Sport	5-7	5330	6000
4007	Limousine	5-7	5650	6045

Series — Eleventh	Bore & Stroke — 3 3/16 x 5
Name — Eight	H.P. AMA — 32.5
Produced — 8-21-33 to 8-30-34	Brake — 120 x 3200
Cars produced — 5,120	Motor # — 374,000 to 379,148
Models — 1100-1-2	Vehicle # — BTPPN

Body Type		Passenger	Shipping	8-21-32		
				Factory	Delivered	Delivered
Number	Style	Capacity	Weight	List	Price	Price
					Standard Equip.	DeLuxe Equip.
Model 1100	(129" wheelbase)					
703	Sedan	5	4640	$2350	$2550	$2725
Model 1101	(136" wheelbase)					
710	Touring	5-7	4400	2590	2845	2973
711	Phaeton	4	4359	2570	2825	2953
712	Sedan, Formal	5	4760	3285	3555	3683
713	Sedan	5	4660	2585	2840	2968
716	Sedan, Club	5	4730	2670	2954	3082
717	Coupe	5	4580	2640	2896	3024
718	Coupe	2-4	4580	2640	2804	2932
719	Coupe, Roadster	2-4	4430	2580	2835	2963
721	Phaeton, Sport	4	4430	2830	3030	3205
723	Sedan, Convertible	5	4680	3090	3355	3484
727	Victoria, Convertible	5	4710	2980	3243	3371
Model 1102	(141" wheelbase)					
714	Sedan	5-7	4945	2655	2911	3039
715	Sedan, Limousine	5-7	5000	2790	3049	3177

Series — Eleventh		Bore & Stroke — 3 1/2 x 5				
Name — Super 8		H.P. AMA — 39.2				
Produced — 8-21-33 to 8-30-34		Brake — 145 x 3200				
Cars produced — 1,920		Motor # — 752,000 to 754,999				
Models — 1103-4-5		Vehicle # — BTPPN				

Body Type		Passenger Capacity	Shipping Weight	Factory List	Delivered Price (8-21-33)	Delivered Price
Number	Style				Standard Equip.	DeLuxe Equip.
Model 1103 (135" wheelbase)						
753	Sedan	5	4890	$2950	$3229	$3371
Model 1104 (142" wheelbase)						
750	Touring	7	4720	3180	3466	3610
751	Phaeton	4	4645	3090	3374	3518
752	Sedan, Formal	5	5010	3800	4099	4243
756	Sedan, Club	5	4985	3255	3570	3714
757	Coupe	5	4885	3180	3466	3610
758	Coupe	2-4	4800	2980	3262	3406
759	Coupe, Roadster	2-4	4680	3070	3354	3498
761	Phaeton, Sport	4	4740	3350	3639	3783
763	Sedan, Convertible	5	4930	3790	4088	4233
767	Victoria, Convertible	5	4875	3640	3935	4079
773	Sedan	5	4910	3200	3515	3659
Model 1105 Standard (147" wheelbase)						
754	Sedan	5-7	5245	3290	3587	3731
755	Sedan, Limousine	5-7	5275	3480	3781	3925
Model 1105 Dietrich (147" wheelbase)						
4068	Coupe, Stationary	2-4	4955	5445	5780	5925
4070	Sedan, Convertible	5	5055	5800	6142	6286
4071	Runabout, Convertible	2-4	4920	5365	5698	5842
4072	Victoria, Convertible	4	4770	5345	5648	5792
4182	Sedan, Sport	5	5380	6295	6648	6792

Model 1105 LeBaron (147" wheelbase)					
280	Phaeton	4	4755	7065	7435	7578
858	Cabriolet, All-weather	5-7	5205	5450	5785	5930
859	Town Car, All-weather	5-7	5265	5450	5785	5930

Series — Eleventh	Bore & Stroke — 3 7/16 x 4
Name — Twelve	H.P. AMA — 56.7
Produced — 8-21-33 to 8-30-34	Brake — 160 at 3200
Cars produced — 960	Motor # — 901,600 to 902,586
Models — 1106-7-8	Vehicle # — BTPPN

8-21-33

Body Type		Passenger	Shipping	Factory	Delivered	Delivered
Number	Style	Capacity	Weight	List	Price	Price
					Standard Equip.	DeLuxe Equip.

Model 1108 Dietrich (147" wheelbase)						
4002	Town Car, All-weather	5-7	5715	5695	6160	6313
4068	Coupe, Stationary	2-4	5405	6185	6650	6808
4069	Phaeton, Sport	4	5400	5180	5645	5798
4070	Sedan, Convertible	5	5505	6555	7026	7185
4071	Runabout, Convertible	2-4	5370	6100	6562	6721
4072	Victoria, Convertible	4	5220	6080	6542	6701
4182	Sedan, Sport	5	5130	7060	7541	7700

Model 1108 LeBaron (147" wheelbase)						
858	Cabriolet, All-weather	5-7	5655	6155	6620	6788
859	Town Car, All-weather	5-7	5655	6155	6620	6788
280	Phaeton, Sport	4	5130	7065	7435	7578

Series — Eleventh	Bore & Stroke — 3 7/16 x 4
Name — Twelve	H.P. AMA — 56.7
Produced — 8-21-33 to 8-30-34	Brake — 160 at 3200
Cars produced — 960	Motor # — 901,600 to 902,586
Models — 1106-7-8	Vehicle # — BTPPN

8-21-33

Body Type		Passenger	Shipping	Factory	Delivered	Delivered
Number	Style	Capacity	Weight	List	Price	Price
					Standard Equip.	DeLuxe Equip.
Model 1106	(135" wheelbase)					
275	Runabout, Spdst. LeBaron	2	5400		$7746	
Model 1107	(142" wheelbase)					
730	Touring	5-7	5415	$3980	4398	$4557
731	Phaeton	4	5325	3890	4307	4465
732	Sedan, Formal	5	5630	4660	5092	5251
733	Sedan	5	5530	3960	4378	4537
736	Sedan, Club	5	5660	4060	4508	4666
737	Coupe	5	5530	3990	4409	4568
738	Coupe	2-4	5585	3820	4235	4394
739	Coupe, Roadster	2-4	5330	3850	4266	4425
741	Phaeton, Sport	4	5400	4190	4613	4771
743	Sedan, Convertible	5	5470	4750	5180	5338
747	Victoria, Convertible	5	5440	4590	5021	5179
Model 1108 Standard	(147" wheelbase)					
734	Sedan	7	5700	4185	4603	4762
735	Sedan, Limousine	7	5750	4385	4807	4966

Series — Twelfth	Bore & Stroke — 3 1/4 x 3 7/8
Name — One Twenty	H.P. AMA — 33.8
Produced — 1-5-35 to 9-23-35	Brake — 110
Cars produced — 24995	Motor # — X-1500 - 27499
Models — 120A	Vehicle # — BTPPN

Body Type		Passenger Capacity	Shipping Weight	Factory List & Date Effective
Number	Style			
Model 120A	(120" wheelbase)			1-5-35
898	Coupe, Business	2	3400	$ 980
899	Coupe, Convertible	2-4	3385	1070
895	Coupe, Sport	2-4	3435	1020
894	Coupe, Touring	5	3455	1025
893	Sedan	5	3510	1060
896	Sedan, Club	5	3515	1085
892	Sedan, Touring	5	3550	1095

Series — Twelfth	Bore & Stroke — 3 3/16 x 5
Name — Eight	H.P. AMA — 32.5
Produced — 8-30-34 to 8-10-35	Brake — 130 x 3200 RPM
Cars produced — 4,781	Motor # — 385,000 to 390,499
Models — 1200-1-2	Vehicle # — BTPPN

Body Type		Passenger	Shipping	Factory List &
Number	Style	Capacity	Weight	Date Effective
Model 1200	(127" wheelbase)			8-30-34
803	Sedan	5	4780	$2385
Model 1201	(134" wheelbase)			
195	Cabriolet, LeBaron, All-weather	5-7	5185	5240
807	Victoria, Convertible	5	4835	3100
811	Phaeton	5	4475	2670
812	Sedan, Formal	5	5035	3285
813	Sedan	5	4935	2585
816	Sedan, Club	5	4845	2580
817	Coupe	5	4700	2560
818	Coupe	2-4	4625	2475
819	Coupe, Convertible	2-4	4555	2580
Model 1202	(139" wheelbase)			
194	Town Car, LeBaron, All-weather	5-7	5225	5385
810	Touring	5-7	4400	3170
814	Sedan	5-7	5075	2755
814	Sedan, Commercial	5-8	4985	2630
815	Limousine	5-7	5125	2890
815	Limousine, Commercial	5-8	5150	2765
863	Sedan, Convertible	5	4800	3200

Series — Twelfth	Bore & Stroke — 3 1/2 x 5
Name — Super Eight	H.P. AMA — 150 x 3200
Produced — 8-30-34 to 8-10-35	Brake — 39.2
Cars produced — 1,392	Motor # — 755,000 to 756,999
Models — 1203-4-5	Vehicle # — BTPPN

Body Type Number	Style	Passenger Capacity	Shipping Weight	Factory List & Date Effective	
Model 1203	(132" wheelbase)			8-30-34	5-21-35
843	Sedan	5	4985	$2990	
Model 1204	(139" wheelbase)				
195	Cabriolet, LeBaron, All-weather	5-7	5300	5670	
841	Phaeton, Sport	5	4875	3450	
847	Victoria, Convertible	5	5000	3760	
851	Phaeton	5	4775	3190	
852	Sedan, Formal	5	5150	3800	
856	Sedan, Club	5	5100	3170	
857	Coupe	5	5015	3080	
858	Coupe	2-4	4920	2880	
859	Coupe, Convertible	2-4	4800	3070	
Model 1205	(144" wheelbase)				
194	Town Car, LeBaron, All-weather	5-7	5525	5815	
850	Touring	5-7	4729		$3690
854	Sedan	5-7	5375	3390	
854	Sedan, Commercial	5-8	5320	3265	
855	Limousine	5-7	5400	3580	
855	Limousine, Commercial	5-8	5380	3455	
883	Sedan, Convertible	5	5050	3910	

Series — Twelfth	Bore & Stroke — 3 7/16 x 4 1/4
Name — Twelve	H.P. AMA — 56.7
Produced — 8-30-34 to 8-10-35	Brake — 175 x 3200 RPM
Cars produced — 721	Motor # — 903,000 to 903,999
Models — 1207-8	Vehicle # — BTPPN

Body Type		Passenger	Shipping	Factory List &	
Number	Style	Capacity	Weight	Date Effective	
Model 1207 (139" wheelbase)				8-30-34	5-21.-35
195	Cabriolet, LeBaron, All-weather	5-7	5930	$6290	
821	Phaeton, Sport	5	5550	4290	
827	Victoria, Convertible	5	5590	4790	
831	Phaeton	5	5475	3990	
832	Sedan, Formal	5-7	5780	4660	
833	Sedan	5	5700	3960	
836	Sedan, Club	5	5800	4060	
837	Coupe	5	5680	3990	
838	Coupe	2-4	5635	3820	
839	Coupe, Convertible	2-4	5480	3850	
Model 1208 (144" wheelbase)					
194	Town Car, LeBaron, All-weather	5-7	5950	6435	
830	Touring	7	5415		$4490
834	Sedan	7	5800	4285	
835	Limousine	7	5900	4485	
873	Sedan, Convertible	5	5620	4950	

Series — Fourteenth	Bore & Stroke — 3 1/4 x 4 1/4
Name — One Twenty	H.P. AMA — 33.8
Produced — 9-23-35 to 9-3-36	Brake — 120
Cars produced — 55042	Motor # — X-27500-99000
Models — 120-B	Vehicle # — BTPPN

| Body Type | | Passenger | Shipping | Factory List & |
Number	Style	Capacity	Weight	Date Effective
Model 120-B	(120" wheelbase)			9-23-35
998	Coupe, Business	2	3380	$ 990
899	Coupe, Convertible	2-4	3525	1110
895	Coupe, Sport	2-4	3455	1030
894	Coupe, Touring	5	3475	1040
893	Sedan	5	3505	1075
896	Sedan, Club	5	3495	1090
997	Sedan, Convertible	5	3660	1395
892	Sedan, Touring	5	3560	1115

Series — Fourteenth	Bore & Stroke — 3 3/16 x 5		
Name — Eight	H.P. AMA — 32.5		
Produced — 8-10-35 to 9-3-36	Brake — 130 x 3200		
Cars produced — 3,973	Motor # — 390,500 to 395,499		
Models — 1400-1-2	Vehicle # — BTPPN		

Body Type Number / Style	Passenger Capacity	Shipping Weight	Factory List & Date Effective
Model 1400 (127" wheelbase)			8-10-35
903 Sedan	5	4815	$2385
Model 1401 (134" wheelbase)			
294 Cabriolet, LeBaron, All-weather	5-7	5185	5240
907 Victoria, Convertible	5	4810	3200
911 Phaeton	4	4890	3020
912 Sedan, Formal	5-7	5030	3285
913 Sedan	5	4978	2585
916 Sedan, Club	5	4815	2580
917 Coupe	5	4745	2560
918 Coupe	2-4	4735	2470
919 Coupe, Roadster	2-4	4740	2730
Model 1402 (139" wheelbase)			
295 Town Car, LeBaron, All-weather	5-7	5225	5385
910 Touring	5-7	5060	3270
914 Sedan	5-7	4955	2755
914 Sedan, Business	5-8	4985	2630
915 Limousine	5-7	5045	2890
915 Limousine, Business	5-8	5150	2765
963 Sedan, Convertible	5	5140	3400

Series — Fourteenth	Bore & Stroke — 3 1/2 x 5
Name — Super Eight	H.P. AMA — 39.2
Produced — 8-10-35 to 9-3-36	Brake — 150 x 3200
Cars produced — 1,330	Motor # — 757,000 to 759,000
Models — 1403-4-5	Vehicle # — BTPPN

| Body Type | | Passenger | Shipping | Factory List & |
Number	Style	Capacity	Weight	Date Effective
Model 1403	**(132" wheelbase)**			8-10-35
943	Sedan	5	5080	$2990
Model 1404	**(139" wheelbase)**			
294	Cabriolet, LeBaron, All-weather	5-7	5300	5670
941	Phaeton, Sport	5	5200	3650
947	Victoria, Convertible	5	5122	3860
951	Phaeton	5	5080	3390
952	Sedan, Formal	5	5245	3800
956	Sedan, Club	5	5178	3170
957	Coupe	5	5010	3080
958	Coupe	2-4	4933	2880
959	Coupe, Roadster	2-4	4993	3070
Model 1405	**(144" wheelbase)**			
295	Town Car, LeBaron, All-weather	5-7	5525	5815
950	Touring	5-7	5200	3690
954	Sedan	5-7	5300	3390
954	Sedan, Business	5-8	5320	3265
955	Limousine	5-7	5380	3580
955	Limousine, Business	5-8	5380	3455
983	Sedan, Convertible	5	5390	4010

Series — Fourteenth   Bore & Stroke — 3 7/16 x 4 1/4

Name — Twelve   H.P. AMA — 56.7

Produced - 8-10-35 to   Brake — 175 x 3200
          9-3-36

Cars produced — 682   Motor # — 904,000 to 905,000

Models — 1407-8   Vehicle # — BTPPN

Body Type		Passenger	Shipping	Factory List &
Number	Style	Capacity	Weight	Date Effective
Model 1407	(139" wheelbase)			8-10-35
294	Cabriolet, LeBaron All-weather	5-7	5900	$6290
921	Phaeton, Sport	5	5785	4490
927	Victoria, Convertible	5	5585	4890
931	Phaeton	5	5480	4190
932	Sedan, Formal	5	5735	4660
933	Sedan	5	5695	3960
936	Sedan, Club	5	5640	4060
937	Coupe	5	5495	3990
938	Coupe	2-4	5495	3820
939	Coupe, Roadster	2-4	5495	3850
Model 1408	(144" wheelbase)			
295	Town Car, LeBaron, All-weather	5-7	5950	6435
934	Sedan	5-7	5790	4285
935	Limousine	5-7	5890	4485
930	Touring	7	5460	4490
973	Sedan, Convertible	5	5945	5050

Series — Fifteenth   Bore & Stroke — 3 7/16 x 4 1/4

Name — Six (One Ten)   H.P. AMA — 28.36

Produced — 9-3-36 to   Brake — 100
          9-20-37

Cars produced — 65,400   Motor # — T-1500 - 68000

Models — 115-C (110)   Vehicle # — BTPPN

| Body Type | | Passenger | Shipping | Factory List & | |
Number	Style	Capacity	Weight	Date Effective	
Model 115-C (115" wheelbase)				9-3-36	8-9-37
1088	Coupe, Business	2	3140	$ 795	$ 960
1089	Coupe, Convertible	2-4	3285	910	1075
1085	Coupe, Sport	2-4	3215	840	1005
1084	Coupe, Touring	5	3235	860	1025
1083	Sedan	5	3265	895	1060
1086	Sedan, Club	5	3275	900	1065
1082	Sedan, Touring	5	3310	910	1075
1060	Station Wagon	8			1295

Series — Fifteenth	Bore & Stroke — 3 1/4 x 4 1/4
Name — One Twenty	H.P. AMA — 33.8
Produced — 9-3-36 to 9-20-37	Brake — 120
Cars produced — 50,100	Motor # — X-100,000 - 150,300
Models — 120-C, CD	Vehicle # — BTPPN

Body Type Number	Style	Passenger Capacity	Shipping Weight	Factory List & Date Effective 9-3-36	8-9-37
Model 120-C (120" wheelbase)					
1098	Coupe, Business	2	3340	$ 945	$1130
1099	Coupe, Convertible	2-4	3485	1060	1250
1095	Coupe, Sport	2-4	3415	990	1175
1094	Coupe, Touring	5	3435	1010	1200
1093	Sedan	5	3465	1045	1235
1096	Sedan, Club	5	3455	1050	1240
1097	Sedan, Convertible	5	3630	1355	1550
1092	Sedan, Touring	5	3520	1060	1250
1070	Station Wagon	8	3590		1485
Model 120-CD (120" wheelbase)					
1094CD	Coupe, Touring	5	3465	1220	1415
1096CD	Sedan, Club	5	3485	1260	1455
1098CD	Sedan, Touring	5	3550	1270	1465
Model 138-CD (138" wheelbase)					
1090CD	Limousine, Touring	5-7	3900	1840	2050
1091CD	Sedan, Touring	5-7	3835	1690	1900

Series — Fifteenth	Bore & Stroke — 3 3/16 x 5
Name — Super Eight	H.P. AMA — 32.5
Produced — 9-3-36 to 9-29-37	Brake — 135 x 3200
Cars produced — 5,793	Motor # — 395,000 - 403,000
Models — 1500-1-2	Vehicle # — BTPPN

Body Type		Passenger	Shipping	Factory List &	
Number	Style	Capacity	Weight	Date Effective	
Model 1500 (127" wheelbase)				9-3-36	9-29-37
1003	Sedan, Touring	5	4530	$2335	$2630
Model 1501 (134" wheelbase)					
L-394	Cabriolet, All-weather, LeBaron	5-7	4965	4850	5050
1007	Victoria	5	4650	3150	3460
1012	Sedan, Formal	5	4795	3235	3550
1013	Sedan, Touring	5	4670	2535	2835
1016	Sedan, Club	5	4600	2530	2830
1017	Coupe	5	4595	2510	2810
1018	Coupe	2-4	4585	2420	2715
1019	Coupe, Convertible	2-4	4580	2680	2980
Model 1502 (139" wheelbase)					
L-395	Town Car	5-7	5360	4990	5190
1014	Sedan, Touring	5-7	4700	2705	3010
1014B	Sedan, Business	5-8	4755	2580	2880
1015	Limousine, Touring	5-7	4815	2840	3145
1015B	Limousine, Business	5-8	4925	2715	3020
1063	Sedan, Convertible	5	4945	3350	3665

Series — Fifteenth	Bore & Stroke — 3 7/16 x 4 1/4
Name — Twelve	H.P. AMA — 56.7
Produced — 9-3-36 to 9-10-37	Brake — 175
Cars produced — 1,300	Motor # — 905,500 to 908,000
Models — 1506-7-8	Vehicle # — BTPPN

Body Type		Passenger Capacity	Shipping Weight	Factory List & Date Effective	
Number	Style			9-3-36	8-9-37
Model 1506	(132" wheelbase)				
1023	Sedan, Touring	5	5335	$3490	$3870
Model 1507	(139" wheelbase)				
L-394	Cabriolet, All-weather, LeBaron	5-7	5740	5700	5925
1027	Victoria	5	5345	4490	5015
1032	Sedan, Formal	5	5550	4260	4655
1033	Sedan, Touring	5	5525	3560	3940
1036	Sedan, Club	5	5520	3660	4045
1037	Coupe	5	5415	3590	3970
1038	Coupe	2-4	5255	3420	3920
1039	Coupe, Convertible	2-4	5255	3450	3950
Model 1508	(144" wheelbase)				
L-395	Town Car, All-weather, LeBaron	5-7	5790	5900	6130
1034	Sedan, Touring	5-7	5600	3885	4270
1035	Limousine, Touring	5-7	5660	4085	4475
1073	Sedan, Convertible	5	5680	4650	5150

Series — Sixteenth	Bore & Stroke — 3 1/2 x 4 1/4
Name — Six	H.P. AMA — 29.4
Produced — 9-20-37 to 9-20-38	Brake — 100
Cars produced — 30,050	Motor # — A-1500 - 31,660
Models — 1600	Vehicle # — None

Body Type		Passenger	Shipping	Factory List &	
Number	Style	Capacity	Weight	Date Effective	
Model 1600 (122" wheelbase)				9-20-37	2-4-38
1188	Coupe, Business	2	3450	$1075	$ 975
1185	Coupe, Club	2-4	3425	1120	1020
1189	Coupe, Convertible	2-4	3500	1235	1135
1184	Sedan, Touring, 2 Door	5	3475	1145	1040
1182	Sedan, Touring, 4 Door	5	3525	1175	1070

Series — Sixteenth	Bore & Stroke — 3 1/4 x 4 1/4
Name — Eight	H.P. AMA — 33.8
Produced — 9-20-37 to 9-20-38	Brake — 120
Cars Produced — 22,624	Motor # — A-300,000 - 322,751
Models — 1601-1D-2	Vehicle # — BTPPN

Body Type		Passenger Capacity	Shipping Weight	Factory List & Date Effective	
Number	Style				
Model 1601 (127" wheelbase)				9-20-37	10-26-37
1198	Coupe, Business	2	3570	$1225	
1195	Coupe, Club	2-4	3550	1270	
1199	Coupe, Convertible	2-4	3625	1365	
1197	Sedan, Convertible	5	3775	1650	
1194	Sedan, Touring, 2 Door	5	3600	1295	
1192	Sedan, Touring, 4 Door	5	3650	1525	
Model 1601-D (127" wheelbase)					
1172	Sedan, Touring, 4 Door	5	3685	1540	
Model 1601 (139" wheelbase)					
1665	Cabriolet, All-weather Rollston	5-7	NA	$4810	
1669	Town Car, All-weather Rollston	5-7	NA	4885	
1668	Brougham, All-weather Rollston	4	NA	5100	
Model 1602 (148" wheelbase)					
1190	Limousine, Touring	5-7	4245	1955	
1191	Sedan, Touring	5-7	4195	2110	

Series — Sixteenth	Bore & Stroke — 3 3/16 x 5
Name — Super Eight	H.P. AMA — 32.5
Produced — 9-20-37 to 9-20-38	Brake — 130
Cars produced — 2,478	Motor # — A-500,000 to 504,527
Models — 1603, 04 and 05	Vehicle # — BTPPN

Body Type		Passenger	Shipping	Factory List &
Number	Style	Capacity	Weight	Date Effective
Model 1603 (127" wheelbase)				9-30-37 10-11-37
1103	Sedan, Touring, 4 Door	5	4530	$2790
Model 1604 (134" wheelbase)				
1107	Victoria	5	4650	3670
1112	Sedan, Formal	5	4795	3710
1113	Sedan, Touring, 4 Door	5	4670	2995
1116	Sedan, Club	5	4600	2990
1117	Coupe	5	4595	2965
1118	Coupe	2-4	4585	2925
1119	Coupe, Convertible	2-4	4580	3210
Model 1605 (139" wheelbase)				
1114	Sedan, Business	5-7	4815	$3165
1115	Limousine, Business	5-7	4815	3305
1143	Sedan, Convertible	5	4945	3970
Model 1604-05 (139" wheelbase)				
494	Cabriolet, All-weather, Rollson	5-7	NA	5790
495	Town Car, All-weather, Rollson	5-7	NA	5890
3086	Cabriolet, Touring, Brunn	5-7	NA	7475
3087	Cabriolet, All-weather, Brunn	5-7	NA	7475

Series — Sixteenth	Bore & Stroke — 3 7/16 x 4 1/4
Name — Twelve	H.P. AMA — 56.7
Produced — 9-10-37 to 9-20-38	Brake — 175
Cars produced — 566	Motor # — A-600,000 to A-600,620
Models — 1607-08	Vehicle # — BTPPN

Body Type		Passenger Capacity	Shipping Weight	Factory List & Date Effective	
Number	Style				
Model 1607 (134" wheelbase)				9-20-37	10-26-37
1127	Victoria	5	5345	$5230	
1132	Sedan, Formal	5	5550	4865	
1133	Sedan, Touring, 4 Door	5	5525	4155	
1136	Sedan, Club	5	5520	4255	
1137	Coupe	5	5415	4185	
1138	Coupe	2-4	5255	4135	
1139	Coupe, Convertible	2-4	5255	4370	
Model 1608 (139" wheelbase)					
1134	Sedan, Touring	5-7	5600	4485	
1135	Limousine, Touring	5-7	5600	4485	
1153	Sedan, Convertible	5	5680	5390	
Model 1607-08 (139" wheelbase)					
494	Cabriolet, All-weather, Rollson	5-7	5740	$6730	
495	Town Car, All-weather, Rollson	5-7	5735	6880	
3086	Cabriolet, Touring, Brunn	5-7	5725	8510	
3087	Cabriolet, All-weather, Brunn	5-7	5730	8510	

Series — Seventeenth	Bore & Stroke — 3 1/2 x 4 1/4
Name — Six	H.P. AMA — 29.4
Produced — 9-20-38 to 8-8-39	Brake — 100
Cars produced — 24,350	Motor # — B-1,500 - 27,000
Models — 1700	Vehicle # — BTPPN

Body Type		Passenger	Shipping	Factory List &	
Number	Style	Capacity	Weight	Date Effective	

				9-20-38	5-1-39
Model 1700 (122" wheelbase)					
1288	Coupe, Business	2	3295	$1000	$ 888
1285	Coupe, Club	2-4	3365	1045	944
1289	Coupe, Convertible	2-4	3385	1195	1092
1284	Sedan, Touring, 2 Door	5	3390	1065	964
1282	Sedan, Touring, 4 Door	5	3400	1095	995
	Station Wagon	7	3652		1404

Series — Seventeenth   Bore & Stroke — 3 1/4 x 4 1/4

Name — One Twenty   H.P. AMA — 33.8

Produced — 9-20-38 to   Brake — 120
          8-8-39

Cars produced — 17,647   Motor # — B-300,000 - 319,000

Models — 1701-2   Vehicle # — BTPPN

| Body Type | | Passenger | Shipping | Factory List & | |
Number	Style	Capacity	Weight	Date Effective	
Model 1701	(127" wheelbase)			9-20-38	5-1-39
1298	Coupe,				
	Business	2	3490	$1200	$1099
1295	Coupe, Club	2-4	3535	1245	1145
1299	Coupe,				
	Convertible	2-4	3545	1390	1288
1297	Sedan,				
	Convertible	5	3780	1700	1600
1294	Sedan,				
	Touring,				
	2 Door	5	3595	1265	1166
1292	Sedan,				
	Touring,				
	4 Door	5	3605	1295	1196
1293	Station				
	Wagon	7	3850		1636
Model 1702	(148" wheelbase)				
1290	Limousine,				
	Touring	7	4185	1955	1856
1291	Sedan,				
	Touring	7	4100	1805	1702

Series — Seventeenth

Name — Super Eight

Produced — 9-20-38 to
          8-8-39

Cars produced —3,962

Models — 1703-5

Bore & Stroke — 3 3/16 x 5

H.P. AMA — 32.5

Brake — 130

Motor # — B 500,000 to 505,000

Vehicle # — BTPPN

Body Type		Passenger	Shipping	Factory List &
Number	Style	Capacity	Weight	Date Effective
Model 1703	(127" wheelbase)			
1272	* 4 Door Sedan, Touring	5	3930	$1732
1275	* Coupe, Club	2-4	3860	1650
1277	* Sedan, Convert-tible	5	4005	2130
1279	* Coupe, Convertible	2-4	3870	1875
Model 1705	(148" wheelbase)			
1270	Limousine, Touring	5-7	4510	2294
1271	Sedan, Touring	5-7	4425	2156

*   Non-classic unless fitted with meritorious coachwork.

Series — Seventeenth	Bore & Stroke — 3 7/16 x 4 1/4
Name — Twelve	H.P. AMA — 56.7
Produced — 9-20-38 to 8-8-39	Brake — 175
Cars produced — 446	Motor # — B 600,000 to 601,000
Models — 1707-8	Vehicle # — BTPPN

Body Type		Passenger	Shipping	Factory List &
Number	Style	Capacity	Weight	Date Effective
Model 1707	(134" wheelbase)			9-20-38
594	Cabriolet, Rollston, All-weather	5-7	4950	$6730
1227	Victoria	5	5570	5230
1232	Sedan, Formal	5	5745	4865
1233	Sedan, Touring	5	5670	4155
1236	Sedan, Club	5	5590	4255
1237	Coupe	5	5425	4185
1238	Coupe	2-4	5400	4185
1239	Coupe, Convertible	2-4	5540	4375
Model 1708	(139" wheelbase)			
595	Town Car, Rollston, All-weather	5-7	5075	6880
1234	Sedan, Touring	5-7	5750	4485
1235	Limousine, Touring	5-7	5825	4690
1253	Sedan, Convertible	5	5890	5395
4086	Cabriolet, Touring, Brunn	5	5845	8355
4087	Cabriolet, All-weather, Brunn	6	5845	8355

Series — Eighteenth	Bore & Stroke — 3 1/2 x 4 1/4
Name — One Ten	H.P. AMA — 29.4
Produced — 8-8-39 to 9-16-40	Brake — 100
Cars produced — 62,300	Motor # — C-1500 - 65,000
Models — 1800	Vehicle # — BTPPN

Body Type		Passenger	Shipping	Factory List &	
Number	Style	Capacity	Weight	Date Effective	
Model 1800 (122" wheelbase)				8-8-39	7-1-40
1388	Coupe, Business	2	3110	$ 867	$ 867
1385	Coupe, Club	2-4	3150	924	940
1389	Coupe, Convertible	2-4	3230	1087	1104
1384	Sedan, Touring, 2 Door	5	3190	944	964
1382	Sedan, Touring, 4 Door	5	3200	975	996
1383	Station Wagon	8	3380	1195	1200

Series — Eighteenth   Bore & Stroke — 3 1/4 x 4 1/4

Name — One Twenty   H.P. AMA — 33.8

Produced — 1-18-40   Brake — 120

Cars produced — 28,158   Motor # — C-300,000 - 330,000

Models — 1801   Vehicle # — BTPPN

Body Type		Passenger Capacity	Shipping Weight	Factory List & Date Effective	
Number	Style				
Model 1801 Standard	(127" wheelbase)			1-18-40	7-1-40
1398	Coupe, Business	2	3350	$1038	$1038
1395	Coupe, Club	2-4	3405	1095	1111
1399	Coupe, Convertible	2-4	3485	1258	1277
1396	Sedan, Club 4 Door	5	3460	1217	1239
1397	Sedan, Convertible	5	3640	1550	1573
1394	Sedan, Touring, 2 Door	5	3440	1115	1135
1393	Station Wagon	8	3590	1397	1407
1392	Sedan, Touring, 4 Door	5	3450	1146	1166
700	Victoria, Convertible, Darrin	5	3826	3800	
Model 1801 DeLuxe	(127" wheelbase)				
DE1395	Coupe, Club		3405	1145	1161
DE1399	Coupe, Convertible		3485	1299	1318
DE1396	Sedan, Club		3460	1292	1314
DE1392	Sedan, Touring		3450	1225	1246

Series — Eighteenth	Bore & Stroke — 3 1/2 x 4 5/8
Name — Super Eight One Sixty	H.P. AMA — 39.2
Produced — 8-8-39 to 9-16-40	Brake — 160
Cars produced — 5,662	Motor # — C-500,000 - 507,000
Models — 1803-4-5	Vehicle # — BTPPN

Body Type		Passenger	Shipping	Factory List &	
Number	Style	Capacity	Weight	Date Effective	
Model 1803 (127" wheelbase)				8-8-39	7-1-40
1378	Coupe, Business, 2 Door	2	3665	$1524	$1524
1375	Coupe, Club	2-4	3735	1595	1614
1379	Coupe, Convertible	2-4	3795	1775	1797
1376	Sedan, Club, 4 Door	5	3780	1717	1740
1377	Sedan, Convertible	5	3990	2050	2075
1372	Sedan, Touring, 4 Door	5	3825	1632	1655
Model 1804 (138" wheelbase)					
1362	Sedan, Touring, 4 Door	5	4070	1895	1919
Model 1805 (148" wheelbase)					
1370	Limousine, Touring	7	4460	2154	2179
1371	Sedan, Touring	7	4350	2026	2051

Series — Eighteenth	Bore & Stroke — 3 1/2 x 4 5/8
Name — Custom Super Eight One Eighty	H.P. AMA — 39.2
Produced — 8-8-39 to 9-16-40	Brake — 160
Cars produced — 1900	Motor # — CC 500,000 to 503,000
Models — 1806-7-8	Vehicle # — BTPPN

Body Type		Passenger	Shipping	Factory List &
Number	Style	Capacity	Weight	Date Effective

Model 1806 (127" wheelbase)

Number	Style	Capacity	Weight	Date Effective
700	Victoria, Convertible, Darrin	5	4121	$4570
1356	Sedan, Club, 4 Door	5	3900	2243

Model 1807 (138" wheelbase)

Number	Style	Capacity	Weight	Date Effective
694	Rollson, All-weather, Cabriolet	7	4050	4450
710	Sedan, Convertible, Darrin	5	4050	6300
720	Sedan, Sport, Darrin	5	4215	6100
1332	Sedan, Formal	5	4210	2840
1342	Sedan, Touring 4 Door	5	4175	2410

Model 1808 (148" wheelbase)

Number	Style	Capacity	Weight	Date Effective
695	Rollson, All-weather, Town Car	7	4175	4574
1350	Limousine, Touring	7	4585	2669
1351	Sedan, Touring	7	4510	2541

Series — Nineteenth	Bore & Stroke — 3 1/2 x 4 1/4
Name — One Ten	H.P. AMA — 29.4
Produced — 9-16-40 to 8-25-41	Brake — 100
Cars produced — 34,700	Motor # — D-1,500 - 38,000
Models — 1900	Vehicle # — BTPPN

Body Type		Passenger	Shipping	Factory List &	
Number	Style	Capacity	Weight	Date Effective	
Model 1900 Standard	(122" wheelbase)			9-16-40	6-26-41
1488	Coupe, Business	2	3150	$ 907	$ 927
1485	Coupe, Club	2-4	3200	1000	1020
1489	Coupe, Convertible	2-4	3310	1175	1195
1484	Sedan, Touring, 2 Door	5	3245	1024	1010
1482	Sedan, Touring, 4 Door	5	3250	1056	1076
1483	Station Wagon	8	3460	1231	1251
1462	Taxicab	5	3950	NA	
Model 1900 DeLuxe	(122" wheelbase)				
1485DE	Coupe, Club, DeLuxe	2-4	3205	1038	1058
1489DE	Coupe, Convertible, DeLuxe	2-4	3315	1209	1229
1484DE	Sedan, Touring, DeLuxe 2 Door	5	3270	1084	1070
1482DE	Sedan, Touring, DeLuxe 4 Door	5	3270	1126	1136
1463DE	Station Wagon, DeLuxe	8	3470	1291	1326

Series — Nineteenth	Bore & Stroke — 3 1/4 x 4 1/4
Name — One Twenty	H.P. AMA — 33.8
Produced — 9-16-40 to 8-25-41	Brake — 120
Cars produced — 17,100	Motor # — D-300,000 - 319,000
Models — 1901	Vehicle # — BTPPN

Body Type		Passenger	Shipping	Factory List &
Number	Style	Capacity	Weight	Date Effective

				9-16-40	6-26-41
Model 1901 (127" wheelbase)					
1498	Coupe, Business	2	3385	$1112	$1142
1495	Coupe, Club	2-4	3430	1205	1235
1499	Coupe, Convertible	2-4	3585	1377	1407
1497	Sedan, Convertible	5	3725	1725	1753
1494	Sedan, Touring, 2 Door	5	3504	1230	1260
1492	Sedan, Touring, 4 Door	5	3510	1261	1291
1493	Station Wagon	8	3720	1436	1466
1473	Station Wagon, DeLuxe	8	3730	1496	1541

Series — Nineteenth   Bore & Stroke — 3 1/4 x 4 1/4

Name — Clipper   H.P. AMA — 33.8

Produced — 4-1-41 to   Brake — 125
              8-25-41

Cars produced — 16,600   Motor # — D-400,000 - 418,000

Models — 1951   Vehicle # — BTPPN

Body Type		Passenger	Shipping	Factory List &	
Number	Style	Capacity	Weight	Date Effective	
Model 1951 (127" wheelbase)				4-1-41	6-26-41
1401	Sedan, Touring	5	3725	$1375	$1420

Series — Nineteenth   Bore & Stroke — 3 1/2 x 4 5/8

Name — Super Eight One   H.P. AMA — 39.2
       Sixty

Produced — 9-16-40 to   Brake — 160
           8-25-41

Cars produced — 3,525   Motor # — D-500,000 - 505,000

Models — 1903-4-5   Vehicle # — BTPPN

Body Type		Passenger	Shipping	Factory List &	
Number	Style	Capacity	Weight	Date Effective	
Model 1903 (127" wheelbase)				9-16-40	6-26-41
1478	Coupe, Business, 2 Door	2	3875	$1594	$1639
1475	Coupe, Club	2-4	3800	1709	1754
1479	Coupe, Convertible	2-4	3965	1892	1937
1479DE	Coupe, Convertible DeLuxe	2-4	3985	2067	2112
1477	Sedan, Convertible	5	4140	2180	2225
1477DE	Sedan, Convertible DeLuxe	5	4160	2405	2450
1472	Sedan, Touring, 4 Door	5	3865	1750	1795
Model 1904 (138" wheelbase)					
1462	Sedan, Touring, 4 Door	5	4305	2009	2054
Model 1905 (148" wheelbase)					
1470	Limousine, Touring	7	4570	2289	2334
1471	Sedan, Touring	7	4495	2161	2206

Series — Nineteenth	Bore & Stroke — 3 1/2 x 4 5/8
Name — Custom Super Eight One Eighty	H.P. AMA — 39.2
Produced — 9-17-40 to 8-25-41	Brake — 160
Cars produced — 930	Motor # — CD 500,000 to 502,000
Models — 1906-7-8	Vehicle # — BTPPN

Body Type Number	Style	Passenger Capacity	Shipping Weight	Factory List & Date Effective
Model 1906	**(127" wheelbase)**			
1429	Victoria, Convertible, Darrin	5	4040	$4595
Model 1907	**(138" wheelbase)**			
794	Cabriolet, All-weather, Rollson	7	4075	4695
1422	Sedan, Sport, Darrin	5	4490	4795
1432	Sedan, Formal	5	4380	3095
1442	Sedan, Touring 4 Door	5	4350	2632
1452	Brougham, Sport, LeBaron 4 Door	5	4450	3545
Model 1908	**(148" wheelbase)**			
795	Town Car, All-weather, Rollson	7	4200	4820
1420	Limousine, Touring, LeBaron	7	4850	5595
1421	Sedan, Touring, LeBaron	7	4740	5345
1450	Limousine, Touring	7	4650	2913
1451	Sedan, Touring	7	4590	2769

Series — Twentieth   Bore & Stroke — 3 1/4 x 4 1/4

Name — Clipper Six 110   H.P. AMA — 29.4
      Special and Custom

Produced — 8-25-41 to   Brake — 105
      2-7-42

Cars produced — 11,325   Motor # — E-1500 - 14000

Models — 2000-10-20-30   Vehicle # — BTPPN

| Body Type | | Passenger | Shipping | Factory List & | |
Number	Style	Capacity	Weight	Date Effective	
Model 2000 (120" wheelbase)				8-25-41	11-29-41
1588	Coupe, Business	3	3365	$1180	$1248
1585	Sedan, Club	6	3415	1215	1285
1582	Sedan, Touring	6	3435	1250	1318
Model 2010 (120" wheelbase)					
1505	Sedan, Club	6	3440	1270	1353
1502	Sedan, Touring	6	3460	1303	1388
Model 2020 (122" wheelbase)					
1589	Coupe, Convertible	5	3315	1385	1468
Model 2030 (133" wheelbase)					
1584	Taxicab, New York Special	6	3980	NA	

Series — Twentieth	Bore & Stroke — 3 1/4 x 4 1/4
Name — Clipper Eight 120	H.P. AMA — 33.8
Produced — 8-25-41 to 2-7-42	Brake — 125
Cars produced — 19,199	Motor # — B-300,000 - 321,000
Models — 2001-11-21	Vehicle # — BTPPN

Body Type Number	Style	Passenger Capacity	Shipping Weight	Factory List & Date Effective	
Model 2001 (120" wheelbase)				8-25-41	11-29-41
Clipper Special					
1598	Coupe, Business	3	3490	$1235	$1303
1595	Sedan, Club	6	3540	1270	1338
1592	Sedan, Touring	6	3560	1305	1373
Model 2011 Clipper Custom (120" wheelbase)					
1515	Sedan, Club	6	3565	1325	1405
1512	Sedan, Touring	6	3585	1360	1443
Model 2021 (127" wheelbase)					
1599	Coupe, Convertible	5	3585	1495	1578

Series — Twentieth   Bore & Stroke — 3 1/2 x 4 5/8

Name — Super Eight One   H.P. AMA — 39.2
        Sixty

Produced — 8-25-41 to   Brake — 165
        2-7-42

Cars produced — 2580   Motor # — E-500,000 - 504,000

Models — 2003-4-5-23-25   Vehicle # — BTPPN

Body Type		Passenger	Shipping	Factory List &	
Number	Style	Capacity	Weight	Date Effective	
Model 2003 Clipper	(127" wheelbase)			8-25-41	11-29-41
1575	Sedan, Club	6	3985	$1635	$1753
1572	Sedan,				
	Touring	6	4005	1695	1814
Model 2023	(127" wheelbase)				
1579	Coupe,				
	Convertible	5	3905	1795	1917
Model 2004					
1562	Sedan,				
	Touring	6	4090	1905	2029
Model 2005	(148" wheelbase)				
1570	Limousine,				
	Touring	5-7	4445	2175	2306
1571	Sedan,				
	Touring	5-7	4325	2050	2176
Model 2055	(148" wheelbase)				
1590	Limousine,				
	Business	5-7	4435	2025	2152
1591	Sedan,				
	Business	5-7	4315	1900	2024

Series — Twentieth	Bore & Stroke — 3 1/2 x 4 5/8
Name — Custom Super Eight One Eighty	H.P. AMA — 39.2
Produced — 8-25-41 to 12-30-41	Brake — 165
Cars produced — 672	Motor # — CE500,000 to 503,366
Models — 2006-7-8	Vehicle # — BTPPN

Body Type Number	Style	Passenger Capacity	Shipping Weight	Factory List & Date Effective
Model 2006 (127" wheelbase)				11-29-41
1522	Sedan, Touring, Clipper styling	6	4030	$2346
1525	Sedan, Club, Clipper Styling	6	4010	2244
Model 2006 (127" wheelbase) 700 x 16				
1529	Victoria, Convertible Darrin	5	3920	4783
Model 2007 (138" wheelbase)				
897	Cabriolet, All-weather Rollson	7	4075	5079
1532	Sedan, Formal	6	4390	3201
1542	Sedan, Touring	6	4280	2602
Model 2008 (148" wheelbase)				
895	Town Car, All-weather, Rollson	5-7	4200	5172
1520	Limousine, Touring LeBaron	5-7	4850	6012
1521	Sedan, Touring, LeBaron	5-7	4740	5756
1550	Limousine, Touring	5-7	4540	2817
1551	Sedan, Touring	5-7	4525	2689